VOICES FROM
RAW RECRUITS:

"IT'S A CESSPOOL, AND WE START THE PROCESS."
> —Sonny Vaccaro,
> Nike basketball kingpin

"YOU CAN'T TAKE A STAND IF YOU WANT TO STAY IN THE BUSINESS. IT'S BETTER TO STAY QUIET. BETTER TO STAY IN A TOTAL DENIAL POSITION."
> —Tates Locke,
> Indiana State coach

"ALL HANDS ARE OUT. A PAIR OF NIKES AND A SWEAT SUIT TO A SIXTH-GRADER IS LIKE $100,000 TO A COLLEGE KID."
> —Pat Barrett,
> L.A. summer league coach

"THE STREET BROKERS' SECRET IS CONTROLLING THE PRODUCT EARLY. IT'S LIKE SLAVERY. MODERN-DAY SLAVERY IS WHAT IT IS."
> —Rudy Washington,
> Iowa assistant coach

"SOMETIMES I WONDER WHAT DISHONESTY IS. IS IT DISHONEST FOR A KID TO BE PAID . . . OR IS IT JUST AGAINST THE RULES?"
> —John Thompson,
> Georgetown coach

RAW RECRUITS

ALEXANDER WOLFF AND ARMEN KETEYIAN

POCKET BOOKS

New York   London   Toronto   Sydney   Tokyo   Singapore

POCKET BOOKS, a division of Simon & Schuster
1230 Avenue of the Americas, New York, NY 10020

ISBN: 0-671-70428-1

First Pocket Books paperback printing January 1991

10 9 8 7 6 5 4 3 2 1

Cover photo by SIGRID ESTRADA

Printed in the U.S.A.

For Tates Locke,
who came clean and came back

Contents

events or exchanges, we have provided the version we believe to be the most accurate and plausible.

In some instances we have used information and quotes that aren't attributed to sources by name. The Code, which is explained in the following pages, prevents many who currently make their living in basketball from going on the record. Like medicine, anonymous resources are distasteful but sometimes necessary. We have tried to avoid using them wherever possible, but where we have found them to be credible, and their reasons for insisting on anonymity to be persuasive, we have not flinched from obscuring attribution.

To help pull so many disparate strains into a single narrative, we have relied on maps—previous reporting that covered areas over which we travel. Journalists who will find their work reflected in the story we tell here include Virginia Anderson, John Carroll, John Clay, Cheri Collis, David Green, Valarie Honeycutt, Gene McLean, Billy Reed, Joseph Stroud, and, in particular, Jerry Tipton of the Lexington *Herald-Leader*; Bill Brubaker of the Washington *Post*, and, previously, the New York *Daily News* and *Sports Illustrated*; Rick Bozich, Hunt Helm, Scott Fowler, Todd Murphy, and Richard Wilson of the Louisville *Courier-Journal*; Brian Malloy of United Press International; Mike Embry of the Associated Press; Johnette Howard, Mick McCabe, and Scott Walton of the Detroit *Free-Press*; Joel J. Smith of the Detroit *News*; Chris Dufresne, Steve Elling, Mal Florence, Irene Garcia, Myron Levin, Bill Libby, and David Morgan of the Los Angeles *Times*; Tom Keegan of the Orange County *Register*; John Henderson of the Las Vegas *Review-Journal*; Mark Bradley of the Atlanta *Journal-Constitution*; Jeff Gordon, Vai Gregorian, and Jim Thomas of the St. Louis *Post-Dispatch*; Mike Fish of the Kansas City *Star-Times*; Sandra Fish, Gene Frenette, and Don Yaeger of the Florida *Times-Union*; Mark Barnhill, Beth Barrett, Doug Cress, Eric Sondheimer, and Jim Tranquada of the Los Angeles *Daily News*; Michael Dobie of *Newsday*; Taylor Bell and Marty Walsh of the Chicago Sun-Times; Jim Drinkhall of The Wall Street Journal; Steve Wieberg of USA Today; Bill Bruns of Money; Hank Nuwer of Sport; Mike Douchant of The Sporting News; Rick Ball of Basketball Times; and, of course, Jeffrey Marx and Michael York of the Lexington Herald-Leader. Many of them generously shared their time and wisdom with us.

Work done by current or erstwhile colleagues at Sports Illustrated, among them Morin Bishop, John Feinstein, Larry Keith, Curry Kirkpatrick, Jack McCallum, Rick Reilly, Steve Rushin, Bruce Selcraig, Robert Sullivan, and Sam Toperoff, helped point the way, as did reporting by Gary Apple of KMOV in St. Louis and Bob Hensley of WTVQ in Lexington. Several books, including Tates Locke and Bob Ibach's Caught in the Net, Charley Rosen's The Scandals of '51, Stanley Cohen's The Game They Played, Jerry Tarkanian and Terry Pluto's Tark, Dave Kindred's Basketball: The Dream Game in Kentucky, and Rick Pitino and Bill Reynolds' Born to Coach, served as Baedekers. We consulted Allen Sack's study of attitudes toward NCAA legislation, published in the Journal of Sport and Social Issues. In addition, Elliott Almond, David Barrett, Frank Burlison, Peter Carry, Martin F. Dardis, Mike Dardis, Dan Doyle, Kevin Ellison, Randy Hanson, Michael Jaffe, Aram Janoyan, Jay Jennings, Jerry Kirshenbaum, Tom Konchalski, Stefanie Krasnow, Mark Mulvoy, Frank Pace, Sandy Padwe, Leslie Robinson, Jay Thomas, Jack Tobin, and Chuck Wielgus all made substantial and timely contributions, as did Basil Kane, Leslie Wells, Jack Romanos, Irwyn Applebaum and Eric Rayman, who saw this project through.

Some people who helped us prefer not to be recognized publicly. We thank them without making eye contact.

A small portion of this book appeared in different form in Sports Illustrated.

A.W.
A.K.

RAW RECRUITS

PROLOGUE

THE MAN unfurls a steel folding chair, then sets himself down in a hallway outside a gym at the University of Nevada in Las Vegas. The spot he chooses is hard by a pay phone, which he will use a dozen times in the next half-hour. "This," he says, "is my office."

This is also his city. The people here have seen him down and out, and seen him triumphant too—yet he's not UNLV basketball coach Jerry Tarkanian. Some call him one of the college game's power brokers, yet he's neither Big East founder Dave Gavitt nor Indiana coach Bob Knight. He's connected by blood to the director of one of the biggest sports books in town, but he has legitimacy that the touts and sharpies can only hope for. And although he's best friends with Georgetown coach John Thompson, he's so unimposing and self-deprecatory in manner that he calls himself "a fat dago from Pittsburgh."

Of Pittsburgh someone once said, "Open any window and you'll get a smoke-filled room." But there is nothing conspiratorial about this man or his bearing. He wears Nikes and a disarmingly open expression. He has prospered by invoking friendships formed in good faith over the years. The most powerful college coaches are his collaborators; the best college players share confidences with him long before they arrive on a campus.

Yet something leaves this man ill at ease. There's trouble in his most substantial holdings, deep trouble. He knows it, and knows, too, that he's partly responsible for it. "It's a cesspool," he says. "And we start the process."

For four days a high-school summer tournament has been raging here, showcasing the best adolescent ball players in the land. College recruiters have made their predatory way to the desert, to a city whose economy depends on visitors losing. The event that attracts them belongs to this man, even as he wishes it didn't.

"I've gone on record," he says. "I think all-star games should be banned. There should be no all-star camps. The AAU scene is a cesspool. The all-star games are a cesspool. In reality, our camp, even if we try to do it right, is a cesspool, because we cater to 120 kids. I know these kids. I've watched them over twenty-five years, and I see the harm that's done."

He knows all this, yet still he carries on. There are hundreds more like him, only most keep their qualms, if they have any, to themselves. They are players in the game. And they have to keep playing the game.

— 1 —

Pandora's Package

THE ENVELOPE was like any one of millions carried by overnight delivery services each business day. Made of cardboard and slightly smaller than a record-album jacket, it began its journey on the afternoon of March 30, 1988, when an employee of Emery Worldwide air freight fetched it from the basketball office in Memorial Coliseum on the campus of the University of Kentucky. Around 9:30 P.M. the envelope left Lexington by truck, bound for Emery's hub in Dayton, where it was sorted and ultimately routed onto a red and white DC-8 that touched down at Los Angeles International Airport shortly before 6 A.M. Pacific time. Within hours this innocent-looking parcel would spill forth troubles that promised to change forever college basketball's winningest program.

Emery's distribution center near LAX is a vast two-story warehouse the size of half a city block. Like a bakery or the newsroom of an evening paper, it's abuzz early. As dawn breaks, the building is already a bazaar of moving conveyor belts and loaded shipping pallets. Forklifts scurry about. "Splitters" sort through offloaded shipments and route them to the appropriate "rollers," which carry parcels to areas where "pickers" perform second sortings. On a Thursday morning, in the midst of this animated scene, Eric Osburn is in his cluster area, sorting about one hundred overnight envelopes into three boxes.

The NCAA's 50th Anniversary Final Four is just two days away, but Osburn, a father of two who has been with Emery for ten years, doesn't much care. He's not a basketball fan. As a driver for the company—they're known in-house as territory representatives, or "T.R.'s"—he spends several hours picking before taking his truck out on its daily route. It's some time past 7:30, about two hours into his shift, when Osburn notices the flap on a Courier Express Urgent envelope has come open.

A picker will run into open envelopes every now and then, perhaps several a week. There will be no rip, crease, or tear, and no evidence of force or tampering; either the gum sealing the flap fails, or the contents of the package strain the flap until it pops open. An Urgent envelope is designed to hold standard 8½-inch by 11-inch pieces of paper totaling up to eight ounces, but the flap is more likely to come open if the contents are bulkier. As Osburn examines this particular parcel, he suspects that the VHS videocassette inside has pushed the envelope open.

But then Osburn notices something else. Between the tape and its cardboard sleeve he recognizes the distinct outline of paper money. Then the five and zero of a fifty-dollar bill. Then the bulk of a wad.

"Hey," he says to no one in particular. "Look at this."

Emery doesn't accept cash for shipment, nor will it ship guns, watches, or precious gems. So Osburn calls over his supervisor, Paul Perry, and shows him what he has found.

"Shit," Perry says.

Perry summons a few more T.R.'s and counts the money

4

in front of them. There are twenty fifties in all, a cool thousand. At this point no one has noted the name of the shipper, Dwane Casey, a Kentucky assistant coach, or the addressee, a C. Mills. Indeed, Osburn has seen only the cash and a label on the videocassette reading "Fax vs. Kennedy." Money and sports, he thinks. Must be tied into gambling. Somebody paying off a debt.

Perry and Osburn take the package to Steve Nelson, another supervisor, who watches Perry count the money again. Then Nelson summons the security man on duty, Clarence Bullerman, who works for Security Experts, Inc., a private firm contracted by Emery to secure its LAX facility. Once again the money is counted, this time by Bullerman.

Bullerman also examines the envelope. He has no reason to suspect anything untoward. The package came from a university. The air bill is typed and the cost prepaid, characteristics that don't match the profile of shipments of contraband. It's noteworthy that money is present, not that any is missing. So Bullerman decides not to file a report.

That appears to be that. Together, Perry and Bullerman reseal the package securely with packing tape. A T.R. won't necessarily deliver the same parcels he has sorted, and the address on this particular one—in the Fairfax section of town, just south of West Hollywood—isn't on Osburn's route this morning. So Perry vouchsafes it to the proper T.R., David Jones, for delivery. There's cash inside, he tells Jones. Deliver this package first, and be sure to get a legible signature.

It's now just past eight A.M. In light of the considerable sum in the envelope, Steve Nelson has called the consignee, Claud Mills. Nelson thinks he has awakened him. "We have a shipment of one thousand dollars coming to you," he says. "It's from the University of Kentucky. Will someone be home to sign for it?"

"Who's this playing with me?" Mills says. "I'm expecting two videotapes. Why in the hell would the University of Kentucky send me a thousand dollars?"

"I don't know," Nelson says. "We got a videotape, but evidently somebody sent you a bonus of a thousand dollars. We need to check the address. Are you at 1547 South Orange Drive?"

"Yes," Mills says.

Nelson tells Mills of Emery's policy not to accept currency, and asks him to inform the shipper not to send cash in the future. Mills wants to know whether he can have the shipment returned.

"Sorry," Nelson says. "It's our policy. If you want to send it back, you'll have to use some means other than Emery."

Mills is furious. "I don't care what you do with the money," he tells Nelson. "You can stick it up your ass if you want to."

Claud Mills would later say he was upset because he sensed the implications of the call. "I'm familiar with recruiting rules. I'm not gonna talk with some white person on the phone, some stranger, about my son and some kind of illegal anything, saying 'Yeah, yeah, yeah' early in the morning. I don't care if he's black as tar, I'm not talking to anybody on the phone about something like that."

And so that morning Claud Mills phoned Emery's 800 number to complain. "Some damn body," he told the operator, "is playin' with me in Los Angeles, California."

Meanwhile, out on the road, David Jones is having a problem. He can't find the address on the package. The air bill is only faintly legible, and there's no such house number on South Orange Drive. Jones calls back in, asking Perry to check Emery's computer and get him a good address. By midmorning a dispatcher sets him straight: the proper street is South Orange *Grove*. Claud Mills had erroneously confirmed the bad address in the confusion of Nelson's eight A.M. phone call.

Four, perhaps five, times Jones makes contact with the LAX facility about the Mills shipment. Listening over the driver-dispatcher radio, he's hearing quite a hubbub, all over this one package. First there was the confusion in pinning down the address. Now the voice of Richard Flanders, the dispatcher, crackles back. He has radioed to tell Jones to deliver the package as soon as possible. The consignee has phoned in. He was "freaking out, irate," Flanders would recall.

"What business do you have opening my packages?" Claud Mills yelled at Flanders. He demanded to talk to a supervisor. Flanders switched him over to Nelson, the man who had originally called him.

Mills was calm now. He asked again about sending the money back. Nelson told him once more: he was welcome to return the contents of the package, but not via Emery.

By the time the T.R.'s are ready to hit the road that morning, word of the cash has worked its way around the facility. One Emery driver is sports-minded enough to recognize the names on the air bill and make the connection. Chris Mills is the star basketball player at Fairfax High School, perhaps the finest ever to come out of the city. Last November 11, after a five-way recruiting fight also involving Nevada–Las Vegas, Syracuse, UCLA, and Indiana, he had signed a letter of intent to play at Kentucky. No one needs a copy of the *NCAA Manual* to figure out that sending cash to a recruit is an improper inducement and serious recruiting violation.

"It's not right," says another T.R. The office grapevine was in full swing, recalls John Zaverl, a T.R. whose brother-in-law works at the Los Angeles *Daily News*.

When David Jones finally finds the Millses' apartment, he has no small sense of foreboding. He knows the neighborhood isn't the best, knows the consignee has been raising hell, knows that there's money in the package—although he has no clue why. Yet when he reaches the stoop of Apartment No. 2 at 1547 South Orange Grove shortly before noon, he finds it surprisingly calm.

The door is open. Claud Mills is gone, off to pick up his sister at work. Tracey Mills, Claud's son and a high-school freshman, comes to the door, but Jones decides he's not old enough to accept delivery. Tracey goes off to the bedroom to fetch his older brother.

At 11:55 A.M. Chris Mills, the 6-foot-7-inch reason this package has been sent in the first place, signs for it.

It took exactly two weeks for word to seep out. In its April 14 edition, the *Daily News* broke the news of the extraordinary events of that Thursday morning. A week before, the *News* had contacted officials at the University of Kentucky and the NCAA for their reactions, and each in turn assigned an investigator to the case. In the meantime *News* reporter Mark Barnhill tracked down Dwane Casey in Pittsburgh, where he had gone for the Dapper Dan Roundball Classic, a high-school all-star game in which Chris was participating.

Casey first denied sending the Millses any package. When Barnhill told him the *News* had an air bill bearing his name, he acknowledged sending Claud Mills a tape. It would ultimately come out that Casey had left the videocassette on the desk of Larnetta McDowell, a secretary in the basketball office, before heading to Louisville on business around one P.M. on March 30. McDowell would tell the NCAA that the tape and an empty Courier Express envelope sat on her desk for nearly two hours that afternoon before she put the videocassette in the envelope.

The Kentucky coaching staff often swapped videos with prospects, Casey told Barnhill, so the recruit could look at the Wildcats' style of play, and the 'Cats could in turn monitor his progress. But to the charge that he had put cash in the envelope, Casey paced agitatedly in his room, shaking his head. "This is the most ridiculous thing that's ever happened in my life," he said. "It's a ridiculous accusation. I have never put any money in any package, and I'll say that until the day I die."

Over the next several days, Claud Mills would be no less emphatic. When he returned home around 1:45, he said, the package was lying on a table by the door, where Chris had left it. Claud says the envelope appeared to be partially open at the top. Tracey says "a hole" was open on the side. Neither Claud, Tracey, nor Chris say they saw any money inside—only a videocassette of Chris in action against Kennedy High. "I didn't receive no money from Dwane Casey," Claud Mills would say. "Nobody from Kentucky gave me no money. They sent me a tape, but I don't know nothing about no money.

"I've got the number two or three kid in the country and I'm going to send him somewhere for a thousand bucks?" he said sarcastically. "I've got UCLA begging. USC begging. Las Vegas begging. Indiana begging. Every school in the country, all just begging. And I'm sending him [to Kentucky] because I'm getting a thousand dollars? That makes a whole lot of sense. [My son] could have gone anywhere in the country for fifty or a hundred thousand. What the hell you talking about, a thousand dollars. That's slavery. Chris Mills ain't no thousand-dollar man. He's one of the top players in the nation. He didn't come there for no money. UNLV–Las Vegas has got more money than Kentucky. L.A. has money. If we want money, we would go to one of those places.

"My kid is as good as anybody. When we didn't go to UCLA, they put a hex on my son. It had to be a hex, man, had to be a setup, nothing but a setup. To hurt Chris Mills, to hurt Kentucky, so Chris Mills couldn't go to Kentucky.

"I raised that kid without a wife, I raised him by myself,

and there was nothing ever said about that kid until last week. I wanted him not only to be the best basketball player, but the best person. And he got that way because of only one thing: discipline."

Chris Mills the basketball star is utterly the product of Claud Mills's doting attentions. Thus it's appropriate that no one thinks of them as anything but natural father and son. But whatever it is that binds them isn't blood. Chris Mills was born Christopher Lemont Ford on January 25, 1970, to Carlos Ford and Karen Mallory. When Chris was less than five months old, his mother married Claud Mills. It's unclear today whether Claud is technically Chris's stepfather or his adoptive father, because adoption records are confidential in California. But Chris and Claud have lived together ever since Claud and Karen Mallory Mills split in 1972. In August of 1986, just before Chris's junior year at Fairfax High, Claud filed a petition in L.A. County Superior Court to change Chris's surname from Ford to Mills.

Claud hadn't wanted his son to play for Hamilton High, the school in whose district he lived. Hamilton didn't have any players, he felt, and its coach wasn't "up-to-date." So over the summer before Chris's sophomore year, Claud moved with his two boys into a one-bedroom, $400-a-month apartment in the two-story, ranch-style building on South Orange Grove. Chris would be eligible to attend Fairfax High, which had a young and accommodating coach, Harvey Kitani, and one of the better academic reputations in the city. To assure that Claud would have Kitani's ear, Derick Mills, Chris's half-brother, signed on as a volunteer assistant.

Sean Higgins, the guard on Michigan's 1989 national championship team, was a year ahead of Chris at Fairfax. Coincidentally, he lived with his mother and stepfather in Apartment No. 4 of the same building. Yet even when Sean was a senior and one of the four or five most sought-after recruits in the nation, Chris, his junior teammate, was named L.A.'s Class 4-A Player of the Year. "Sean was a great player, but I always questioned his attitude," says Jalal Abdul-Rahman, the son of former UCLA coach Walt Hazzard, and a summer-league buddy of Mills and Higgins. "He had some altercations with Chris, even though they were on the same team. The thing was, Chris was the MVP Sean's senior year. Sean wasn't even considered for MVP. I think Sean sometimes got a little mad and tried to cut Chris off. Like 'You're taking me out of the limelight.'"

The cognoscenti knew, and deep down no doubt Sean did too: Higgins was spectacular and streaky, a dazzling shooter when the stars were aligned properly. But Fairfax's best all-round talent, the Lions' best basketball player, was the smooth eleventh-grader who lived in Apartment No. 2. Chris played center as a senior at Fairfax, but he was clearly cut out to be a major-college guard. His choice of Kentucky, Claud would tell all who asked, owed itself to "the big-guard spot and [Wildcats coach] Eddie Sutton." At Arkansas, Sutton had made his reputation by taking raw athletes around 6 foot 4—players like Sidney Moncrief, Ron Brewer, Darrell Walker, and Alvin Robertson—and turning them into seamless guards with the size to defend and rebound and the skills to score from inside or out.

Not that Chris needed much work. He had no apparent weaknesses. He was always willing to play a role. He would block five and six shots a game without ever getting in foul trouble. It was as if he had been playing the game all his young life.

In fact, Chris had played in one league or another since he was four. While in junior high, as Claud recuperated from a work-related back injury, Chris lived with the Hazzard family for nearly two years. "He used to call my mom 'Mom,'" remembers Jalal, who joined Chris as a regular at the Queen Anne Rec Center near the Hazzard home, and played with him on the B&B Spurs, a youth-league team that once won 46 of 50 games.

The NCAA would soon intervene, declaring the arrangement an unfair recruiting advantage for UCLA, and Chris moved back in with his father. But he still always had a coach around the house. From Claud and Derick came a steady stream of advice. Claud in particular would critique the most picayune detail of Chris's game, down to how the ball rolled off his fingertips when he let it fly. The videocassette in the Emery package was just one of many that Claud himself had made at Lions games, and part of a collection that he still guards jealously today. "I don't know how he can stand it," Chris said late in his senior year. "I mean, he watches a Fairfax game on tape every night. I usually just watch the replay the night after the game. I'll rewind for all the good plays. Then he shows me all the bad plays."

Ordinarily there weren't very many bad ones to show. Chris was a diligent student, too, whose academic credentials never gave college recruiters pause. Before he graduated, the school honored him as it does very few of its athletes. No one at Fairfax will ever wear No. 42 again. "I always told Chris, 'Books first, ball second, and I take care of the business,'" says Claud.

As Chris began shopping for a college, he and his family knew how they *didn't* want to go about it. In November 1986, Sean Higgins had signed a letter of intent to attend UCLA, only to claim later that his stepfather had coerced him into doing so. The Pac-10 office investigated Higgins's claim and ultimately decided to void the letter, freeing Sean to sign with Michigan and play near his father, Earle, a Detroiter. The Higgins drama, which Sean said involved his stepfather threatening him with a baseball bat, touched the Mills family. Some of the quarrels over Sean's future spilled out of Apartment No. 4 and wafted through the Millses' window. "We saw what Sean went through from five yards away," said Derick Mills. "No one wants to go through that." Thus, Derick said, the family resolved that the choice of college would be entirely Chris's.

Colleges began contacting Chris as early as ninth grade, but most recruiters first saw the full breadth of his abilities over the summer of 1987, before his senior season. At the Kentucky Prep All-Star Festival in Lexington over the July 4 weekend, Chris was spectacular, scoring 30 points. Eddie Sutton spotted UNLV assistant coach Mark Warkentien at the game. "Tell Tark," Sutton told him, referring to Jerry Tarkanian, Warkentien's boss, "that I've got to have that kid."

Sutton singled out Warkentien, knowing what most of the basketball world knew—that UNLV had the inside track on Mills. Chris had been a special project of Tarkanian's, a player so rare that Tark called virtually every day to talk with him, Claud, or Derick. In the trade this is known as "baby-sitting." You get "in" on a prospect, close enough to monitor every aspect of his life, phoning and writing the family so fastidiously that no one else can gain a foothold. Eventually the signing date comes and, through sheer ubiquity, you get your man. Some schools pay neighbors to note the license plate numbers of any cars pulling into the prospect's driveway, and cross-check them with the Department of Motor Vehicles, just to see who's making home visits when. Others have been known to pay off a hotel operator to "forget" a rival assistant's wake-up call on signing day. Recruiting can be a cutthroat business.

A week after speaking with Sutton in Lexington, Warkentien was back in L.A. to watch Chris play summer ball in the Fairfax gym. He noticed Dwane Casey standing off in a corner. "It was like it's a clear day and everything's okay," Warkentien says. "Then all of a sudden a MIG fighter flies overhead."

As the summer wore on, Tarkanian noticed changes in Claud. Veteran baby-sitters can sense these things, the way a nanny knows when an infant has an attack of colic coming on. Claud was behaving differently, Tark thought. He seemed more distant over the phone. And he was keeping the company of a Beverly Hills lawyer and onetime sports agent named Al Ross.

Ross had gotten to know the Mills family in 1985, when he agreed to represent Fairfax High in a dispute with the L.A. Unified Schools District Interscholastic Athletic Committee. The school had been barred from taking any out-of-state trips because of students' rowdy behavior at a track meet, and the Lions had two trips scheduled that year—to Las Vegas and Louisville. One of the players' parents asked Ross to help Fairfax appeal the probation. His efforts failed, but Ross left his business card with a number of the parents, and over time he and Claud Mills struck up a friendship. They were seen together several times thereafter: at the Dunes Hotel in Las Vegas for a Super Bowl party in January 1987; at a UNLV game in Southern California during the 1986–87 season; and at Chris's games, where they often sat together. "Midcourt, man," says one observer. "Side by side. Ross has been hanging around the Millses for a long time. . . . I assumed they were friends. [Ross] had a very big interest in Chris. I never saw Claud sit consistently with anyone else."

Tarkanian knew Ross too—from a conversation the two had had that spring. Ross told Tarkanian he was interested in representing Armon Gilliam and Freddie Banks, the two best seniors on UNLV's 1986–87 Final Four team. If he could sign Gilliam and Banks as clients, Ross told Tarkanian, he would be able to help out Claud Mills financially. To Tarkanian, it didn't sound as if Ross was saying he could actually deliver Chris Mills. It sounded rather as if Ross was positioning to make the youngster's father beholden to him. If Ross succeeded, Tark knew, Ross would wield the kind of influence that no recruiter could afford to ignore.

Ross's involvement troubled Tarkanian enough that he

stopped calling the Mills household completely. Twelve days went by with no contact. Then Derick Mills called Tark. Chris and Claud hadn't heard from Vegas. They were worried. What was up?

Tarkanian told Derick his misgivings about Ross. Claud Mills called back a short time later. "You know, you're right," Claud told Tark. "I won't have anything more to do with him."

And so UNLV remained confident that Chris would be a Runnin' Rebel. Why, Chris had come to town in July with a summer-league all-star team for the Las Vegas Invitational, a big AAU tournament, and had a grand time. He and Shawn Kemp, the high-school star from Elkhart, Indiana, who would also sign with Kentucky, teamed up to win the whole thing, and were seen tooling around town together in a late-model sports car. Claud made the trip too. He played twenty-five-dollar chips at the blackjack tables at the Dunes, where a pit boss approached him, handed him his business card, and said, "If there's anything I can do . . ."

Even when Tarkanian ran into Syracuse coach Jim Boeheim at a Nike coaching clinic in Orlando in early October, and Boeheim warned him that UNLV wasn't going to sign Mills, Tarkanian didn't believe it.

Just to be sure, he called the Mills home. "Everything's fine," Claud said.

Claud Mills grew up in Ashdown, Arkansas, a little town near the Texas and Oklahoma borders, where he was a star guard in that state's segregated high-school leagues of the late fifties. "Dusty," they called him, for the way the net kicked up dust when his jump shots swished through. Except for chronic back troubles, even today he's in superb shape for someone pushing fifty. He's built squat but powerfully, with the blunt features of a pug.

Since coming to L.A. in the early sixties, Mills has survived on blue-collar jobs and disability benefits while weathering a multitude of legal and financial problems. Rosa Mills, Claud's first wife and the mother of Derick and another son, Dewayne, charged in her 1966 divorce complaint that Claud beat her often. After she and Claud split, Claud failed to make child-support payments on numerous occasions, and four times warrants were issued for his arrest. In 1983 he was hit with an earnings withholding order to recover back rent, and at the time of Chris's recruitment Claud still owed the state of California more than $1,100 for an unpaid tax lien. As recently as August 1986, his circumstances were so modest that his request to have Chris's surname changed was filed in *forma pauperis* —meaning the state waived the $99 court fee because he couldn't afford it.

Yet in spring 1987, the Millses' lot brightened considerably. Their living room, always a shrine to Chris's achievements, was cluttered with more and more basketball trophies—but it also had new furniture. Claud traveled to Arkansas and Pennsylvania to watch Chris play, as well as to Las Vegas, where he enjoyed the so-called "power of the pen" in at least one casino. At the start of his senior season at Fairfax, several weeks after signing with Kentucky, Chris began driving a 1984 Datsun 300ZX Turbo with tinted windows, new Pirelli tires, and, until his father told him to remove it, a cellular phone.

The car cost $7,416.69. Claud says he paid for it and his new furniture with money he received in workman's compensation for another back injury, one suffered on the job in the records section of L.A.'s Cedars Sinai Medical Center in April 1986. The mishap left him unable to lift more than fifteen pounds. Indeed, Claud received about half of a $24,465 workman's comp settlement in November 1987, and Chris's 300ZX was purchased on December 3. Claud has said he came into another $7,000 for "pain and suffering" after an auto accident occurring in March 1987. Further, he says, Derick and Dewayne Mills have become wealthy dealing in California real estate. "They're worth as much as Coach Sutton or any of them," he says. "Why would I sell Chris Mills down the drain for a seven-thousand-dollar car or one thousand dollars?"

On closer inspection, however, the family income Claud claims doesn't entirely stand up. Derick Mills has said he has invested in single-family homes, but that neither he nor his brother became wealthy as a result. "I'm wealthy in mind," Derick said. "That's it." Of the $7,000 Claud says he received for "pain and suffering" after his car was rear-ended by an uninsured driver, he paid about $3,100 to his attorney and physician.

As for Claud's payments from Cedars Sinai after his accident there, he received temporary disability checks to tide him over—$448 every two weeks, the maximum allowable. But those payments stopped in late May 1987, soon after Claud was pronounced physically unfit to return to his job at the medical center. Between mid-May and the beginning of September, the only money Cedars Sinai paid him was in July—a $1,000 advance against his final workman's comp settlement, still several months off.

As summer 1987 began, Chris Mills was about to become the most sought-after basketball property in the land. But Chris's father had no regular source of income. He needed a job.

And so, on May 4, 1987—at a time when recruiting gurus had Chris ticketed for UNLV—Claud began work as a storeroom clerk at Lorimar Telepictures in Culver City, processing orders for food to be distributed to studio sets. There in the storeroom, Claud openly attributed his getting the job to the good graces of a man named Molasky.

At the time, Irwin Molasky was a vice president and director of Lorimar. He's also a Las Vegas developer and UNLV season ticket holder who, along with comedienne Whoopi Goldberg and casino maven Steve Wynn, sits in

"Gucci Row," courtside at Runnin' Rebels home games. His son, Andy Molasky, is a Lorimar executive, with an office in Culver City.

For a school or booster to arrange a job for a member of a prospect's family is an improper inducement under NCAA rules. Both Irwin and Andy Molasky say they had no influence in Claud Mills's getting a job at Lorimar, nor any knowledge of Claud even working there until it was brought to their attention by a reporter. Jerry Tarkanian says, "[Claud] had mentioned something to Warkentien about being laid off, but it was no big deal. I think somehow Wark talked to Irwin. But Irwin wasn't involved. We didn't arrange a job for him." Claud says he got work at Lorimar on his own, and was paid no more than $7 an hour.

A source at Lorimar, however, questions that. "It was a different deal. Paychecks normally came once a week, on Thursdays, by interoffice mail. Claud would go over to the producer's building [to get paid]." Sources describe Mills as working irregularly and occasionally clashing with his department head. "It didn't matter," says one. "Basically he was an untouchable. If he didn't feel like working, he didn't. If he did, he did."

Claud took trips to Las Vegas three or four times during his stint at Lorimar, the sources say, and boasted that he could arrange for free hotel suites and travel. And he carried large bills that he would flash when he had the chance. "He never said so-and-so gave me this," one source says. "But he had a lot of money in his pocket all the time. Three, four hundred dollars, sometimes more . . . He'd leave work at twelve o'clock on different occasions to meet different schools. He would say if the school didn't make a good deal, he wouldn't bother with them."

As August and September wore on, Claud began missing more and more days of work. In mid-September his supervisor told him he would be laid off on October 1. Instead, he quit on September 25. But before leaving, the same source says, Claud declared himself "happy with" Kentucky.

"I asked him, 'What about Vegas? They set you up here. What are they gonna say when they find out [Chris is] going to another school?' Claud said, 'Kentucky's talking a little bit better'—not those exact words, but to that extent. He knew people wanted his son, and he was trying to get the best deal and situation."

While Claud was allegedly casting about for a good deal, so was Chris, according to players at Indiana who escorted him around campus during his official visit to Bloomington that fall. The Hoosiers are conspicuous among Chris's five final choices as a school widely thought to be above reproach. Their coach, Bob Knight, is an irascible man, but one who speaks often of abiding faithfully by NCAA rules. Chris reportedly asked several Hoosiers whether IU players were paid, and said he had to have a car, cash, and an off-campus apartment. Mark Robinson, the Indiana player who was one of Chris's hosts for the weekend, has said he asked Chris how much money he thought he needed.

"Thousands," Robinson says Chris told him.

Robinson and two other Indiana players, Keith Smart and Rick Calloway, told Chris that no one at Indiana got anything. "He asked, 'Why doesn't everyone have cars?'" Robinson says. "We said because they don't give us anything but financial aid. That's all you get.

"He just said, 'I know you guys get stuff. You're just not talking.' He kept saying, 'You guys are lying. You can tell me. You can tell me. After I sign, is it any different?'"

Mills ticked off benefits players at the other schools he had visited—schools Robinson declines to name—told him they received. He asked Smart, whose dramatic jumper against Syracuse won for IU the 1987 NCAA title, what he had been given for hitting the shot. "Nothing," Smart told him.

And he raised the issue of improper benefits again when

Calloway asked him whether he would choose Indiana.

"Man, I don't know. I like the school. I like the coach. And you guys always win. But I got to have things."

"If you're not going to come, just tell us," Calloway said as he and Robinson were about to take Chris to a campus party. "We can just go out and party and we won't have to worry about asking you anymore."

"I don't think so," Chris said.

The Monday after Mills flew back to L.A., Robinson told Indiana assistant coach Dan Dakich that the Hoosiers weren't going to get Chris. "He's going to go somewhere where they give him something," Robinson said, "because he needs some things to come to school."

Dakich relayed Robinson's comment to his boss. Knight was surprised. In their meetings, Claud had insisted that he and his son weren't looking for anything improper. (Indeed, they dispute the accounts of the Lorimar employees and the Indiana players.) Perhaps Chris had just been trying to impress his potential teammates; maybe he was simply trying to feel them out on what life would be like in Bloomington. Knight decided to give Chris the benefit of the doubt, and keep recruiting him.

But Tates Locke, another Indiana assistant, had sat in on the visit to the Mills home, and he felt otherwise. Locke had left the profession after being involved in recruiting scandals as the head coach at Clemson during the seventies, and Knight had hired him partly as a rehabilitation project. Despite his time in uncontaminated Bloomington, Locke and his olfactories could still recognize that certain aroma. "Once you've been involved in that stuff, as I was at Clemson, you just smell it. The air is very obvious. Through the summer I told Coach, 'We have no chance.' Once someone puts it on the table, it takes an unbelievably strong kid to turn away from it, particularly an inner-city kid who thinks he's upgrading his standards."

* * *

One game and two men mark the beginning of college basketball's metamorphosis during the eighties from a regionalized pastime into a profit-driven, coast-to-coast obsession. The game was the 1979 NCAA championship between Michigan State and Indiana State, which drew more television viewers than any other college game had before or has since. The men, the Spartans' Earvin (Magic) Johnson and the Sycamores' Larry Bird, would go on to the NBA and resuscitate that wheezing league with their charisma and genius.

To the colleges, it was as if the departure of Magic and Bird created a giant vacuum that sucked the sport into a prosperous new era. Everything seemed to happen at once. Cable TV turned college hoop into a nightly wintertime fixture. The Big East, and a raft of other demographics-conscious conferences with names sounding like trucking lines, generated for their member schools enormous interest and money. Meanwhile the spectacle of the college game had never been better, particularly the showcase, the three-week-long NCAA tournament.

In 1981, over a single Saturday in March, NBC's Bryant Gumbel was like the captain on the bridge of a college hoops fantasy starship. From his New York studio set, he whipped around the country from one breathtaking second-round game to another. Here was Kansas State's Rolando Blackman shooting down favored Oregon State with a corner jumper at the buzzer. There was lightly regarded St. Joseph's upsetting mighty DePaul with a last-minute rush up the court. And here was Arkansas beating Louisville with a half-court heave, and making the Razorbacks' coach, a curly-coiffed man named Eddie Sutton, deliriously happy.

Watching it all happen, the folks at CBS knew it made for splendid TV. They readied a staggering bid of $16 million to commandeer this grand event. Every few years since 1982, the NCAA and CBS have renegotiated their deal, with each new pact pushing the figures higher, from $16 million to $32 million to $55.3 million a year. In November 1989 they reached agreement on a seven-year, $1-billion contract that, beginning in 1991, would pay out an average of $143 million annually.

All the money pouring into the sport was blindingly new. The NCAA plowed some of it back into drug education and drug testing, some into its administrative budget, even a little bit into enforcement. Most of it, however, went back to the participating schools. At the beginning of the decade, 48 teams qualified for the NCAAs; by the end, 64 would. Most tournament teams had to share their takes—by 1989 you made almost $275,000 for a first-round loss and $1.374 million for reaching the Final Four—with other members of their leagues. But the mighty conferences now sent five and six schools to the NCAAs, and thus had fortunes to divvy up among themselves; others sent one team, and had to split a first-round loser's share as many as ten ways. More and more it was boom or bust, the rich getting richer and the poor failing to keep pace.

Basketball players have been bought for as long as colleges have pursued them, since back before games were ever nationally televised and the term "Final Four" was even coined. Indeed, forty percent of the college players polled in a 1964 National Association of Basketball Coaches survey said they had been plied with cash, cars, or clothing. But all this new money increased incentives to cheat, and its warped distribution only quickened the urge further. At the top end, among the elite conferences, the escalating stakes turned recruiting into a desperate arms race. For the midmajor and smaller schools, the imperative was to make the tournament, and recruiting became a matter of survival.

And then came another change. In 1986 the NCAA membership began enforcing the provisions of Proposition 48, which ruled that freshmen athletes not meeting prescribed minimums on their core courses and college boards had to sit out a season. A coach could recruit the marginal student, and risk the wrath of the president or faculty representative to whom he reported. But if—for reasons of ego, competitive pride, or job security—he needed to win right away, a Prop 48 case would be of no use. Thus recruiters went to great lengths to sign the rare ones, the kids like Chris Mills, who were both great players and Prop 48 qualifiers. Coaches took their struggle to dangerous outer limits, enlisting opportunistic outside parties in their cause, or jockeying for the blessing of the summer-league character or shoe-company representative who had the most influence with their quarry.

Picture it: Millions and millions in TV money flowing into the sport. All 290-odd schools in Division I scrambling desperately to gain one of 64 berths in the tournament. The pool of useful talent shrunk drastically by new academic standards. Interest in the college game, and thus the passions of boosters, never higher. And respect for NCAA rules, which continued to ban any remuneration for athletes, even in this era of plenty, never lower.

Simple principles of economics hold that under such conditions, prices will rise. Unless, of course, the commodity can't have a price because legislation won't permit it. In which case the market will go underground.

But the bidding, the high-stakes play for the jackpot young superstars, was still going to go on. And in the go-go eighties, those stakes were going to go up, further than they had ever gone before.

Sometime past midnight on October 27, 1985, Eddie Sutton lingered outside the offices of the Lexington *Herald-Leader*, waiting to be handed an early-run copy of that Sunday's paper. Sutton hadn't yet coached a game for the Wildcats. He had been hired the previous spring, and was enjoying the honeymoon a new coach—even one in college basketball's most withering hot seat—is traditionally accorded. But Lexington is a town through which rumors run like current through a wire. And like everyone else in the Bluegrass, he had heard scuttlebutt about the newspaper preparing an exhaustive series of articles on NCAA rules violations in the Kentucky program under his predecessor, Joe B. Hall. On this raw night, as curious as anybody, Sutton was getting an early look.

What he read was astonishing. The reporters, Jeffrey Marx and Michael York, had interviewed thirty-three current or former Kentucky players. Thirty-one said they knew of improprieties during their careers as Wildcats, and twenty-six said they took part in them. The violations ranged from acceptance of free meals or discounted clothes to sugar-daddy arrangements and postgame locker-room "hundred-dollar handshakes" with prominent boosters.

The stories demonstrated how the program "paired off" Wildcats with fat cats, and implicated one of Hall's closest friends, Cecil Dunn, in a scheme to scalp players' tickets—this when Dunn was an attorney in the county prosecutor's office, which is responsible for enforcing Kentucky's ticket-scalping law. "Boy, I want to vomit when I read that stuff," said former DePaul coach Ray Meyer. "Twenty-six players, and they're admitting that things like that went on. Then all those wins at Kentucky don't mean a damn thing."

In the following days, Sutton seemed to alternate between being unsettled by the charges and being unfazed by them. The series would win a Pulitzer Prize, and Sutton had a right to be out of sorts. If this were all true, he had come into a pretty rancid situation. Indeed, Lute Olson, the coach at Arizona, had turned down the Kentucky job precisely because he believed the boosters were out of control.

Yet Sutton hadn't been responsible for any of the detailed improprieties either. Shortly after the *Herald-Leader* articles appeared, he said he didn't want to pass judgment on the prior regime. "But with its tradition and stature, this program doesn't have to cheat," Sutton said. "We should be like North Carolina, like Indiana."

NCAA investigators had come to know the road to Lexington well. In 1976 they pursued reports that recruits were offered cash and cars. But they couldn't pin down much more than a few pairs of free sneakers, and docked the school only a couple of scholarships. In 1978 the NCAA looked into reports of free meals for basketball players at Cliff Hagan's Ribeye, a restaurant owned by the UK athletics director. No sanctions were levied when Hagan and Hall denied the allegation. Later that year the NCAA investigated whether Dwight Anderson, a star guard, had played while academically ineligible. UK certified that Anderson had indeed been eligible, and the NCAA closed its case.

With the *Herald-Leader*'s detailed charges as their guide, investigators swooped in for what should have been an easy mop-up operation. Nearly two and a half years later, on March 3, 1988, the NCAA announced it had found no evidence of wrongdoing within a four-year statute of limitations. Kentucky was rebuked for not fully cooperating with the probe, yet once again dodged sanctions. "Everyone is frustrated," said David Berst, who directs the NCAA's enforcement division, to the press that day. "But out of thirty-three individuals quoted in the articles, sixteen told us they were either misquoted or quoted out of context. It's not fair to convict somebody on third-hand newspaper quotes when these quotes are denied to us in face-to-face conversations.

"You can look at it two ways. If the newspaper article was correct, then there were forces at work that caused us not to get the full story. That would be an embarrassment for us. Certainly, if the stories were incorrect, that would be an embarrassment to the Pulitzer award. As to which of us should be embarrassed, I'll leave that to the judgment of others."

In the judgment of many within the commonwealth of Kentucky, the NCAA's findings only proved the *Herald-Leader* stories had been complete fabrications. Why was the newspaper refusing to release tape recordings of its interviews? There was only one solution to resolve the matter, according to Oscar Combs, editor and publisher of *The Cats' Pause*, a newspaper devoted to Kentucky sports that referred to the charges as "the alleged allegations": play the tapes. But the paper declined to, citing their privileged and private nature. And so March 3 wiped the slate clean, beginning for Sutton what he would eventually call his "forty days of sunshine."

In background and style, Eddie Sutton was a departure from the two previous suzerains of Kentucky basketball. Where Adolph Rupp and then Hall had ruled in almost dynastic fashion, Sutton was a parvenu, a man who had devoted his entire professional life to building programs. His first head college job was at the College of Southern Idaho, a two-year school whose president more or less threw down a campus and hired Sutton to assemble a basketball team that would spread the institution's name. Next stop was Creighton, a sleepy Catholic college in Omaha, with horizons that were quickly outstripped by Sutton's talents and ambitions. By the time Sutton had finished at Arkansas, the Razorbacks were a national power, and the only school in the Southwest Conference where the basketball coach could hold truck with his football counterpart. Sutton never seemed more the arriviste than when, upon taking the UK job, he declared himself so delighted he would "crawl all the way" to Lexington. It was an ill-chosen phrase that folks in Arkansas came to resent.

But in Kentucky, while the coach is big, the program is bigger. Through Sutton's first two recruiting seasons, even with the threat of NCAA sanctions hidestrapping the Wildcats, Kentucky brought in enormous hauls of talent. Leonard Hamilton, an assistant left over from the Hall regime, assembled the first class, which featured Rex Chapman, an in-state marvel considered to be the best high-schooler in the land. The second recruiting class, featuring Eric Manuel, another consensus Top Five player, was the work of Dwane Casey, who joined the staff when Hamilton left in the spring of 1986 to become head coach at Sutton's alma mater, Oklahoma State.

Casey had never known anything but Kentucky. Born in the western town of Morganfield, he had been a popular reserve guard on the 'Cats' 1978 national championship team. He spent one season, 1980–81, as a graduate assistant on the UK staff before taking a job at Western Kentucky under Clem Haskins. He left coaching briefly in the fall of 1982, to sell ads for a Lexington TV station, before rejoining the Hill- toppers.

Casey had a chance to move with Haskins to Minnesota, but the UK vacancy lured him back to Lexington again. Like Hamilton, he was black and glib, but unlike Leonard, who sometimes got his back up, Casey was unfailingly charming. He could work a set of white parents as easily as black ones, and related to the press as well as he did to any of his fellow coaches. Sutton and his staff would soon be working for a new president, David Roselle, who wanted to see academic values, not athletic interests, set the university's agenda. Casey seemed to fit in perfectly. He had been a good student, and had proven he could make it in the world outside basketball. And he seemed an innocent. "Dwane Casey," a former teammate remembers, "wouldn't have had a girl in his room without leaving the door open." If UNLV's Mark Warkentien knew Casey, he surely wouldn't have likened him to a MIG fighter that day in the Fairfax gym.

2

The Endless Summer

THE CAMPUS of Dominguez High School sits in Southeast Los Angeles, perilously close to the front lines of that city's gang wars. Few respectable organizations have the clout to recruit against the Crips and the Bloods on their own turf. But on this early-summer evening, on an untidy concrete slab ringed by dented garbage cans, Isadore (Issy) Washington has convened a meeting of one that does—the Slam-N-Jam basketball program he cofounded and now directs.

Most of the sixteen backboards in the Dominguez school yard have a forlorn look, their chain nets either gone or hanging limp like Spanish moss. A handful of parents sits on an adjacent stoop as Washington runs practice. These kids are the Slam-N-Jam's pride, the twelve-and-under and thirteen-and-under all-star teams. Like his charges, Washington is wearing a Reebok T-shirt and Reebok shoes. His instruction is pointed, and to such good effect that in the most recent age-group playoffs for Southern California, Issy's kids swept all six divisions.

A whistle stops play. Someone isn't keeping his hands up on defense. As Washington thumbs the youngster off the court, the boy mutters something, but Issy will brook none of it. A trim man pushing fifty, Washington has a voice that crackles. "You can get out of here right now if you want!"

Soon the Twelves will be off to a national tournament in Salt Lake City, and the Thirteens headed for another event, in Indianapolis. Thus Washington's appeal to the parents as the workout winds down and dusk settles over the school yard. Money. Could they come up with some more to help send assistant coaches along?

The parents balk. They want to know why Reebok can't foot that bill.

"All Reebok gives me is a few shoes and some T-shirts and that's it," Washington says, as if by rote.

And another sponsor?

"We're working on that. . . ."

Washington takes the initiative. "What about you?" he asks a father. "All those musicians you know in that record company."

The parents are unmoved. They have already sold raffle tickets, staged bake sales, gone door-to-door. Washington senses defeat.

"Okay," Issy says. A look of resignation begins to work its way across his face. "Papa Washington will dig into his pocket to pay for his coaches."

Through the sixties and into the seventies UCLA controlled Los Angeles. If John Wooden didn't make sure of it by winning eleven NCAA championships over thirteen seasons, then real estate developer Sam Gilbert, the Bruins' spendthrift sugar daddy, did. But today the City of Angels is a city bereft of allegiances. Eight Division I schools dot the L.A. basin, from the University of California's Irvine campus in Orange County, on up to UC–Santa Barbara, a few hours' drive to the north. Every one, even UCLA, counts itself lucky when it can prevail upon a local high-school star to stay home.

Outside influences began to win over schoolboy ball players in Southern California around the time of the Bird-Magic watershed. At the other end of the country, in Bristol, Connecticut, a television entrepreneur named Bill Rasmussen was starting up a twenty-four-hour, all-sports cable network called ESPN. The new network had a voracious appetite for live programming, and college basketball fit that need perfectly. It was cheap to produce. It appealed to upscale viewers. Games fit neatly into two-hour blocks during the winter months, when the largest share of what would become a subscriber base of more than 53 million TV sets was in use. ESPN shrewdly cut deals with all the top hoops conferences and syndicators. To the ACC and SEC, the Big Ten, Big East, and Big 8, the meager rights fees the network paid out didn't much matter; the exposure more than made up for them. The regular time slot the Big Ten and Big East carved out on Monday nights would eventually take its place as a sort of midwinter *Monday Night Football*, with analyst Dick Vitale a love-him-or-hate-him figure analogous to Howard Cosell.

Yet the network's influence didn't fully come clear until the 1985–86 season, when the Big Ten left ESPN for an over-the-air syndicated package concentrated in the Midwest. That season the league's recruiters found they could still get players out of Chicago, which hadn't yet been wired for cable; but when they went into homes elsewhere they were alarmed at what they saw. Their targets, members of the vid-kid generation, knew all sorts of arcana about the Big East and ACC, and that Old Dominion started three freshmen, and that Bradley sent weak side help into the post. But they hadn't seen the Big Ten's best—Iowa at Purdue, or Illinois versus Ohio State, or Indiana-Michigan.

By taking itself off cable, the midwestern land-grant giants had essentially ceded both coasts. A few more years of this and the conference would get clobbered trying to recruit nationally. Big Ten commissioner Wayne Duke re-signed with ESPN for the following season, and ever since, with its fortress mid–prime-time slot on "Big Monday" following the featured Big East game, the league has consolidated its position as one of college basketball's three preeminent conferences.

Out west, leagues like the Pacific-10, the Western Athletic Conference, and the Pacific Coast Athletic Association (now the Big West) were getting their slices of the ESPN pie too—but with one important condition. West Coast cablecasts would come on at 11:30 P.M. in the population centers of the East, when viewers were inclined to choose Carson or bed. Those late games, often played before desultory crowds, weren't likely to hold an audience, particularly an east-of-the-Mississippi high-school ball player on a school night.

Even more ominous, the best schoolboys in the West now had piped into their homes the equivalent of video recruiting brochures for basketball powers back east. An L.A. high-school star would get home from hoops practice around dinnertime, flip on the tube, and see 30,000 orange-clad crazies in Syracuse's Carrier Dome, with Vitale loosing his adenoidal hyperbole in the background. He would see a game between North Carolina and Duke, schools within ten miles of each other, and learn that the students had slept outside the gates of Cameron Indoor Stadium the night before to get in. He didn't have to watch TV to discover that the women nearly outdrew the men at Southern Cal, or that UCLA's season-ticket base was at its lowest ebb since the early days of the Yorty administration. He already knew that.

Wooden had put together his remarkable run at UCLA by hanging on to the best California kids, and inducing the occasional superstar from the East Coast or the Flyover—Lew Alcindor from New York City; Lucius Allen from Kansas City, Kansas; Mike Warren from South Bend, Indiana—to come west. Now the flow was running the other way. It reached its peak in 1986 when, of the best players in L.A., two, Earl Duncan and Stephen Thompson, chose Syracuse; a third, Scott Williams, enrolled at North Carolina; and another, Elden Campbell, picked Clemson. All indicated that TV had played a part in their decision, or that they felt the game in the West was "down." Duncan, who rarely missed an ESPN game, even maintained a library of homemade videocassettes to compare the styles of the schools he was considering. "If a West Coast kid went east, there used to be a fifty-fifty chance you'd get him back as soon as he saw the snow on the ground," said Jerry Tarkanian with a trace of nostalgia. Yet here they were, actually choosing Syracuse winters. Horace Greeley had pulled a 180.

The defection of the best of the Class of '86 was a terrible blow to college basketball in the West, one from which it is just now recovering. But it was an advertisement for the new curators of the L.A. game—Los Angeles's public schools, summer leagues, and street agents. Suddenly sweat-suited recruiters from every corner of the land were touching down at LAX, turning their attention to youngsters as early as age eleven or twelve. The college hoops boom of the eighties may not have touched UCLA or Southern Cal or Long Beach State, but the raw materials fueling it were all over town.

Hundreds of thousands of school-age boys populate the Greater L.A. area, and most of them are bedazzled by basketball, thanks to the success and showmanship of the NBA's Lakers. The high-school season lasts from December through March, and as soon as it ends the summer leagues kick in. For eight months neither the schools nor the NCAA has any jurisdiction as the two primary programs, Washington's Slam-N-Jam and its archrival, Rich Goldberg's American Roundball Corporation (ARC), fight over L.A.'s basketball-playing youth. And into that breach of supervision—a Sargasso Sea of sultry heat and rented gyms and packs of outsized teens in tank tops, sometimes navigating one hundred miles of freeway to play a single game—step the middlemen, the brokers and "uncles" and sundry third parties who inhabit the netherworld of player procurement.

"Summer's the time," says one big-time college coach. "The kids are out of school, free, no constraints, no control. It's like burglars. Burglars know in the summer everybody's on vacation. That's the time to rob the house."

Rich Goldberg and Issy Washington claim lofty motives for founding their respective leagues. Certainly much of the urban self-help and civic utopianism that show up in literature for American Roundball Corporation and the Slam-N-Jam is sincere. Both sponsor tutorials to prep youngsters for their college boards. ARC awards a scholar-athlete jacket to any league player who strings together two semesters with a B average. Slam-N-Jam's parent is an organization called Athletes for Academic Success, and Washington ticks off the national letter of intent signing dates, in April and November, with a glint in his eye. "Those are my birthdays," he says. "That's when I see how many of my kids get scholarships to college."

Washington is a retired Air Force major, a garrulous man who'll deal digits to a stranger. Born in Mississippi and schooled in the Pacific Northwest, he handled the subcontracting for the B-1 bomber before starting Slam-N-Jam in the late seventies. From simple beginnings as a pro bono inner-city youth program run out of Compton High, Slam-N-Jam grew to encompass eighty teams in ten different leagues, from first grade to college, based in neighborhoods up and down the state, from North San Diego County clear on up to the Bay Area. Now as many as forty Slam-N-Jammers get free rides to Division I schools in a typical year. For a flat $120, which he charges all but the needy, Washington provides kids with terrific competition and a pair of Reeboks in which to take it all on. "In the middle of a ghetto, from nine A.M. to seven P.M. on Saturday and Sunday, instead of being in gangs and out on the street selling drugs, they're inside playing basketball, doing something positive," he says. "We have a waiting list of people from Mission Viejo [a ritzy Orange County suburb] wanting to get into beautiful downtown Compton." The irony makes him laugh.

At about the same time Washington was cofounding Slam-N-Jam, ARC took root in the more affluent San Fernando Valley. Rich Goldberg invokes the same reason— the kids—for starting his league. A high-school English teacher with a half interest in a Burbank sporting goods store, Goldberg comes off as more entrepreneur than educator. In his mid-forties, with hair combed strategically over, he likes to boast of his Brooklyn roots. An outer-borough attitude didn't abandon him when he made his way west to go to college. After bouncing around the broadcasting industry for a while, Goldberg coached at Calabasas High School and in recreation programs in L.A. With Nike's help he has nurtured ARC, extending it into Las Vegas, the Bay Area, Seattle, and Indiana, and is making plans to take over another twenty markets. ARC's presence in Southern California alone includes 200 teams in spring and summer programs, from fifth grade through college.

"Summer league" is a misnomer, for neither ARC nor Slam-N-Jam is ever really out of season. Few L.A. school districts can afford to field full-scale junior-high teams, so the younger kids play for Rich or Issy over the winter. Then, in the spring, high-school ball players sign up for "summer" leagues as soon as their regular seasons are over. Come June, the very best muster into all-star teams, which travel the nationwide summer circuit, competing in every corner of the country. The L.A. leagues sponsor important stops on that tour: the Slam-N-Jam National Invitational and the ARC Future Stars Showdown.

Washington himself could tell you that the budget for a summer league—rent the gym, pay the refs, take out the insurance, and buy the uniforms—is fairly modest. Summer basketball is nevertheless big business. The NCAA sanctions nearly 250 such programs nationally. Start with several hundred teams, at ten kids a team, at $65 to $120 a year per kid. Then fold in the stakes of the shoe companies—Nike funds ARC with $125,000 a year; Reebok gives Slam-N-Jam $40,000 in cash and at least as much again in merchandise—and a league can gross hundreds of thousands of dollars.

Yet while Nike and Reebok require an accounting of how their investment is spent, any other income goes unaudited. And there is other income. College coaches say they make donations to summer leagues in the form of shoes or cash for future considerations. Help fund a summer league, says Iowa assistant Rudy Washington, a Los Angeles native who's no relation to Issy Washington, and "you get names, phone numbers, addresses of all the players. And you want players. See, the league director can legitimately make contact with all the kids. He's constantly pumping them. He takes them to college games. He gets with the parents. He says, 'Let me sit in on the home visit, I've got the kid's best interests at heart.' The kid ends up going to the university that funded the league and never even knows it."

At the pinnacle of each league is its summer flagship team. Washington's is L.A. Team Reebok. Goldberg's is the Nike ARC Mid-Valley All-Stars. The league directors act as impresarios, sending them off to AAU tournaments around the country in hopes of spreading the Slam-N-Jam or American Roundball name and, with a respectable showing, adding a little more luster to it. The value of these road victories isn't in generating more hardware for the Washington den or Goldberg rec room. It's in flogging the league to the parties that count—the youth of Los Angeles at the bottom end, and the executives of the sponsoring shoe company at the top end.

As the summer programs rake in more and more money, as they expand their horizons and consolidate their bases of power, Goldberg and Washington have come to detest each other. Only a few years ago they maintained an uneasy peace. Now one will spirit away the other's best players in an instant. Promises of international travel, generous meal money, free shoes and gear are aids in that competition, but kids beget kids too. Better players want to test themselves against the very best. It's a kick just running with a blue-chipper, something to tell your friends. Lure to your league the right youngster, a Chris Mills or a Sean Higgins, and a Pied Piper effect kicks in.

What's known locally as the "Issy-Goldberg feud" has forced the top players in Southern California to choose sides. To switch leagues is to forsake one's past and jeopardize friendships. One day after Chris Mills's sophomore year, shortly after he had jumped from Slam-N-Jam to ARC, Mills was playing pickup ball at Hollywood High when Issy Washington tooled up to the gym. He opened the trunk of his silver Mercedes 450SL to reveal a stash of virgin Reeboks, and proceeded to try to induce Mills into jumping back to Team Reebok. Mills didn't bite.

Nor did Earnest Killum, a talented 6-foot-4-inch senior at Lynwood High, when Goldberg phoned his home, pleading with him to abandon Slam-N-Jam for ARC. "He just kept bugging me," says Killum. "He said, 'Earnest, it's better if you play for us. We go to places all over.' He said I'd get Nike stuff. As a team he was going to take care of us. Keep money in our pocket. I told him I didn't want to do that. It's better to play for Team Reebok. Team Reebok has class."

Goldberg likes to point out how Washington dallied in paying a bill of $18,000 owed UCLA for rent on Pauley Pavilion after a summer tournament there a few years back. When Westwood proved too expensive, Issy moved his week-long Slam-N-Jam Invitational to Long Beach State, a midmajor program that would charge him only $833 a day to rent the gym. For his part, Washington says that the ARC attitude is "win at all costs." Indeed, Goldberg's perennial obsession is to cop that diamond of the summer circuit, the Las Vegas Invitational, the five-day basketball bacchanal that attracts sixty-four of the best high-school all-star teams in the nation.

In 1984 Goldberg flew to Vegas such stars as Tom Hammonds (from Pensacola), Lowell Hamilton (from Chicago), and Mike Jones (from Phenix City, Alabama) to join the ARC Mid-Valley All-Star team that already featured Los Angelenos Sean Higgins and Trevor Wilson. (Goldberg's mercenaries were so tuckered out by the rigors of their visit that the Mid-Valley team flopped badly, and Hamilton was seen dozing off on the bench during a game.) In 1987 he brought in Shawn Kemp from Indiana to join Mills on the Mid-Valley team. (This time the ARC flagship did win the LVI title.) ARC entrants have reached the finals in Vegas seven times in eleven years, although not since tournament director John Farrell, after fielding the complaints of teams furious at Goldberg for loading up, outlawed the use of ringers in 1988.

Both L.A. programs have carried their battle north to the Bay Area, where a realtor named Rick Lynch runs his ten-year-old Nor-Cal Basketball League, well aware of the battles being waged to the south. In 1988 Goldberg offered to turn Nor-Cal into an ARC franchise. He proposed that Lynch charge ARC's standard $65 fee, and forward $55 of it to him. In return, ARC would kick in $2,000 for rent, refs, and administrative expenses, and provide each youngster with a Nike T-shirt and game jersey—both of which Goldberg gets for free. Yet Lynch already had 290 kids in his spring league. For $90, each got a $40 pair of Avia shoes and a jersey. Lynch says, "I told Rich, 'Sixty-five times three hundred is a lot of money.' [It's nearly $20,000.] Why should I give my league to him?" All along, Lynch says, one of ARC's men in the Bay Area has tried to lure away Nor-Cal's best players with the usual inducements—shoes, sweats, and meal money on trips.

Nonetheless, says Lynch, "Issy might be worse than Goldberg." Lynch says that Washington set up Nor-Cal's deal with Avia, which Reebok owns. As part of that agreement, Lynch says he ultimately discovered, Washington had received $11,500 from Avia that was earmarked to cover Nor-Cal's promotional and operating costs in 1988 and 1989. "He kept about $3,000 of the money," says Lynch. "When I confronted Issy about it, he said, 'Yeah, well, I set up the deal.' I told him that's a pretty steep finder's fee."

Washington says he gave Lynch all but a contingency of $2,900, which he kept for travel and "cash flow" problems. Avia executive Barry Davis, who arranged the Nor-Cal sponsorship deal with Washington, calls the dispute "a touchy subject," adding "whatever happened is between Issy and Rick."

It's hardly necessary to bring in an outsider to bad-mouth the L.A. summer-league directors, for Washington and Goldberg cut each other up quite well enough on their own. Washington, says Goldberg, is an opportunist, in it primarily for the money. Goldberg, says Washington, is an elitist, in it primarily for the ego rub. Partisans of both leagues charge the other with dangerously raising the expectations of young stars by comping them with shoes, gear, and travel. The summer leagues, California assistant coach Gary Colson says, stake out their turf "just like gangs. It's like in the movie *Colors*, only without the violence."

Not yet, anyway. "I get Issy and Rich together to fight," says UCLA coach Jim Harrick, shaking his head in wonder, "and I could make out like Don King."

The ARC Future Stars Showdown is nearing its climax on a hazy afternoon in the gym at Cal State–Northridge. A cacophony of sneaker squeaks, whistles, and irregular thumps is white noise behind the East Coast inflections of Rich Goldberg's voice. "Look at Issy," he says. "He charges one hundred and twenty dollars, and tells kids who can't afford it, 'Give me forty or fifty dollars and I'll give you a pair of shoes.' Well, he gets the shoes for free. I've talked to some pretty reliable people, and doing some figuring, he must make around a hundred and fifty thousand a year."

Goldberg says that college coaches who came by Washington's summer all-star tournament in Pauley a few years ago grumbled about parking and admission fees. Nike basketball promotions man Sonny Vaccaro heard the complaints, and promised Goldberg funding if ARC were to set up its own week-long showcase. "The first year we got all the better players and Issy got very upset," Goldberg says. "But I had to do it. Because he was charging too much money and not giving the kids enough in return.

"The difference between us is, basically, I'm a straight-forward, direct New Yorker. I don't have ego problems. I think he's got a little bit of an ego, and sometimes it gets the best of him."

An hour's drive away, night has fallen. Issy Washington is on his turf, on Compton's mean streets, in his parked Mercedes—a 1977 model he's quick to point out has 200,000 miles on it. Washington will in one breath downplay the money at issue in the summer-league business, calling it "fool's gold," and insisting he's taking such a financial beating that he'll soon give it all up; in the next breath he'll talk about starting a national summer tournament to rival the Las Vegas Invitational. "All these other leagues want to knock me off, but they can't," he says. "I'm black. I can relate to the kids. The others, they're afraid to operate here."

It's not in him to refer to Goldberg by name. Washington dances around his rival with pronouns, descriptive phrases, and arch looks. "Every year he comes out with a trick. A trick a year. The trick one year"—the year ARC lured Chris Mills away from Slam-N-Jam—"was he was going to send them to Europe. I told the kids, 'Look, if there were recruiters in Europe in August, I'd go too. But since there aren't, Issy's staying right here in beautiful downtown Compton.' The kids went to him anyway, but they never did go to Europe. This year he tells the kids, 'If you don't play in my league, you can't go to Vegas.' [Nike sponsors the Las Vegas Invitational, and in 1989 Farrell, the tournament director, tried unsuccessfully to turn the LVI into a "closed shop" for Nike-sponsored summer teams only.] Well, we're going to Vegas.

"Even with all that money he spent, I whipped his ass twice. In the national tournament in Vegas, and over here. He sat out in the car for two hours after we won. He couldn't figure out *what* was going on. If he got someone who could coach, they'd probably kick my ass. But I don't care if he's got Kareem. If he's coaching, I'm in the ball game."

Washington lets out a satisfied laugh. "You start paying thirteen-year-old kids, that's why you have problems like the Mills situation," he says.

Paying thirteen-year-old kids?

"Yeah. I know one kid."

Paid?

"Fifteen thousand."

Come on.

"One kid. Fifteen thousand."

Bullshit.

"My archrival. Supposed to be a loan to the kid's old man, so the family can move from where they live now, in Santa Ana, to the Valley. Then the kid ends up playing for him all year.

"I'm going to let you talk to Bob Gottlieb about it. If I say something, it sounds like sour grapes. But one kid—thirteen-year-old Samoan, about six-two, hell of a player—got fifteen big ones. I believe Bob. He was hurt. Because it hurt his team."

Bob Gottlieb is one of those people the game lets go of but who can never quite let go of the game. For six seasons he was a head coach at Jacksonville and Wisconsin–Milwaukee, and did a tour as an assistant at Creighton under Eddie Sutton. When the college game passed him by, he settled in Orange County, contenting himself with coaching his two sons, Gregg and Doug, in an age-group hoops program. But the coach's instinct still lingered in him, and when he first saw the youngster on Doug's twelve-and-under team, it was as if he were back in the big time, viewing a blue-chip prospect.

Lorenzo LeuLuai (it's pronounced LEE-oo-eye) was indeed six feet two and 180 pounds, with strong hands and passing and shooting skills well beyond his age. Many people considered him the best twelve-year-old in the state. He's the eldest of six children of David LeuLuai, a poor and devout Mormon of Samoan descent.

Lorenzo spent 1988 playing for Gottlieb in a variety of tournaments, including the Slam-N-Jam Invitational. But in September, David told Gottlieb that Lorenzo was thinking of playing for an ARC age-group team—this despite the long drive from Santa Ana to Hollywood High, where the team would practice. Then he mentioned the possibility of buying a house up that way—in Inglewood, perhaps. "It seemed like every week it was a different story," Gottlieb says. "So I got fed up one time and said, 'Why not be honest with me?'"

At that, Gottlieb says, David LeuLuai opened up. He told him that Rich Goldberg had come by his house earlier that fall. Goldberg told him how much he liked Lorenzo and the family, how he knew they were poor. He wanted to help them put a down payment on a new house, help them buy a new car. He offered David $15,000.

Lorenzo did indeed join the Mid-Valley All-Stars full-time in September, and played in ARC's fall and winter leagues with some of L.A.'s finest junior-high-schoolers. Goldberg offered to fly Lorenzo to Las Vegas to watch the older kids play in their big summer tournament. He took him to a UCLA–Notre Dame game at Pauley, trundling him into the locker room afterward to meet the Bruins' Trevor Wilson, Darrick Martin, and Don MacLean. "Stay with this man," UCLA's Harrick told Lorenzo, gesturing at Goldberg. "He'll help you a lot."

Gottlieb, however, didn't despair of somehow getting LeuLuai back. He ran into Lorenzo and his father in January, during halftime at Gregg Gottlieb's high-school game. "I had almost begun thinking there was no way Goldberg gave them fifteen thousand dollars," Gottlieb says. "One of the first things I said to the father was, 'I bet you never got that fifteen thousand.' He replied, 'I got five already.'

"I'd asked the father whether he thought he'd have been offered that money if his son wasn't a basketball player. And he said, 'Yes. It's a miracle. Goldberg giving us this has nothing to do with my son being a player. It's because he wants to help me, because I'm a poor man. What's wrong with that?'"

Bob Gottlieb is hardly a disinterested party. He had Lorenzo and, to his disappointment, lost him. But, he says, "This is exactly what the father told me. This whole experience has soured me on youth basketball. Goldberg has taken the evils of college recruiting and brought them down to the level of twelve-year-old boys."

Nine people—David, his wife, their six children, and David's mother—are shoehorned into the LeuLuais' two-bedroom, single-story home in Santa Ana. The porch sags. The front door is missing a handle. The living room is tidy but spare. The only bright fixtures on the property are Lorenzo's basketball trophies, and the brand new Dodge Caravan in the driveway. In spring 1989, after Lorenzo began playing for ARC, David took about $5,000 out of his savings plan at work to buy it.

David is a broad-shouldered and warm man who speaks English with more confidence than nuance. But as a doting parent he has picked up a sophisticated knowledge of where his boy fits in the hoops pecking order. He understands fully why high-school coaches have been calling his home. What's more, he knows that people would render harsh judgments upon hearing that five figures were exchanged over a seventh-grader. "I don't want anybody to offer money for my son, even though I'm poor," he says. "If they give me something for my boy, I tell them I will slap your face. I don't want to receive a penny. It's only seventh grade, you know what I'm saying. It's only seventh grade . . . it's so young."

David LeuLuai says that Gottlieb, when it became apparent he was going to lose Lorenzo, suggested he could find a way to help out the family. "We talk about maybe I find that Hilton man."

Was he talking about Stan Castleton, a basketball fan who owns the Anaheim Hilton?

"That's the one. I tell Gottlieb I know lot of people who have more money than [Castleton].

"[Gottlieb] thinks [Goldberg] offers me money because

Lorenzo is a good player. Sometimes someone might offer me money because when he comes to look at my house, I have six kids and I am very poor.

"If they give me like five thousand dollars, you know, it's like, you give me this money for what reason? If they offer [it so] Lorenzo [will] play over there, not for that. But if they give me presents because I am poor, I will take it. You know what I mean. As a gift from somebody else. If it's Nike's money or from his pocket, I will take it as a gift for my family, because he came inside my house. He looked around. He looked at the outside. 'There is poor.' But I don't care how poor I am. One day the Lord will bless me."

Did He bless you through Rich Goldberg?

"No, this is just an example, like I said. But if someone says to me, 'David, not for Lorenzo, but for your family, it's a token for you to buy something for your family,' I will take it.

"Just like you—you're in my house, you feel the spirit. I will take the money from you today."

Rich Goldberg says he didn't give the LeuLuais a thing. "I heard that rumor," he says. "I laugh it off, it's so absurd. Unscrupulous people will say anything. Where am I supposed to get that kind of money? I take money out of my own pocket for ARC to keep it going, to help these kids make these trips. Anything more, I couldn't do that. Issy could. I couldn't."

Forget for a moment the question of whether Goldberg gave the LeuLuai family any money. Why would it be worth anyone's while to offer $15,000 for a seventh-grader?

Lorenzo LeuLuai would assure a league's credibility in an entire class, citywide, over a half-dozen years. If LeuLuai's presence were to attract an average of just twenty additional players a year before he goes off to college, the investment would pay off. And if a college recruiter, eager to gain access to a LeuLuai, were to find it worthwhile to contribute to ARC or Slam-N-Jam, the investment would be all the more shrewd.

Goldberg says Nike budgets about $10,000 as a stipend for his time and trouble in administering its summer leagues, and he thinks he's grossly shortchanged. "Last year that ten thousand went to pay the bills we incurred sending these kids on trips," he says. "I didn't make a penny. [According to public records, ARC, a nonprofit corporation, had a surplus of $19,000 in 1987.] I don't get shoes. I don't get cash. I don't have it. I'm a teacher. The money we make goes to help these kids take those trips. If we don't have enough, I generally wind up taking money out of my own pocket—to my wife's chagrin, because we have two kids of our own.

"Look at the car I'm driving. [Goldberg drives a 1984 Buick LeSabre.] Look at the car my wife is driving. [Rhonda Goldberg drives a 1979 LeSabre.] We're having trouble making our house payments." [In 1987 the Goldbergs bought a $268,000 home in Van Nuys. He says years of frugality allowed him to make a $67,000 down payment, even though recent California public records don't show him to have had any previous home equity. A year later he and Joseph Dunn, a high-school coach in Burbank, each sank $30,000 into opening Mid-Valley Sporting Goods. "He had his (money) and I had mine," says Dunn. "Mine was my life savings. . . . How he got his, I don't know."]

"All these people are jealous because I maintain honesty around the program," Goldberg says. "We've had kids stolen away from us because they're given more. Slam-N-Jam is giving them shoes, warmups, giving them this and that. That's the wrong values. I don't want to perpetuate those values to kids."

Yet ARC's all-star trips are all-expenses-paid. During the 1987 Future Stars Showdown, Goldberg lodged the ringers on his famous "M&M" team—the one featuring Chris Mills and UCLA's Martin—at the Westwood Holiday Inn, a place so high rent that Lute Olson refuses to stay there when his Arizona Wildcats come to town. And stories circulate around town of Goldberg offering inducements to other youth-league stars to join ARC.

Even for junior-high kids, summer basketball in L.A.— whether with Slam-N-Jam or ARC, whether based in beautiful downtown Compton or the serene San Fernando Valley—is a gravy train, a dizzying few months of trips and tournaments. "By the time he gets to high school," says Bill Foster, who left his coaching position at Miami in March of 1990, "a good player has been to Vegas, Hawaii, traveled the U.S. and stayed in nice hotels, just like NBA guys. What else is there to look forward to?"

Terry (Fat Chance) Kirkpatrick grew up in L.A. during the Wooden years. In accordance with the rites of passage of that era, he sneaked into Pauley Pavilion to watch UCLA practice. Sneaking in must have been no mean feat, from the look of him today: Kirkpatrick weighs upwards of 250 pounds. Yet he picked up his nickname not for his girth, but for a knack for signing recruits his rivals gave him a "fat chance" of ever landing. As an assistant at Houston, Kirkpatrick recruited the Phi Slama Jama teams that made three straight trips to the Final Four during the early eighties.

In his day, when he sat the Cougars' bench next to head coach Guy Lewis, he cut a Falstaffian figure that players sometimes snickered at. The school let him go for undisclosed reasons in 1984, and Kirkpatrick has been out of the procurement game ever since. But no one worked the streets, particularly the mean ones of L.A., the way Fat Chance did. And he didn't like what he saw. "When I was at Houston, guys in L.A. would come up to me and say, 'Either you donate to my summer league or you're on my shit list,' " he says. "It may be a hundred and fifty or two hundred dollars just not to be on the shit list. I was approached for five hundred a couple of times. Other universities helped out with uniforms or shoes. I went back and told Guy who was involved. We weren't doing it. But if you don't play with the power brokers, they try and label you. That's what they tried to do with me. I laughed because they couldn't destroy my power base. I grew up in Los Angeles."

Today, most recruiters can't afford to be so defiant. The summer leagues form their alliances, and colleges must do a certain amount of kowtowing if they expect to compete. As much influence as ESPN has had in that eastward flow, the decline of the West is also attributable to the ascendancy of third parties. "Power brokers are pushing kids east," Kirkpatrick says. "It's like a shark to a wounded animal. They smell blood. There's no reason UCLA should go into a ten-year drought in recruiting. Kids like Scott Williams and Stevie Thompson don't have any business leaving L.A.

"What kids in L.A. have to learn is it's not their power broker who brings recruiters to town. It's their game, their test scores, their being a good person. You mean to tell me we wouldn't have known about Sean Higgins if he hadn't played in a summer league? Hell, he could have played in a church league and we would have found out about him. The summer leagues are good, but the trouble is after you leave the floor and before you get on."

Kirkpatrick uses the term "power brokers," but that's too grandiose a label for many of the characters who frequent the city's parks and gyms. Some slink through doorways, or peer through the chain-link fence. Others sit silently in the gym, scoping out the scene. Most come without portfolio. Some don't even bother to introduce themselves. "They'd just shake your hand after a game," says Iowa guard James Moses, who got his first pair of free shoes as a sixth-grader, from Rich Goldberg. "Then they'd talk about the benefits

I'd receive. If you go here, you'll benefit off this, a car—anything to blow your mind."

The street agents hone their negotiating skills around the summer leagues. If a league really wants a kid, it may go through someone it has deputized into its cause. The middleman is staked to a stash of, say, twenty pairs of shoes, gratis. Top-of-the-line sneakers run upwards of $100 a pair, and a typical city kid will go through five or six in a year. If a member of the "community" is keeping him in shoes at deep discounts, a youngster is going to listen to a sales pitch for the summer league wearing that brand.

Once the summer league gets the kid, the broker gets something too—his hooks into a prospect who'll have colleges pursuing him a few years down the road. Eventually the street agent transfers the youngster's allegiance from summer league to school. It happens almost seamlessly, and the one factor common to both is usually the sponsoring shoe. Nike summer-league kids virtually always go to Nike schools. Reebok summer-league kids are more likely to go elsewhere. "The brokers are like leeches," Kirkpatrick says. "They see he needs shoes, but they say, 'I want you to talk to this guy [from a certain school].' They're just high-class pimps. Kids growing up here have three pairs of socks to their name, and now all of a sudden they're getting shoes. If you have a choice between your old Chuck Taylors and new Air Jordans, which would you take?"

The scouting of high-school ball players used to have about it the majesty of a state visit. A college coach would sneak out of practice on a Friday afternoon, park at a snowy airstrip on the edge of town, and hop a private plane on loan from some booster. He would touch down a few hours later and, just before tipoff, make a grand entrance into a little gym. A frisson of recognition would ripple through the crowd. Locals would throw nervous side glances the coach's way after the hometown hero's every move, in hopes of gauging—from the visitor's body language, perhaps, or the times he would make notes on the back of his program—how their boy was doing.

The process couldn't be more different today. Recruiting is now a summer activity. Only a smattering of fans and family members watch as teenagers play themselves into or out of scholarships; the other faces are those of coaches from virtually every school in America. AAU jamborees like the Las Vegas Invitational are part of this summertime road show. So are the competition summer camps, from Nike's academics-and-basketball convocation at Princeton, to the hoops-only gatherings like Howard Garfinkel's Five-Star and Bill Cronauer's B/C All-Stars. "All these camps are just the preview for the auction," says one college coach. "They strut the horses out, and everybody looks at the teeth and the hooves, checks the heartbeat and the bloodlines. Then they go back and figure out what it's going to cost."

Nothing has been more responsible for this revolution in the process of evaluating and wooing players than the November early-signing period. Ironically enough, when the Collegiate Commissioners Association introduced the rule in 1982, it hoped to add a measure of sanity to recruiting. The longer the process lasted, the reasoning went, the more likely improprieties would creep in. By cutting the process short, you relieve the pressure. If a youngster knows where he wants to go to school, now he can say so in the fall and be left to spend his senior year in peace.

It hasn't quite turned out that way. Recruiters are indeed laying off the senior early signee, but instead they turn their attention to youngsters when they're juniors and younger, bringing to bear all the head-inflating flatteries that much earlier. The November signing date's corollary is a six-week "dead" period in January and February, when coaches are forbidden to watch high-schoolers play. That means most evaluations of seniors-to-be must be made in the summer, primarily during an intense three-week period in July. Youngsters know this. For a typical teenager hoping to play college ball, his choice of summer league, AAU team, or showcase camp is much more important than anything he'll do in high school. He must figure out how best to sell himself, how to spend those twenty-one crucial days. Should he go to Five-Star? Or enter an AAU tournament and run the risk of his team bombing out? Whatever his answers, the youngster is already thinking of himself as a commodity. His summer coach may be a notorious street hustler, and his high-school coach a certified educator. But it's the summertime guy who's on the scene—feeding him, driving him, lodging him, advising him, and stroking him—when a kid's future is on the line.

Ernie Carr taught psychology and anthropology and coached at Dominguez High for a dozen years until 1989, when he left to become an assistant at UC-Irvine. He trolls the summer circuit now with an acute ambivalence. For those three weeks he has his clipboard out and pen ready, doing his job. But he was once a high-school coach, and knows well the process of alienation that's taking place while school's out. "I hated to have my kids play with somebody else during the summer. He comes back to you in the fall and thinks he's more important than the team. Thinks he's more glamorous. Thinks going to Vegas is more important than winning the league championship. He sure isn't thinking about running a mile in six minutes on the first day of practice.

"There's a kid from Crenshaw High named Danny Griffin. He played jayvee ball there as a tenth-grader and was ineligible almost his entire junior year. His senior year he was seventh man. But he played well for a summer team at a tournament in Kentucky before his senior season, and Pittsburgh gave him a full scholarship. And he's never started a high-school game. He has no background. No structure. [Like all five of the Panthers' freshman class of '93, Griffin didn't meet Proposition 48 requirements; he spent the 1989–90 season at Antelope Valley Junior College.] This can do that, make kids demigods before they prove they can be good high-school players."

Carr also knows how tenuous are the loyalties that keep the Los Angeles high-school athlete true to his school. He has seen them crumble, seen athlete after athlete, including some of his own, leave one of the city's forty-nine secondary schools and resurface at another. Why, Verbum Dei's 1985–86 team was a splendid group, ranked among the nation's best by *USA Today*. But it crumbled a year later when each of its stars transferred to other schools.

In theory, you're required to live in a district to attend its high school, and there's a rule barring "undue influence"— read, recruiting—to get a youngster to switch. But in practice the residency requirement isn't rigorously policed, and recruiting goes on all the time. In the inner city, where families are more inclined to rent than own, jumping teams is as easy as getting out of one lease and signing another. All of this somehow befits Los Angeles, the citadel of the mobile society. Everyone comes from somewhere else, so there's little trauma in uprooting.

Can an L.A. kid be bought for as little as bus fare? "Parents think corruption is the norm," says former L.A. summer-league coach David Benezra, now an assistant coach at Northern Arizona. "When a school tells them no, they actually get insulted. People out here don't believe that schools don't cheat."

Adds a college coach, "Isn't it amazing that all the big names in Southern California in the past few years have been involved in recruiting controversies?"

He means that question rhetorically, because he knows it's not. It's not amazing at all.

* * *

Virtually every year since 1984, at least one Los Angeles high-school star has gone off to college leaving behind a curious storyline, a motley cast of hangers-on and the footprints of NCAA gumshoes. Yet until the Bills 'n' Mills affair, not one of these young men had been sanctioned for anything surrounding his recruitment. Each tale has its own bizarre plot twists, intrigue, and characters. The same elements recur: at least one third party—someone other than the youngster's natural parents or high-school coach —hovered around the blue-chip star. The suitor colleges all came from among the usual suspects, a group that would be well represented if David Berst ever called for a police lineup down at the NCAA precinct house.

The case of John Williams remains the L.A. standard. When he came out of Crenshaw High in 1984, Williams already showed signs of becoming what he is today, a starter with the NBA's Washington Bullets. A 6-foot-8-inch positionless monster, a player with both power and finesse, Williams was the first L.A. high-school star with a style clearly influenced by the Lakers' Magic Johnson. He announced his decision to attend Louisiana State in April, at a three-minute-long press conference in the Crenshaw gym, or, rather, his spokesman announced it—this spokesman being a corpulent, fiftyish Caucasian in dark sunglasses and a white Panama hat who had once made his living selling, among other things, decorative walrus penises.

The man said his name was Stan Ross. It turned out his name was Stan Rothe, but he did go by Stan Ross, as well as by Stan Vukovich, Steve Best, Steve Boston, Jack Ross, and "Stan the Man," or so show law-enforcement records, which also indicate that Rothe spent twenty-two months in prison during the early sixties for receiving stolen property. He was released early, but in 1968 returned to prison for another twenty-five months for parole violations.

It turned out that Rothe was a mutual acquaintance of LSU coach Dale Brown, who's known as a sort of connoisseur of eccentrics, and Mable Marie Mathews, Williams's mother. Brown had met Rothe at a Wayne Newton show in Las Vegas. Mathews knew him from L.A. area racetracks, of which she and he were habitués. Soon after Brown learned of the connection, Rothe and young John began making regular trips to the track together.

Rothe wasn't the only remora attaching himself to Williams. There was Kenneth Miller, then a young sportswriter for *The Sentinel*, a newspaper serving L.A.'s black community. Through his work covering prep sports he grew close to Williams and his mother, who soon trusted him enough to have him screen calls at their home. Miller admits he solicited considerations from schools in return for steering Williams their way. He says Tarkanian offered to make him "the main man of Vegas" if Williams signed there, and that a UCLA booster promised him a car and cash—toward the college degree Miller, now an office clerk for a Century City securities firm, still doesn't have—if Williams matriculated at Westwood. Before Mathews joined her son in Baton Rouge, Miller says, "She told me, 'John and I are going to be taken care of. If you want to come, you'll be taken care of.'"

Miller was fired by *The Sentinel* over his role in the affair, and gets choked up with regret for having tried to broker Williams, for he feels it ruined his life. Yet, he says, "You look at South Central Los Angeles—all the poverty—and we've always pounced on any opportunity we could."

Barry Easton's motives for sidling up to Williams were different. A white kid in his early twenties, he had been a star high-school baseball player and would soon become president of the San Diego Friars, a World Team Tennis franchise his family co-owned. Williams was still at Crenshaw when Easton befriended him, taking him around town, to Lakers games and the regular spots on the West L.A. party circuit. Easton has told *Sports Illustrated*'s Bill Brubaker he hoped someday to be Williams's agent, and has said he gave John a used Toyota because "someone in the news shouldn't be riding a bus." Williams in turn would ultimately bring Easton east to Baton Rouge, where he was so ubiquitous—he sat beside Williams in class and slept in his dorm room—that LSU players began calling him the White Slave. Within a couple of months Brown, believing that Easton was trying either to persuade Williams to turn pro or transfer to UCLA, would ask him to leave.

And there was Don Fields, father of former UCLA star Kenny Fields. He sat in on a meeting between Williams's mother and a representative of UNLV, who says Fields laid out stark terms: $50,000 in cash, a new Datsun 280ZX Turbo, a $600-a-month allowance, a no-show summer job, and spending money for the senior prom if John were to choose the Runnin' Rebels. "The allowance will have to be paid with dignity," Fields said. "When Kenneth was at UCLA, when he went to get his, he always had to go over to some booster's house, sit around, have a Coke or a sandwich and talk with the guys, like he was a little lap dog begging for his food. So with John . . . I just want him to come and see you and you hand him an envelope."

The man from Vegas staggered out of the meeting. He said his school didn't do such things, but promised to relay the particulars to his school anyway. But just as he was getting into his car, Fields called back to him.

"Listen," he said. "You know, the fifty thousand dollars is so she can buy a house to get out of this one. Fifty doesn't really do any good anymore. We need about sixty-five."

Fields won't comment on the exchange today, saying, "I don't want to make a lot of trouble for people." Mathews won't discuss any aspect of her son's recruitment.

UNLV would drop out of the chase at this point. If he had signed Williams, Tarkanian says, NCAA investigators "wouldn't have waited for the plane to land—they'd have come down in parachutes."

Louisville coach Denny Crum had an appointment with Mrs. Mathews and her son just before the signing date, but was stood up. He went home. All Crum will say for the record today is: "I was surprised, real surprised, he signed with LSU. He told us he was coming to Louisville."

UCLA, with Walt Hazzard having just succeeded Larry Farmer as coach, was playing catchup and never really got in the running. "John made some comment that if we had gotten to UCLA two weeks earlier, he'd have signed with us despite all the suitcases," says a former Bruins assistant coach. "That one was beyond anyone's belief. That's why Farmer quit. He had a three-year contract and just said, 'Fuck it, I can't win.'"

As for Houston, Terry Kirkpatrick, the redoubtable Fat Chance, says he told Williams, "You don't want to sell yourself. We spent five hundred years as a people trying to get ourselves to the point where you can do things off respect. . . . Don't cheat yourself, because if you can be bought, you can be sold." (This is exactly what Kirkpatrick said he told former Villanova star Ed Pinckney after Pinckney, in 1981, said Fat Chance had offered him a Datsun 280Z, a charge Kirkpatrick denies.)

And then there was LSU. Brown claims he landed Williams partly because the Bayou Bengals refused to get involved in a bidding war, and Mrs. Mathews found that so refreshing. Why, when he heard stories of what Williams was being offered, Brown even discussed with LSU chancellor James Wharton and athletic director Bob Brodhead plans for a dramatic charade: He would pack a suitcase with $150,000 and place it in front of Williams and his mother. Then he would lay a dollar bill on top. "There," he would say. "That makes me the highest bidder. The meat truck will be outside to pick you up in an hour, John."

Wharton and Brodhead talked Brown out of the plan, believing it would be too easy to misinterpret. If indeed no cash was involved, a combination of Brown's iconoclastic manner, a rapport that developed between Williams's mother and Brown's assistant, Ron Abernathy, and the remarkable coincidence of Mr. Brown's and Mrs. Mathews's common friend, Stan Ross/Rothe, conspired to send John to Baton Rouge. Says Miller, "Everyone else fell by the wayside when Mable began making decisions for her son. Had it not been for Mable, someone else would have wound up getting a piece of the pie off John, because John Williams, as much as I love him and respect him, is not your Phi Beta Kappa kid. He's a good kid, but he never really made a decision for himself."

For twelve days after signing the letter of intent, Mrs. Mathews kept news of her son's college choice secret. At one point, Miller says, she told him, "Kenny, they're thinking of putting you and Barry Easton in the trunk of a car. Don't worry about it, Kenny. Just get in my car and I'll protect you." Miller doesn't know whom she meant by "they," but John's mother spoke vaguely to others of threats directed at her family by parties representing the losers in the derby. Her remarks hardly endeared her to the runners-up. Brown, however, stood by her. "They said Mrs. Mathews had smoke coming out of her ears, fire coming out of her nostrils," Brown said. "Well, she didn't have a For Sale sign around her son's neck."

Several years later, long after John had left LSU early to turn pro, the phone rang one day in Jerry Tarkanian's office. It was Mable Mathews on the line, calling from the Barbary Coast down the Strip. She wondered if Tark could lend her some money.

"I'm sorry, but I really can't do that," Tarkanian said. "But, say . . . why don't you call Dale Brown?"

It has never been proved that John Williams or his mother ever took anything improper from anyone—even a white-hatted ex-con—representing LSU. Yet Williams is still known around the Southeastern Conference as the Louisiana Purchase. His bizarre recruitment ushered in L.A.'s big-bucks era, and raised expectations all around the city.

* * *

One day in 1982, for reasons that have never been fully explained, Tom Lewis left forever the home of his mother and stepfather in San Juan Capistrano. Lewis, then a freshman at Capistrano Valley High, made his way to Garden Grove and moved in with the Capo Valley sophomore basketball coach, a man named Pat Barrett.

Lewis was a blossoming star. Barrett had come to know him a couple of years earlier, soon after Tom and his divorced mother, Judy, came west to Orange County from Boston. Lewis was 6 foot 3 and barely 150 pounds, a gangly and unpolished package of basketball energy, when Barrett first saw him in a summer-league game. Barrett, then twenty-seven, was burly and blond, with a nervous tic and a junk-food habit. He had played briefly at San Jose State and fancied himself a coach. He took Lewis on as his project, opening the Capo Valley gym on weekends to engage his young find in instructional games of one-on-one.

The two needed each other. Lewis was snorkeling academically and desperately searching for a father figure. Barrett had a varsity letter but no degree, and just as sorely needed a vocation. Soon there developed between them what Stan Morrison, the coach at Southern Cal who eventually signed Lewis, calls "a Pygmalion situation."

"Tommy's parents didn't care if he lived, died, or swam," says Barrett. "They never called, never offered money to help." After Lewis's freshman season, when Barrett became an assistant at Mater Dei High, Lewis followed him there.

Tom, soon to be a wiry and strong 6 foot 7, was now a real prospect. In his senior season he would average thirty-two points a game for the Monarchs, who went 29–0. Barrett handled everything. He fielded recruiters' inquiries. When the college boosters came calling, boasting of their wealth and leaving the impression, as Barrett says, "that it was going to be a bed of roses," Lewis's surrogate father was at the door like a maître d', taking names.

"Wherever Tom was going, I was going to watch him in school," says Barrett. "He didn't want to go by himself. He needed a support system. Tom had a lot of family problems. I was going to go where he was, to be supportive, like a dad. Obviously, it didn't take a rocket scientist to figure out that wherever Tom was going, I wasn't going to go and apply for a four-seventy-five-an-hour job."

Each school laid out what it could offer Lewis. One described a total package well into the six figures, Barrett says—covering clothes, car, insurance, phone, rent, and spending money. Then the school made a separate offer to Barrett. "I told Tom what every situation was, and what my job offer was," says Barrett. "It was his decision. [Lewis agrees that he, not Barrett, chose Southern Cal.] But I wasn't going to go someplace with a lot of uncertainties, where you had to read between the lines. They had to be specific. 'Pat, you'll work at so-and-so and make so many dollars.' *Boom, boom, boom.* Then I was comfortable. I didn't want to go somewhere and struggle. If I had to come home, Tom would have had problems."

Lewis liked Syracuse, but while the Orangemen were prepared to house Tom, his girlfriend, and their infant daughter, they weren't specific enough—for Barrett's taste, anyway—about how Tom's "support system" would be provided for. "Pat wanted a job, but he didn't want to show up," recalls Syracuse coach Jim Boeheim. "He wanted to travel with the team and go to practice. I told him we couldn't do that, not in Syracuse. Believe me, if we had, the whole town would have known about it. The town wouldn't have stood for it and the kids wouldn't have stood for it. Pat just looked over at Tom and raised his eyebrow. Right then and there I knew it was over."

Barrett liked Arizona State, particularly a Scottsdale businessman and real estate magnate named Jim Hamel. "He was the only person of all the boosters who really liked

Tommy," says Barrett. "Everyone else looked at him like, 'How many points is he going to score,' like he was a piece of meat."

One college coach says Barrett asked for a car, an apartment, and a no-show job. That coach says he told him, "Get in line, buddy. Because if that shit's handed out, I'm going to be *first*."

Says Tarkanian, "Pat Barrett is the biggest whore I ever met. We pulled out because of him. Tom had narrowed his choices to us and Syracuse. As far as Pat was concerned, I told him he could come in as a manager on scholarship and sit in on all the practices if he really wanted to get into coaching like he said. But to tell you the truth, I'm glad we lost Tommy. I didn't want a son of a bitch like Pat Barrett around here for four years.

"Pat was telling people he was going to make so much money off Tommy he was going to have to build a safe in his garage. That he was going to dig a hole in his garage floor, build a safe, then pull his car over it to protect his money. Stan Morrison is a good guy, an honorable guy, but USC bought Tom Lewis. I remember Pat watching [a USC] practice once. Pat kept [second-guessing] Stan. Cutting Stan down before they even played a game.

"I got a phone call at seven A.M. [on the signing date] and Warkentien told me, 'Coach, you'll never believe this, but Tommy's going to USC.' USC! They weren't even entered in the race. It was a two-horse race and they weren't even entered."

Just before signing day, Tarkanian said Lewis would go to UNLV "unless something bizarre happens." And if not UNLV, the grapevine had it, then surely he would choose Syracuse, Kentucky, or Arizona State.

"I knew better," says Morrison. The Southern Cal coach had flown to Dallas for the McDonald's High-School All-America Game. Though the game was sold out, Morrison scalped a nosebleed seat, then used his size and dress suit to con his way down to the floor. "I see a seat at the end of press row, right near the bench, walk in, and sit down like I belong there. Tommy sits at the end of the bench, right next to my seat. I couldn't have planned it any better. He sees me and does a double-take.

"He smiled. That's all. He just smiled. Sitting on the plane back to L.A., I had this shit-eating grin on my face. Hell, I could have flown back to L.A. without the plane. Two days later he called and said he wanted to be a Trojan. I asked him why, and he said, 'You didn't give up.'"

Morrison, now coach at San Jose State, says Southern Cal did nothing improper to sign Lewis. But Barrett did indeed become a ubiquitous presence in the L.A. Sports Arena, attending Trojan practices and making road trips.

Barrett denies he ever made any remark about building a safe in his garage, but admits he thought about putting his ward on the block. "For a while, yeah, I was twenty-seven, twenty-eight years old and everyone was so interested in doing things for me to get the kid," he says. "Hell, it was going to be easy. A college goes, 'We want the kid to come here, what do we have to do?' It's a broad question and the mind wanders. It could mean anything.

"USC was the compromise choice. We decided on the last day. Morrison did a great job. All the support systems were there."

Lewis liked the booster network, the opportunities for summer jobs, and the contacts he would presumably make in Southern California, where he hoped to spend the rest of his life. And the most crucial support system of all, Barrett, liked being part of the picture.

At Southern Cal, Lewis led the nation's freshmen in scoring. But he never got accustomed to the losing, and Morrison was fired after a season of turmoil. Then Lewis joined two freshman teammates, Bo Kimble and Hank Gathers, in asking the USC athletic department for a voice in hiring Morrison's replacement. They didn't get it, and

Southern Cal's new coach, George Raveling, gave each a month to decide whether he wanted to stay. All three announced they would transfer.

To outsiders, it was a baffling chain of events. Why would three starters leave all of a sudden, just because of the arrival of a new coach? Why would the new coach essentially read them an ultimatum? There seemed to be only one explanation. Raveling wasn't going to make good on promises that had been made to his young stars, least of all the arrangement allowing Barrett to provide "support" at practices and on road trips.

Barrett denies there was any special deal. But in May 1986 Lewis announced he would transfer to UC-Irvine. Then, come September, he enrolled at Pepperdine. Did he change his mind, students of college hoops in the Southland wondered, because UCI had denied Michael Fielder, a friend and ex–Mater Dei teammate, admission? Or because Lewis and several Anteaters had played pickup ball over the summer and not gotten along? Irvine coach Bill Mulligan says it was for both reasons—and because "Pat expected us to help him with employment."

Barrett currently works for Stan Castleton, "that Hilton man" David LeuLuai referred to. Castleton is a Pepperdine booster and good friend of UCLA's Jim Harrick, who coached him at Morningside High before Harrick moved on to Pepperdine. Barrett is an instructor at the Performance Training Institute, a sports and fitness center based in the Anaheim Hilton. Twice a week he picks up Castleton's young son and teaches him basketball. Says Barrett, "I started working for him, obviously, when Tom went [to Pepperdine]."

Meanwhile Tom Lewis, his college career interrupted and scrutinized more than most, is still a Wave. He's living, Barrett says, in a beachside apartment in Malibu. Lewis's guardian won't say explicitly that his protégé is getting anything improper. But he will say, "How in the hell is a kid supposed to live off campus in Malibu on six hundred twenty-five dollars a month? [Barrett is referring to the approximate cost of living in Pepperdine dormitories, and the amount the school can properly contribute toward housing an athlete who chooses to live off campus.] You can't find anything under two thousand a month in Malibu. And you've got to pay rent, eat, have a car, car insurance, entertainment.

"I mean, how far is six twenty-five a month going to go?"

Like John Williams, Sean Higgins never made it to school the morning he was supposed to announce his choice of college. Unlike Williams, however, no stand-in wearing a white Panama hat showed up to speak on his behalf.

Sean's mother, Vickie Benson-Bey, had long since mailed invitations to the reporters who mustered at Fairfax High on November 18, 1986. But 7:30 came and went with no sign of Higgins, Vickie, or her husband, Clifford Benson-Bey. Three times Fairfax principal Warren Steinberg phoned the Benson-Beys' apartment at 1547 South Orange Grove. Each time he reached an answering machine.

Finally, at 8:20, Steinberg's secretary slipped him a note. Vickie had called to say she was sorry, but something had come up and the family wouldn't be able to make it. Steinberg could nonetheless go ahead and make the announcement: Sean Higgins would attend UCLA.

A few hours later Vickie reached Steinberg directly. "She said they'd been up most of the night," he recalls. "They were all pooped, so they weren't able to come. She indicated it had been a hard night."

How hard a night would soon come clear. In the dawn of that November morning, Sean would say, he had indeed signed a letter of intent to play at UCLA. But he had done so against his will, and only after being coerced by his 6-foot-8-inch, 250-pound stepfather.

Recruiters sometimes speak colorfully of their business,

throwing around phrases like "baby-sitting" and "getting in the home," terms that evoke images of domesticity. But the recruitment of Sean Higgins was a real-life custody battle, a basketball *Kramer vs. Kramer*. Two schools, UCLA and Michigan, were proxies in a fight between Vickie Benson-Bey and Earle Higgins, her former common-law husband and Sean's father.

Earle Higgins and Vickie Dempsey had met at Eastern Michigan during the sixties, where Earle was a good enough basketball player to earn a brief turn in the ABA. They never married and split soon after Sean was born. Vickie settled with her son in Ann Arbor, where, Sean says, he learned by heart the words to Michigan's fight song. After eleven years in the shadow of Michigan Stadium, Vickie and Sean moved to L.A., where she married Benson-Bey, who drove a bus for the city.

Vickie remained enormously protective of her only child. She had played basketball herself in high school, and took credit for teaching Sean how to shoot. For Earle, who was back in suburban Detroit, she had no use. Sean's father had neglected child support payments during their years in Michigan, and hadn't made more than a few phone calls since Sean came west with her. Then, just before Sean's junior season at Fairfax, Earle showed up at the Slam-N-Jam. Earle would deny he was acting on anyone's behalf. "As far as I'm concerned, Sean could have gone to Little Boot, Mississippi, if that was his choice," he says. But scuttlebutt had him on a mission to sell Michigan, to work the boy's heartstrings.

Whatever was at work, Sean felt Michigan's pull. At the same time he knew he had to keep peace at home. He led UCLA coach Walt Hazzard to believe he wanted to become a Bruin. Meanwhile, Michigan sent him a steady stream of mail at a special post office box, safely away from Vickie and Clifford's prying eyes. Michigan coach Bill Frieder and his assistants wrote often. So did boosters, including a

Detroit attorney named W. Merritt Jones, who began one missive, "As a dedicated University of Michigan basketball supporter, I was really pleased to learn that Michigan is among the schools which you are considering." A smart-looking Wolverines practice jersey even showed up in P.O. Box 35418 one day.

During Sean's official visit to Michigan, he phoned his mother back in L.A. It was dawn in Ann Arbor, three A.M. Pacific time, and Vickie, mortified, was sure he had been out carousing. She held Earle and Michigan—there was no distinction in her mind—responsible. At that point, says someone close to the Benson-Beys, "Vickie said, 'Michigan? No way.' So now Earle's working even *harder* for Michigan."

Trouble boiled over on the morning of the signing date. The night before, Sean had finally told his mother he wanted to sign with the Wolverines. But around dawn, after Clifford left the house to buy some cigarettes, Sean slipped out of the apartment. He made his way to a pay phone, by the Safeway at the end of South Orange Grove, to try to call Earle. Before Sean could get through, Clifford tracked him down and took him home. "Get your ass in the house," Clifford said as his neighbor, Claud Mills, looked on. "I'm tired of you running over your mother."

Once inside, Sean says, Benson-Bey asked him, "Are you going to UCLA or not?" Sean didn't say anything. Benson-Bey slapped him in the face, Sean says, before Sean retreated to his bedroom. A few moments later Benson-Bey appeared, brandishing a baseball bat.

"He had it in his hand, standing over me," Sean would say several months later. "I felt threatened. He'd just slapped me. What else was he going to do to me? He gave me the letter. He had a pen in his hand. He said to sign the letter. I didn't want to sign, but I didn't want to get hit either. That's when I signed. I just signed the thing so he would leave me alone."

Over the next few days, Sean and Earle each wrote the NCAA to ask how they could get the commitment voided. And Michigan assistant coach Mike Boyd sent a letter to Sean's post office box: "Just wanted to drop you a short note to tell you how disappointed I am in the decision that was made by your mother. I know deep down that you wanted to attend Michigan, but it didn't work out that way. But I do understand and I do feel for you."

On December 17, Sean met with representatives of UCLA and the Pac-10 office to tell them how he was coerced. He mentioned the baseball bat, but said nothing when asked about any improprieties committed by the Bruins in their recruitment of him. At about the same time, back in Detroit, Earle Higgins decided to retain an attorney to help spring Sean loose. Mike Boyd recommended a familiar name: W. Merritt Jones.

Jones set right to work. He contacted Pac-10 associate commissioner David Price, who told Jones to write a letter to the National Letter-of-Intent Steering Committee, making the case for coercion as best he could. But Price also told Jones frankly that based on what he knew, he didn't think there was enough evidence to get Sean released from the letter due to duress.

It was now early January. To Michigan, things looked bleak. It was going to be tougher to get Higgins out of his UCLA letter than anyone originally thought. Sean had moved in with relatives, and the Benson-Beys had just bought a new $175,000 home in Inglewood. (Before Clifford could close on the house, he had to pay $5,893.10 to cover two federal tax liens dating back to 1980. According to public records, those liens were officially settled on November 19, 1986—the day after Higgins committed to the Bruins. Investigators who probed the matter could find no evidence that the timing was anything but a coincidence.)

Then, suddenly, Sean had more to say. On January 14, Merritt Jones called David Berst's office. He and Sean had a list of possible UCLA recruiting violations he wanted to discuss with the NCAA. Sean hadn't told investigators these things back on December 17 because representatives of UCLA were present at the time of his interrogation.

In February, Sean told the authors of this book that he had visited the estate of Steven Antebi, a wealthy stockbroker and UCLA booster, before the signing date. There, Higgins said, Antebi offered him a summer job if he came to UCLA, and promised to use his investment acumen to parlay Sean's wages into more money. In addition, Higgins said Antebi told him he would be provided with a car after he signed with the Bruins. (UCLA star Reggie Miller had an arrangement that looked entirely kosher on paper: Miller lived in the chauffeur's quarters on Antebi's estate, and paid rent with generous wages from a cushy summer job. Higgins was to live in the same bungalow.) Not just the offer of a car, but the very meeting itself—an off-campus contact with a booster—would be against NCAA rules.

In spite of Sean's list, the NCAA wouldn't cite UCLA for any serious violations in connection with the Higgins affair. UCLA partisans believe Michigan decided it needed dirt on the Bruins to spring Higgins from his letter, so they handed Merritt Jones a shovel. Hence Sean's sudden willingness—a month after his first meeting with investigators—to talk about NCAA violations committed by UCLA.

In March, the Pac-10 did release Higgins from his UCLA letter, invoking an "extenuating circumstances" clause. "When we made our recommendation, it wasn't on the basis that Clifford wielded a bat," says Price. "We just didn't feel the letter had been signed freely. It was clearly a hostile atmosphere. Clifford himself was outraged that Sean would go against his mother's wishes. He said he was upset enough so he didn't know what he did. After reviewing the atmosphere and consulting with our attorneys, we didn't feel that the letter of intent could stand scrutiny."

The Benson-Beys have always maintained that Clifford

never brandished a baseball bat. There was a bat in the home, they say, but it was really meant for Earle, whom Clifford and Vickie had a paranoic concern was in town and prepared to whisk Sean away. A friend of the Benson-Beys goes a step further: "The baseball bat was just symbolic. Cliff really had something else ready in case somebody would be foolish enough to come into his home and take Vickie's son off to do something she didn't want her son to do."

The prospect of Sean going off to Michigan—to Earle—made the Benson-Beys adamant in their support of UCLA. Vickie and Clifford forcing UCLA on Sean made Earle equally devoted to Michigan. But were UCLA and Michigan making it worth each party's while to be so intransigent?

By most accounts, Ed O'Bannon is one of those rare young stars whose effort always matches his considerable ability. He has a soft, left-handed jump hook, and the sort of effectiveness in traffic that evokes Walter Berry and Wayman Tisdale. But O'Bannon, who began his senior season at Artesia High in fall 1989, would stand out if only because he has an orthodox family life going for him. "Nice kid," college recruiters say with whatever sincerity they're capable of. "Good family."

Ed Senior drives a United Parcel Service truck. Madeleine O'Bannon is a clerk at Harbor Hospital. Young Ed, the third of four boys, has a soft heart belied by his ferocious play, and a head uninflated by his position as L.A.'s finest high-school player, the latest in the line that includes Williams, Lewis, Higgins, and Mills. "He says it sometimes hurts him to put a move on somebody that makes the guy look bad," says Ryan Jamison, a summer teammate. "He's unchanged. Or if he is changed, he's changed in the other way. All the attention has made him more humble."

So far it has been quite a ride for O'Bannon. But it has

been just as heady for Wayne Merino, Artesia's twenty-nine-year-old coach. If you caught a UNLV home game on TV during the 1988–89 season, you could probably pick out Merino, sitting behind the Runnin' Rebels' bench. If you inveigled your way into Seton Hall's closed practice before the national championship game in Seattle that March, you'd have found Merino there, too, as coach P. J. Carlesimo's guest, sitting in.

Precisely because of the stories surrounding the recruitment of Williams, Lewis, Higgins, and Mills, there is a new awareness around the city of what can go wrong when colleges come calling. Merino sees himself as a sentinel, pledged to make sure O'Bannon isn't the next victim. Any school interested in recruiting the Pioneers' star must abide by Merino's rules, arrived at in consultation with the family. Phone calls to the home weren't permitted until the end of summer 1989. Anyone wanting information had to call Merino instead. In theory, a year and a half went by without the youngster or his parents so much as speaking to a college coach. After that prohibition was lifted, coaches could call the O'Bannon home only during a few designated hours in the evening. "If anything, the Mills situation has helped our area because people are more aware of what's happening now," says Merino. "They're more cautious, parents are more informed. 'Wait a minute,' they're saying. 'What's going on?' I send articles over to Ed's parents all the time to keep them up to date."

Merino is saying this in his cramped office at Artesia. He's wearing Ferrari sunglasses, shorts, and a generic T-shirt that had caught the eye of a secretary as he walked in. She teases him. "That's the first time all year I've seen you in a shirt without Nike on it."

Since the sixth grade, O'Bannon has been a faithful Slam-N-Jammer, playing on a summer team Merino coached. He was a freshman on the great 1986 Verbum Dei team that split up. The O'Bannon family moved into

Artesia's district for Ed's sophomore year, the same season Merino became the Artesia coach. Then, suddenly, after O'Bannon's junior year, Merino and O'Bannon abandoned Slam-N-Jam and chose ARC as their summer program.

Why did Merino suddenly move the team?

"The whole intent in switching was so we could do what we wanted, so I could have control," says Merino, who has five members of the Artesia varsity on his ARC team. "I wanted a situation—Ed was going to have enough pressure on him already—where he could play and relax and have fun. I'm coaching my guys in the summer simply because I know I'm not going to distort their value system. I know they're secure. I have a problem with kids having their hands out all the time. If your coaches are bribing you to play, and your parents are saying, 'What did you get today, son?' and encouraging that, then the whole value system is distorted.

"Issy and Goldberg kind of cancel each other out. I don't think you can validate anything either one of them says, and I've known them both for fourteen years. They're going to do what they have to for their leagues to succeed. They're survivors, and they'll survive."

Only one of the scores of recruiters watching from the stands at the Las Vegas Invitational will land Ed O'Bannon. That makes Wayne Merino special, for as coach of the ARC East L.A. team in town this week, he has him. Emboldened by his privileged position, Merino is overcoaching, calling time-out after time-out.

As a high-school coach, Merino would seem to have a legitimacy not shared by many of the uncredentialed people who have brought teams to the desert this week. But one college assistant is unimpressed. "They should put a rule in where summer-league coaches can call only one time-out a game," he says. "So the kids can just play, just showcase their talent. These summer guys are coaching to make a résumé. They look at us and honestly believe they can do a better job than we can. With Merino, it's just a tone of voice. If he can attach himself to one of the five best players in America, he will."

Game's over, and O'Bannon's team has won again. Merino is one of the belles of this ball, greeting what seems like a receiving line of college assistants.

"Hey, Ed," someone says to O'Bannon. "Wayne sure seems to be shaking a lot of hands this week."

O'Bannon's normally even-tempered voice suddenly has an edge to it. "Yeah," he says. "A few too many for my taste."

After an L.A. kid has slipped on his last pair of free shoes and taken his last junket to Vegas and eaten his last comp meal, after all the street leeches and summer leagues have tried and tested his callow loyalties, a ball player's youth is gone, his innocence lost. The star-making machinery has rendered extinct the sleeper or late bloomer. Colleges are making their contacts earlier and earlier. The hangers-on coo at young ball players before girls do, and an attitude of entitlement takes root so firmly that a recruiter determined to play by the rules is laughed out of the gym.

Even Pat Barrett, who stands accused of playing the influence game, is jaded by the attitudes he has seen in his dozen years coaching youngsters in summer leagues around Los Angeles. "Nothing surprises me," he says. "Shoes and sweats, that's where the problem starts. All hands are out. Some of these kids, they could open up a sporting-goods store by the time they get to high school. A pair of Nikes and a sweat suit to a sixth-grader is like $100,000 to a college kid."

Once he leaves secondary school, a youngster will have been coddled and clothed and very possibly corrupted. It hardly matters that the California state assembly passed a bill in 1986 subjecting anyone involved in the improper recruitment of a college-bound athlete to criminal charges. Or that, in its *Guide for the College-Bound Student-Athlete*, the NCAA warns that you're a professional if you "participate on an amateur sports team and receive, directly or indirectly, any salary, incentive payment, award, gratuity, educational expenses or expense allowances other than actual and necessary travel, and room and board expenses for practice and games."

As long as summer leagues are bidding for thirteen-year-olds, schoolboy basketball players simply won't take seriously NCAA-member institutions—part of a consortium that grosses hundreds of millions of dollars annually from its national tournament alone—that offer nothing more than tuition, books, room, and board.

Those who think otherwise live in their own la-la land.

3

Playing Footsie

DERBY DAY is a somber occasion for most sports-minded Kentuckians in 1988. Barely a month has passed since the Los Angeles *Daily News* broke the news of the open Emery envelope. But in Las Vegas on this Saturday in May, as the casinos up and down the Strip merrily take bets on what will transpire at Churchill Downs, the mood is light. And at Bally's, horses aren't the only thing happening. College hoop is too.

Nearly a thousand clipboard carriers are in town for a three-day clinic sponsored by Nike. They pack a second-floor ballroom to hear such coaches as John Thompson and Jim Boeheim discourse on topics like flex offenses and three-quarter-court pressure. Between the presentations of their colleagues, the conferees are treated to a Nike-produced video, *Hooked on Hoop*, running continuously on four strategically placed Sony Trinitron monitors. Dance music blasts. Nike shoe commercials, from the foreboding Charles Barkley–Moses Malone collaboration to the more whimsical ones featuring Michael Jordan and Mars Blackmon, are dropped in stylishly between clips of college and pro action. As George Raveling launches into an exegesis of defensing the three-point shot, Sonny Vaccaro is encamped at the back of the ballroom, surveying the scene. "Everything is us," he says with a satisfied smile. "Everything fits."

Vaccaro is officially the director of Nike's national basketball advisory board, but he forswears titles. He might just as well be *capo di tutti capos*, for all the power he wields; his favored sweat suits might just as well be pinstripe. The athletic shoe business is the single biggest segment of the sporting goods market, grossing more than $2 billion a year. Within it, Nike is preeminent. The Beaverton, Oregon-based firm, named for the Greek goddess of victory, makes more money than the entire U.S. fishing industry, and spends more on promotion alone than most other shoe companies make. The more than $400 million worth of basketball shoes Nike sells each year outstrips runner-up Reebok by some $100 million. (Converse, Avia, and Adidas follow in that order.) The company owes its hegemony in the market to the vision, energy, and instincts of one man, and copious amounts of one thing.

Sonny and money. Since Nike founder Phil Knight introduced them to each other in the late seventies, they have essentially locked up the game. A $3.5-million promotional budget bankrolls Nike's central commitment to college basketball: a clutch of exclusive endorsement contracts with sixty of the top coaches. The most lavish ones belong to the most glamorous names, men like Georgetown's Thompson ($200,000 a year), North Carolina State's Jim Valvano ($160,000), and UNLV's Jerry Tarkanian ($120,000). The money is backed up by a bottomless supply of complimentary shoes, sweats, and bags, all calculated to get the Nike swoosh into the right hands, which is to say onto the most visible feet.

The coaches are ostensibly "consultants," paid to provide the company with "feedback" on the quality of its shoes. But those are awfully big bucks for filling out the occasional questionnaire. The money is, in fact, rent for space on the feet of the coach's players, who, of course, can't accept a cent. The players are like indentured Trojan horses. They take the Nike logo into the big arenas, onto TV, and into the newspaper wirephotos. If one happens to sail in for a dunk on the cover of *Sports Illustrated* in full swoosh, Nike has copped the equivalent of several hundred thousand dollars' worth of advertising, or perhaps more, because of the subliminal power of an otherwise editorial image.

But Vaccaro himself has extended Nike's reach beyond the surface of the college game. He has a grip on its subculture too—the summer leagues and high schools and all-star games; the clinics and camps and cablecasts. On the very same peripheries that colleges find players, Vaccaro first weans them onto his shoes.

Back in 1965, when a "swoosh" was still just the sound a passing Corvette made, he founded the Dapper Dan Roundball Classic in his native Pittsburgh. Today it's still one of the handful of first-rank national high-school all-star games, but of course it's now sponsored by Nike.

In the early eighties Vaccaro rescued from oblivion a languishing summer camp run by a well-meaning but ill-managed outfit called Athletes for Better Education. Held every July on the Princeton campus, the Nike/ABCD camp is devoted equally to basketball and academics. ("ABCD" stands for Academic Betterment and Career Development; for a sobering number of the campers, they and the ensuing twenty-two letters of the alphabet are a revelation.) It's the one summer stop every high-school star wants to make, no matter how overexposed or jaded by the recruiting mazurka he may be. At a cost of about $1,000 a camper, Vaccaro is festooning with the Nike name the 120 best high-school players in the land, all of whom get the usual beswooshed kicks, totes, and knockabout clothes, plus Sonny's unlisted phone number and a heartfelt invitation to call anytime.

For both the Dapper Dan game and the Nike/ABCD camp, final player selections are made by a committee of one, and that committee isn't wearing Cons.

There's more. Vaccaro funds summer leagues in some thirty cities other than Los Angeles, and as Rich Goldberg's ARC spreads east, Nike will be with him every step of the way. The Las Vegas Invitational, that Augusta of AAU tournaments, is another event blessed by the swoosh; Vaccaro someday envisions a national tournament for summer-league champions, to be called the Jordan Cup, after a certain high-profile Nike spokesman. Even Michael Jordan himself, who played in Converses at North Carolina and always liked the feel of Adidases on his feet, credits Vaccaro with persuading him that Nike could design an even better shoe, give him a royalty on every pair sold, and promote the hell out of it. Thus Vaccaro is the Orville and Wilbur Wright of the Air Jordan, even though his responsibilities don't primarily involve the pro game.

Nearly every month Vaccaro convenes a Nike clinic, like the Derby Day gathering in Vegas. Each is a priceless networking opportunity for lower and midmajor college coaches in search of an edge, or high-school coaches looking to move up. Twenty-five of the top high-school teams in the nation get Nikes, gratis, from the Vaccaro stockpile. Nike advertising dominates ESPN's college basketball telecasts, thanks to a $2.5-million deal with the network; even hypemeister Dick Vitale has a contract with Vaccaro for six speaking engagements annually. The National Association of Basketball Coaches' annual all-star game, played over the Final Four weekend when every self-respecting American is thinking basketball, is another steal of a deal—sole sponsorship rights at fifty thou.

But the primary source of Vaccaro's power is his deals

and friendships with the head men, the coaching czars of the college game. Time was when a shoe company might open a hospitality suite at the coaches' convention at the Final Four, dispense coffee, doughnuts, and firm handshakes, and that was about it. Now members of the Nike cabal and their wives are treated to an annual junket, usually to some tropical locale. There they enjoy piña coladas, Vaccaro's annual solo performance of the Isley Brothers' "Shout," and the soothing certainty that in this tenuous profession they have a leg up on all the poor suckers shod in anything else. About fifteen Nike coaches —Boeheim, Arizona's Lute Olson, Arizona State's Bill Frieder, Iowa's Tom Davis, Georgia's Hugh Durham, and Purdue's Gene Keady among them—pull down six figures. Others, like Eastern Michigan's Ben Braun, get nothing more than shoes for their players and the annual trip. Still other, small-time coaches with good "upside potential"— Cincinnati's Bob Huggins, for instance, or Middle Tennessee State's Bruce Stewart—are paid $10,000 a year as an investment on their someday hitting the big time. "My rookie guys," Vaccaro calls them.

One Nike coach says he would have long since left the profession, but the shoe money makes quitting impossible. If you get twice as much from a shoe company as from the school at which you coach, whom do you really work for? "The other companies can't get into me now," says Vaccaro. "No one's into basketball like me. What I've done, what Nike has done, is every time you turn around you run into us. Subconsciously it sets in. It's a mindset."

All told, Vaccaro has purchased incalculable clout. Here he is, moving and shaking:

• Pat Barrett was just an assistant coach at Mater Dei when Tom Lewis, then considering such Nike schools as Syracuse and UNLV, played in the Dapper Dan. Vaccaro named Barrett coach of one of the teams. "I coached the game to make sure Tommy went to Vegas," says Barrett flatly. "I mean, how many high-school assistant coaches coach in a national all-star game? It must have been because of Tom. Tom's playing in it. Sonny's running it. And Pat's coaching in it? You figure it out."

• When Valvano talked to UCLA about replacing Walt Hazzard in 1988, Vaccaro was ready to redress the one apparent hitch in the two parties striking a deal: the prohibitively high cost of housing in Los Angeles. It was worth it to Nike to make up the difference, considering how much more valuable a showman like Valvano would have been in Greater L.A. than the North Carolina Piedmont.

• On the eve of Danny Manning's senior season at Kansas, Vaccaro found out that Jayhawks coach Larry Brown had a $32,000 buyout clause in his deal with Puma. He decided to roll the dice. Vaccaro bought out Brown's contract—"cherry-picked" is the verb Sonny uses—and signed him for one season, figuring it was worth it, what with Manning already a high-profile star and the Jayhawks contenders for a national title. Sure enough, Manning was Player of the Year and Kansas won a national championship, making the Hawks one of an astonishing five Nike schools to win it all during the eighties.

All of this makes Vaccaro the consummate insider. That unpublished phone number is perhaps basketball's worst-kept secret. Calls come in daily from reporters in search of a scoop, parents in need of advice, recruiters in need of a sleeper, and even the odd stumped NCAA investigator hoping for a break in a case. As wired in as Sonny is, he'll have easily identified the top high-schoolers by the time they're sophomores. Suddenly, shoes and warmups begin appearing in their mailboxes—and in all of their team-mates' mailboxes too.

With the coaches who count, the game's majordomos, Vaccaro is as tight as a well-fitted shoe. "I love Sonny dearly," booms Georgetown's Thompson, at whose 1988 Olympic hoops trials the media, but not this shoe salesman, were summarily banned. Vaccaro and Raveling were best men at each other's weddings. Vaccaro and Tarkanian have been close for years, since before they served together as technical advisers on the set of *The Fish That Saved Pittsburgh*, a terrible basketball movie made in the late seventies. Today the Vaccaro kids have jobs all over Las Vegas and the Vaccaro parents live there. Brother Jimmy (a.k.a. Chunce) runs the sports book at Steve Wynn's shimmering new Mirage. When he's through town to visit or do the color on UNLV telecasts, he'll hole up in a back booth of the Barbary Coast coffee shop. The swoosh is a sort of unofficial city crest, and Vaccaro can do anything in Vegas short of levying taxes.

Until he moved into a condo in Pacific Palisades, the top high-school players in the L.A. area would tool by the Vaccaro digs in Santa Monica for sneakers, advice, and more sneakers. Arizona's Brian Williams caught naps on the Vaccaro couch after hoops practice at St. Monica's High down the street. Another frequent visitor, Pasadena native Stacey Augmon of UNLV, says, "Sonny's personality comes in one out of a million born. Every century there's one of those guys who can relate to kids like that." Even Chris, Derick, and Claud Mills learned to avail themselves of the occasional sweat suit or pair of shoes from the endless supply of product he keeps on hand.

Vaccaro shrugs. "Chris would come over and say, 'Can I have something for my dad?' I would do that. He has this friend Randy. He got stuff too. I don't even know Randy. I enjoy doing it. I told Chris if he needed anything else to just take it. If you wrote me a letter, I'd send you a pair of shoes."

(One of Claud's erstwhile co-workers at Lorimar says, "There was a mention of UCLA, but Claud said something about Chris being a Nike-sponsored player and they didn't wear Nikes there. Chris would probably only play someplace where they had a Nike-sponsored team. The impression we got was because Chris was being taken care of by Nike"—by "taken care of," the Lorimar source is referring to the complimentary shoes and sweats out of the Vaccaro closet—"if he went to a Nike-sponsored school, that relationship would continue.")

As long as Vaccaro endows "Nike schools" on the one hand, and befriends the best high-school players in America on the other, suspicions will persist that he's a matchmaker, someone who takes care of his coaches by steering the finest players their way. The notion that Vaccaro can deliver talent dates back to before he took a job with Nike, to 1977, when Dapper Dan participant and Brooklyn product Albert King chose Maryland and Sonny's old buddy, Lefty Driesell. (King turned down UNLV and another Vaccaro chum, Tarkanian.) Then Williams, the cat-napper from the Vaccaro couch, picked Maryland when he came out of St. Monica's in 1987. Cynics point out that Bob Wade, the Terps' coach at the time, was not only a member of the Nike stable, but had been director of the Nike/ABCD Camp while a high-school coach.

Most recently, in November 1987, only days before the early-signing date, Vaccaro touched down in Chesapeake, Virginia, home of Alonzo Mourning, the 6-foot-10-inch shot-blocker considered to be the finest high-school center since Patrick Ewing. Scuttlebutt had Mourning mulling over Georgetown (a Nike school), along with Maryland (ditto) and Georgia Tech (a Converse school at the time), with the Terps closing fast. By now Mourning had spent several summers at the Nike camp, and Vaccaro had long since sent him shoes and sweats, becoming a father figure to him. Even during "dead" periods, when college coaches aren't permitted to contact high-school recruits, Vaccaro and Alonzo would do lunch. "Sonny's a good man," Mourning has said. "Sonny's a friend."

Mourning signed with the Hoyas a few days after Vaccaro's visit. Of course, John Thompson hardly needs anyone's help in selling a black defensive star on Georgetown. But even if, as Vaccaro insists, he didn't intervene on behalf of his good friend the Georgetown coach, his appearance in Chesapeake—which Vaccaro says was solely to secure Mourning's participation in the Dapper Dan—had all of hoopdom wondering. "Because of my relationship with John, that's a logical assumption for anyone to make, friend or foe. I'll accept that inference. But over the time I was in Chesapeake, I never spoke to or saw Alonzo."

"Sonny has interests in Alonzo totally different from ours," Thompson says cryptically. "Alonzo was important [to Nike] to keep their programs—camps, summer leagues —going. I don't bother to defend it. You can't."

Certainly just being with Nike won't get a coach a player. But being with anyone else can keep him out of a very exclusive loop. "No way Sonny would influence a kid to go to one school over another," says Boeheim, "because if we ever found out, we'd be after him." But what's to influence? If the college game is a figure eight, Nike is at its intersection. Everything loops around to one of Vaccaro's interests eventually.

It's said that Vaccaro is obsessed with loyalty, that a coach who leaves the Nike family can count on never, ever being invited back. Villanova's Rollie Massimino left Nike for Puma—and more money—after he won his national title in 1985. But why would any coach leave when everyone in the profession wants in? Georgia Tech's Bobby Cremins switched from Converse to Nike soon after missing out in the Mourning sweepstakes. Perhaps Cremins didn't want to lose the next Nike-bred high-school All-America. Or perhaps he had seen what happened to Walt Hazzard. Soon after Hazzard took the UCLA job, Vaccaro came by Pauley Pavilion to talk contract. He threw out a figure. When Hazzard pointed out that this was considerably less than what a number of other Nike coaches were getting, Vaccaro said something to Hazzard about "paying your dues."

"This is *Walt Hazzard* you're talking to," Hazzard said. "The first banner in this place, it's mine. I won an Olympic gold medal. I spent ten years in the NBA. I was College Player of the Year. I'm not paying any more dues. Fuck you, Sonny."

Hazzard signed with Reebok for $125,000, and tried to persuade his patron to match Nike's giveaways to the top high-school kids. Reebok wouldn't, and Hazzard is no longer in coaching. "I told Walt, 'You're gonna cost us players,'" says one of Hazzard's former assistants. "Sonny's a great guy, but it's an unfair advantage. It's brutal what he can get away with. Everybody knows it, but nobody says anything about it. It's taboo. People don't realize, all the kids in L.A. that we were recruiting were getting Nike stuff. Claud Mills was wearing Nike stuff. If that's legal, if the NCAA allows it, that's scary."

The NCAA does allow it, albeit with an eyebrow raised. "I'm hearing more and more complaints about shoe companies providing merchandise and even cash to players, and in some cases interceding in the recruiting process to direct a player to one institution over another," says enforcement director David Berst. "To the degree that we've been reasonably successful in getting representatives of a school's athletic interests out of the recruiting circle, we've found new, creative efforts on the part of college coaches to find someone else who might be able to influence a prospect. They may be with a summer league, or associated with the major shoe companies. Frankly individuals associated with a summer league or shoe company are more suspect than those associated with an academic institution."

Vaccaro is articulate and passionate in his own defense. Don't confuse what he calls "the business of selling shoes" with friendship. "I don't influence kids," he says. "I don't think anyone should be involved in recruiting except parents and kids. Because of Nike's success, and the success of, say, Sonny Vaccaro, I shouldn't be penalized. If things happen subconsciously, like in *The Manchurian Candidate*, brainwashing, well, I can't control that."

"*The Manchurian Candidate?*" says John Morgan, Reebok's director of marketing. "More like a sledgehammer."

Morgan worked for Nike for fourteen years, until 1986, including a four-year stint in Korea. He wanted to get back into basketball when he returned to the States, but saw the gravy train in place, with Vaccaro driving the locomotive, and declined to board. "[Nike management] liked what he was doing," Morgan says. "I didn't. You've got to have some scruples and integrity in this business. The coaches and elite players get so much, they lose perspective as human beings."

Sonny Vaccaro was born John Paul Vaccaro in Trafford, Pennsylvania, a gritty town outside Pittsburgh. His father, Natale, logged thirty-nine years at the Duquesne steel mill to support the family. "We didn't have," Sonny says, "but we didn't want." His mother, Margaret, gave him his nickname, after his disposition.

The sweat suits don't flatter his body anymore, but they once would have. He was a 5-foot-10-inch, 170-pound, three-sport star at Trafford High, and such a good football player that one Friday night, a truckload of kids from a rival high school turned up at the Vaccaro homestead on Brinton Avenue, fixing to inflict on Sonny bodily harm. Fortunately he was down at Louie's Poolroom. But then, a kid with 10.1 speed always could expect to be one step ahead of trouble. His credentials as a halfback were gaudy enough to interest the Kentucky Wildcats, and he could hit a baseball so well the hometown Pirates offered him a $3,500 contract.

Sonny chose Kentucky's scholarship. As much as he loved baseball, he had promised his father he would get a college degree. Yet his grades were lacking, and the Wildcats had to stash him at Reedley College, a juco near Fresno, where he hurt his back. UK lost interest. Youngstown State stepped in, giving him a scholarship in exchange for his assistance coaching the football and basketball teams. "That changed my whole life," he says. "Otherwise I would have been back working at the mill, a great athlete returning to his hometown a failure. I think that's what gives me a sense of compassion for the kids."

Vaccaro went on to Wichita State, taking a graduate assistantship under Ralph Miller, living in his boss's guest room, recruiting the badlands of greater Wichita until a car accident landed him in the hospital. He had slipped off the narrow gauge of the coaching track.

He went home to Trafford, moved in with his mother, married, and fathered the first of four children. In 1966 the county school district gave him a job teaching health and phys. ed., and assisting with the Trafford High baseball, football, and basketball teams. But his eye always wandered toward distant horizons. A year earlier he had started the Dapper Dan, persuading a local charity to front the seed money in exchange for any proceeds. He tried desperately to lure to the game a New York City youngster named Lew Alcindor, who was the alpha and omega of high-school stars of that era, but for one of the few times in his life the Vaccaro jawbone failed. Yet everyone else came, and the first "Roundball," as the Iron City cognoscenti still call the game, sold out the Civic Arena. Suddenly Vaccaro's was a dog-eared card in the Rolodex of every self-respecting coach.

It was during the late sixties that Vaccaro got to know the Lefty Driesells and George Ravelings, the Hubie Browns and Chuck Dalys. Soon he had scraped together a basketball camp in Seven Springs, Pennsylvania. He would take a dilapidated VW bus into the Pittsburgh ghetto and round up youngsters, most with their belongings stuffed into paper bags, for the ride to the resort town near the Maryland border. The Rolodex gang—most were then college assistants and high-school coaches—served as staff. "He'd have more kids there for free than he had guys paying," says Raveling. "His problem is he operates with his heart, not his head."

When Raveling, then a freshman assistant at Villanova, came through Pittsburgh, he would bunk in at the Vaccaros', sometimes using Sonny's own bed. One morning, when Sonny had left early to do an errand, young Jimmy stuck his head into his older brother's bedroom. Raveling still remembers hearing Chunce's voice: "Mom, some black guy's sleeping in Sonny's bed." It wouldn't be the first time someone would say Sonny Vaccaro was in bed with a college coach.

There followed a stretch in which Vaccaro worked as a rock promoter, selling such quintessentially period acts as Grand Funk Railroad, Edgar Winter, and Frankie Valli. Given the opportunity to book an unknown British vocalist, he dismissed him as a "four-eyed wimp." The singer turned out to be Elton John. But Vaccaro's ability to pick basketball talent was more discerning. In 1970, during the NBA-ABA wars, agents Jerry Davis and Lew Schaffel signed him on as a recruiter. They paid him a flat commission of $2,500 for every player he could bring to the firm. He landed such journeymen as Mickey Davis, Dana Lewis, and John Mengelt, and signed George (Ice) Gervin in a Virginia Beach motel room, roughing out the contract on a cocktail napkin. Next to pre-merger combat, the "shoe wars" of the eighties would be mere bagatelles.

But Vaccaro wasn't delivering enough players to satisfy Davis and Schaffel. He would go into what his bosses called a "post-Roundball fade" every spring after the Dapper Dan. And he was uncomfortable with agenting. To be successful at it you had to make deals, had to go to schools early, had to lead undergraduates to believe a contract was waiting for them. Vaccaro didn't like that. It all came clear when he went through Tuscaloosa to talk to Alabama's Leon Douglas one spring.

Douglas, deep in a card game, looked up at him and said, "Sorry, can't talk now. I'm stuck twenty-five dollars."

If he had fronted Douglas $26, Vaccaro realized, he probably would have gotten him. But he refused to. He felt like a flesh peddler, buttonholing people and taking care of them, even if that's not entirely unlike what he does today legitimately with coaches on Nike's behalf. Nor could he offer other services, for he didn't know from Adam about financial planning. "I could barely manage my own money," he says. Moreover, the life-style was taking its toll at home. In short order he and his wife, Nancy, split, and Sonny took his leave from Davis and Schaffel. In the throes of a midlife crisis, too old to be a coach and too disillusioned to be an agent, he headed west.

For some reason Las Vegas is a sort of refugee camp for expatriate Pittsburghers who love basketball. Sonny and Chunce had bet on fights and played craps while coming up in Trafford—innocent stuff—so action wasn't entirely foreign to them. And they had spent summers in Vegas, visiting Jack Franzi, another Pittsburgher, who was then the oddsmaker at the Barbary Coast.

Chunce had already settled in Vegas when Sonny arrived there. Thus began a dark chapter in Vaccaro's life, "my Ray Milland story, a lost weekend that lasted three years." He drifted. He did some substitute teaching. And he did a lot of gambling, all the while still wending his way back to Pittsburgh each spring to run the Roundball.

Because Vaccaro knew Franzi, Vegas extended to Sonny its welcome. He could eat, sleep, and take in the shows on good will and little else. He became a pseudo-celebrity, scouring the newspapers in the morning, hanging with the cigar guys through the afternoon, playing $500 to $1,000 a day. He put most of it down on baseball games, grinding out a living by playing the percentages at different books around town.

At one point, as any gambler will, he found himself deep in the hole. Jerry Davis says a gentleman presented himself at his New York office one day, looking for Vaccaro. The visitor didn't give a last name. "The situation had gotten totally out of control," says Davis. "Sonny was ex officio with some people. His problem with gambling was he didn't have a big enough stake to take a loss. We arranged for the debt to be written off. It wasn't like he wasn't going to pay. He just didn't have it."

Davis says the debt totaled $70,000. Vaccaro vigorously disputes that figure. He says it was more like $20,000, and no one ever threatened him. "I've lost lots and lots of money," he says. "I've almost blown my life. But I was never afraid physically. It was something I was capable of paying. That's why they called me a good bet. I paid my losses."

One of the benefits of drifting is, even when there seems to be no hope, anything is possible. And Vaccaro knew he knew basketball, knew he knew the streets. He got an old buddy in Trafford, a shoemaker named Bobby DiRinaldo, to cobble up ten pairs of prototype sneakers. They would be different—stylish and a little whimsical—something to turn heads down at the Ozanam Center, and over at East Hills Park, where Pittsburgh's best ball is played. Today some of the designs would be laughable: a backless pair, like sandals; another, with spangles, that Vaccaro calls "my disco shoe." But a few others augured the future in basketball footwear. There were air vents in the front of one, and Velcro on the tongue of another. In fall 1978 he threw them into a knapsack and, with an introduction from Jerry Davis, marched into Phil Knight's office.

The shoes didn't impress, but Vaccaro's gumption and irrepressibility did. Within a year Knight had hired him for a promotions position at $500 a month. "A job of indebtedness," Vaccaro says now. "He never wanted my shoes on the market."

Vaccaro was shrewd enough to realize he had a good thing going with Nike, something a Vegas domicile wouldn't reflect all that well on, and in 1981 he moved to L.A. If he's through Vegas in season, Vaccaro admits he will still make a play on a college game. And Chunce's operation at the Mirage will write up to $250 million in sports and racing action a year. Their relationship begs fundamental questions of propriety that both can understand, but minimize. "There was once an injury at the Final Four that caused a drop in the line of one or two points," says Chunce. "Sonny was at the arena, and it would have been easy for him to call and say, 'Hey, [Indiana's Dean] Garrett's hurt.' But he never did. I've been out to dinner with Dean Smith, with John Thompson, with [Seton Hall coach] P. J. Carlesimo and Sonny, and never once has Sonny brought [betting] up. I consider John Thompson to be one of my two best friends in the whole world. I'd never violate that friendship by asking him a dumb question. I wouldn't jeopardize my career over one stupid basketball game."

Nor would Sonny, Sonny himself says, not after Nike took him in. "I have too much respect for the people I'm dealing with," he says. "I don't do it. I couldn't do it. People have the right to ask that question for the integrity of the game, but I think I answered it when I packed up and left Las Vegas."

Sonny Vaccaro wasn't the first man to buy the sole of college basketball. He only followed in the footsteps of Joe Dean, the grandaddy of the practice. Back in the twenties, Chuck Taylor had stashed boxes of his eponymous Converse All-Stars in the trunk of a Cadillac, passing them out as he criss-crossed the country giving clinics. Dean succeeded Taylor in 1970 as Converse's primary promotions man. At its peak in 1982, Converse's hold on college basketball extended to more than ninety coaches. In Louisville's Denny Crum and the Wildcats' Joe B. Hall, Dean had the state of Kentucky locked up. Indeed, the Converse chevron-and-star insignia was perhaps the only thing the two rival schools could agree on.

But by the early eighties the comfortable world over which Dean lorded had already come under attack. Nike was born in 1976, in the running-mad Pacific Northwest. The company's founders, Knight and Jeff Johnson, knew shoe promotion from track and field. They had witnessed the early shots in the war between Adidas and Puma, which included the slipping of $100 bills inside sprinters' shoes at the 1964 Olympics. "We wanted," Knight says, "to put our shoes on the feet of leaders." As it happened, Vaccaro had hatched a plan to do just that.

Coaches in the late seventies didn't yet expect shoe companies to pay them. "For years we had dealt on friendship and loyalty and good will," says Dean, "on dinner or lunch or doing something for the wives." Many coaches couldn't even command free shoes, getting at best a "one-and-one" deal—buy one pair, get one free.

Vaccaro threw those rules out. Pay the coaches, he said. Give them the shoes. And focus east. Thompson tops the Nike pay scale, and Georgetown is the company's "flagship," because Vaccaro knows well the credibility the Hoyas and their coach have in the inner city, where Georgetown regalia is standard attire. He knows that street styles germinate in the school yards and rec centers of the eastern ghettos, in Harlem and Bed-Stuy and Baltimore and West Philly and D.C., and flow across the continent from there.

The pooh-bahs at Nike, with Stanford MBAs on their walls and bottled water in their fridges, didn't know quite what to make of this roguish character and his brash ideas.

But they sent Vaccaro off on what he calls his "kamikaze sweep." On his first swing across the country he signed up a dozen coaches, including the fast-talking, ambitious young head man at Iona College, Jim Valvano. When the two met at LaGuardia Airport, Vaccaro laid a check for $2,500 on the table. "It was like," Valvano recalls, "we were putting a contract out on somebody."

They were, in a sense. At the end of the first year Nike had twenty-two coaches. By year two the company had ninety. Converse didn't know how to stanch the bleeding. When the Washington *Post* ran a story accusing Nike of buying up coaches, the brass back in Beaverton was mortified. Vaccaro was delighted. "You couldn't buy that kind of publicity," he says. Nike spent three times as much on promotion as advertising during its breathtaking offensive. By 1984 the firm was selling six times as much merchandise as in its first year, and spending more than $30 million on promotions alone.

Then, in 1985, Vaccaro pulled off perhaps his most meaningful deal ever. Eddie Sutton had been Nike's since the beginning of the decade, when Vaccaro wrapped him and his Arkansas team up. But as the coaches gathered in Lexington for the '85 Final Four, Sutton wanted out of Fayetteville. His work there was largely done, and his relationship with Frank Broyles, the Razorbacks' omnipotent athletic director, had deteriorated. Even though he was a Nike man in Converse country, Sutton politicked vigorously around town that week, schmoozing with Kentucky muckamucks, hoping to get consideration for the UK coaching vacancy. Yet Lee Rose, Gene Bartow, and Lute Olson had all been paraded in front of the search committee, and still Sutton hadn't been so much as contacted.

On the Saturday of the national semifinals, just before the end of the Memphis State–Villanova game, Joe Dean left his seat in Rupp Arena. 'Nova had the game won, and Dean was going to beat the rush to the bathroom. But at the top of the stairway, waiting for him, was a desperate man.

Sutton and Dean huddled in an alcove off the Rupp Arena lobby. "Joe, why can't I get an interview here?" Sutton asked.

Dean told him what he knew. Neither Otis Singletary, the school's conservative president, nor athletics director Cliff Hagan much liked him. There was just something about him—even his permed hair—that gave the UK people pause. Indeed, Dean knew how Hagan had reacted when Sutton's name was first broached in a Denver hotel suite the night Joe Hall resigned. "I'm not hiring any coach," Hagan had said, "with a damn Afro."

"Joe, if you can help get me this job, I'll wear your shoes forever," Sutton said.

"I can't get you the job," Dean told him. "But I'll see if I can get you an interview."

That night Dean worked the phones on Sutton's behalf. And when Sutton wound up getting the job, Dean sent him a congratulatory telegram. The message read:

> LOOKING FORWARD TO YOUR WEARING
> CONVERSE SHOES FOREVER.

So began the fight. Dean and his deputy, Al Harden, soon went to Lexington to follow up. Dean says Sutton first told him Kentucky would wear Cons, but then "began to dance." And his dancing shoes had a predictable look.

Vaccaro wasn't going to let slip this chance to get Nike's first real foothold in the Ohio River valley of Kentuckiana, basketball's Fertile Crescent. He knew well that if the 'Cats were wearing Nikes, every kid from Paducah to Prestonsburg would be too.

Kentucky had been a Converse school for as long as anyone could remember, and Harden's son Roger still played point guard on the team. But Vaccaro reminded Sutton of Nike's loyalty to him. Sutton could hardly turn his back on Sonny and his money now—not when Vaccaro had backed him in Fayetteville, and was offering $160,000 a year, with generous incentives to make more. Sutton did let Roger Harden wear Cons for his senior season, out of deference to his father; yet Harden looked like an orphan out on the floor, a felicitous symbol of the waif Converse had become. "Nike built a business of one billion dollars in sales without spending a penny on advertising," says Dean. "You'd walk into a store and it overpowered you mentally. You just got comfortable with that swoosh. We got caught in the 'shoe wars,' and there wasn't a darn thing we could do about it."

The crossfire nicked college administrators, who struggled to justify such payoffs to coaches, many of whom were state employees at institutions ostensibly devoted to higher learning. Shoe retailers were upset, too, particularly those catering to the team trade. They noticed their over-the-counter sales sloughing off, and attributed it to all the giveaways. A few rebels refused to stock Nikes at all in protest.

But promotion sometimes involves taking one step back to go two forward. Soon the corporate yellow ties began noticing a "flow-down effect" from Vaccaro's efforts, and basketball sales took off. There was a brief scare when Reebok, riding the aerobics wave of the early eighties, enjoyed a vogue as the most fashionable brand name in sneakerdom. The Massachusetts-based firm introduced a line of basketball shoes and, even though Vaccaro and his swoosh troops still ruled hoops, in 1986 Reebok actually surged past Nike in overall athletic footwear sold.

It was a valuable lesson for Nike. It vindicated Vaccaro's hunch—that the shoe business is sensitive to all sorts of subjective whims and fancies—and taught the firm that it had to be more responsive to the fashion-driven end of the market. The performance-driven end, what with Nike's superstar stable of Jordan, Bo Jackson, Dwight Gooden, and John McEnroe, has never been a problem. But now Nike follows "planned product life cycles," changing colors and fashion elements in its shoes every six months even as designs remain the same. And in basketball, Nike expanded its clothing line. Two styles, introduced as uniforms during the 1988–89 season, caught every other company snoozing: Nike Flight, a sleek Lycra fabric designed expressly for Syracuse and its above-the-rim game; and Nike Force, a denim-style work cloth conceived just for the flagship Hoyas and their lunch-bucket attitude.

Reebok posted its first earnings decline ever in 1988 as Nike moved back into first place. Converse was a sluggish third, and Joe Dean slid on back to his alma mater, LSU, to become A.D. On the verge of the nineties, Vaccaro was sovereign.

Hang around the game long enough, particularly the shadowy corners of the summertime version, and you'll learn to hold your head a certain way upon entering a gym or school yard. You look straight ahead to see who's who. Then you steal a glance downward to see who's whose, so you can watch the shoe-influence game at work.

It starts with those summer leagues. "Every year it gets worse and worse," says David Benezra, who has fielded summer teams in a number of L.A. leagues during the eighties. "Is it worth it to try to find twelve kids who want to get better at basketball, as opposed to twelve who want to stock their closet? Kids today are tainted before the game is ever played."

A college coach's shoe income is found money, a little rivulet of cash about which only the Internal Revenue Service and, since 1987, the college president need know. Some coaches—Virginia's Terry Holland, for instance, and Bob Knight—turn most or all of it over to the school. Others spend it on furs for their wives or decks for their backyards. But some pump it back into their livelihood. Shoe money can provide a secure slush fund, its use neither accountable to an athletic director nor subject to the indiscretions of some renegade booster.

The cash needn't go directly to the prospect. If a shoe company is giving college Coach A $100,000, and high-school Coach B has three studhorses in the next two recruiting classes, it will behoove Coach A to share some of his loot with Coach B. Coach A may even tell his contact at the shoe company to withhold, say, twenty-five percent of his money this season, and forward the balance to that fine scholastic mentor down in Studsville, Coach B, who would no doubt be right happy to wear the requisite brand of sneakers.

Or a coach may pay with the shoes themselves. Coach A's cache of product is considerable. (Each year a typical big-time college Nike coach gets 150 pairs of shoes, twenty-five gym bags, a $2,000 clothing allowance for his staff, and up to $5,000 worth of T-shirts for basketball camps.) His booty can go directly to Coach B, or Influence Peddler C—a street agent or summer-league coach—whoever happens to be positioned closer to the targeted youngster. "The college coach wants only one kid," explains a college assistant. "He tells the shoe guy that. 'I want him. Take care of this kid.'

"If you see a great player in a certain brand, and you're clean and in another brand, you don't even think about it. You know a shoe company gave Johnny Doe sweats. You know you're wasting your time going after him if you're clean. The player? Hell, he may not see anything except shoes and sweats. But to a seventeen- or eighteen-year-old, that's huge."

Study the list of high schools with shoe contracts. Their distinguishing feature isn't necessarily ten or fifteen years of consistent success or the presence of a veteran, well-respected head coach. Rather, at least one great player is in the program, or has recently come through it. "Louisville had been a Converse school for years," says another college assistant. "Then, a few years back, they switch to Pro-Keds for one year and [Camden High School coach Clarence] Turner's team did the same thing. [The Camden-Louisville pipeline has kept the Cardinals in talent through the eighties.] Now you tell me why a black school in Jersey is wearing Pro-Keds. This way you don't have to cheat. You get it done with shoe money."

From a business perspective, it's all just as the shoe companies want it. There are three cycles to shoe promotion, not unlike those involved in planting, cultivating, and harvesting crops. "Basketball's the only sport where you can tell at an early age that a kid's going to be a great player," Vaccaro says. "In football you can't. In baseball you can't." If the next Michael Jordan wears Nikes through high school and college, who's he going to sign his endorsement deal with when he reaches the NBA?

The next Jordan is out there somewhere, and the odds are Vaccaro has already gotten to him.

It's coming on midnight at the Princeton Marriott, and Vaccaro's friends have come by to pay him their respects. This is just a low-key gathering in the Vaccaro suite to mark midweek at the Nike/ABCD camp. Still, the stars are out, and Boeheim, Cremins, even the hyperactive Valvano, stop by. Vaccaro sits in a straight-back chair in the middle of the room as the coaches genuflect, each in his own way. Then Vaccaro slips off to the bedroom, props himself up against a rack of pillows, and talks about basketball and responsibility.

"Take a look at this," he says, pulling several artboards from a case. It's a logo for Sonny Vaccaro's Hoops That Help. He has the date (January 20, 1990), the teams (Notre Dame and LSU, neither of which wears Nikes), the site (the Superdome), and the TV deal (two years with CBS at

$300,000, which will go to the homeless). Next stop, he says, is the NBA. "I'd like to see every NBA team playing on that day give one dollar of each ticket sold to the homeless in their area."

This isn't Nike, he says. This is Sonny—at the top, but still thinking of the down and out. He has been a poor man and a rich one, an abject gambler and (to hear his friends tell it) a sort of secular saint. He could bury the sport with what he knows, but he won't. In college basketball, as in himself, Vaccaro sees both the good and the bad, both the hypergenerous Seven Springs camp director and the Las Vegas lollygagger. Who is he to judge?

But he will also admit that the summer leagues and camps and city playgrounds—the very precincts Nike owns—are the speakeasies in which the liquor of influence is first served. "We start the whole process. If our money trickles down to touch all levels . . . it's not our intention, and not Reebok's intention, either, for a sixth-grader to be induced or given shoes or be given travel expenses. If that happens, it's wrong."

He'll support the NCAA if it chooses to undo what he has done. "If my competitors quit, I'll quit. If the NCAA were to outlaw all-star games, summer leagues, camps, traveling teams, I would give up mine. All things being equal, kids would probably still be wearing Nikes. Our shoe's a quality shoe. Let's put the game back where it belongs, with the kids, in the neighborhoods."

Vaccaro's offer isn't one to disarm unilaterally. Too many pesos are riding on the status quo for anyone, least of all the triumphant swoosh brigade, to do that.

But what if someone called him on it?

4

Breeding Thoroughbreds

I CAN'T BELIEVE THIS," the old man snarled. "All the money we pay these boys, and they *still* can't get my defense right."

Adolph Rupp watched the 1975 NCAA championship game in the San Diego Sports Arena from a seat just off the Kentucky bench. For three seasons now he had been out of coaching, forced there against his will by a mandatory retirement age people had the temerity to apply to him.

In his own embittered mind, Rupp believed he was still in charge. "Arena's got my name on it," he'd say, referring to Rupp Arena, the shimmering new home of the Wildcats about to open in downtown Lexington. Kentucky and UCLA, the two teams in this final, had between them won more than a third of all the NCAA titles ever contested. Word leaked out after the semifinals that John Wooden, the Bruins' coach, would be stepping down. "It'll be sad if he loses, but he's got enough of those damn trophies," Rupp said before tipoff. "Johnny's in against me tonight."

As it happened, neither Rupp nor Kentucky's three freshman big men could bamboozle the UCLA front line and its center, Richard Washington. The Wildcats just weren't getting Adolph's defense right. The Baron was all the more offended because he felt he had been shunted aside—put out to pasture, in the phrase of the Thoroughbred industry. He thought Joe B. Hall, his former assistant and the current coach, had pulled a power play to get the job. And he told other coaches about improprieties in the Kentucky program, hoping they would turn Hall in. After the Bruins' 92–85 victory, Rupp must have felt the ambivalence that comes with family feuding: sadness at the failure of a team he still considered kin; a perverse pleasure in knowing that it was Hall, after all, who lost.

Rupp descended directly from the founding fathers of the game. He had played for Phog Allen at Kansas, who in turn had been taught by James Naismith, basketball's inventor. He arrived in Lexington in 1930, seven years before the center jump after each basket would be eliminated. By the time his career ended in 1972, Rupp had eclipsed Allen as college basketball's all-time winningest coach.

There will always be skeptics doubting his record, people ready to point out that during Rupp's run the rest of the Southeastern Conference cared about only two sports, the proverbial football and spring football. What the Baron did, in former Notre Dame coach Johnny Dee's words, was "like taking five Canadians and starting a hockey league in Texas." Further, the SEC was all white until the end of Rupp's career.

But then Rupp could have seized a competitive advantage by carrying black players, and he didn't. Give me those Kentucky mountain boys, he liked to say. The coach took to quoting a passage from the Bible: "I will lift up mine eyes unto the hills, from whence cometh my help."

Rupp had the bearing of a man preeminent. His practices were solemn affairs. He lorded over them in starched khakis, while managers policed the periphery of the gym, making sure it was secure from interlopers. His arrogance was a source of his authority. When asked during the interview why UK should hire him, the story goes, he replied, "Because I'm the best damn basketball coach in the nation."

It wasn't until after the war, during the can-do optimism of the Truman era, that Rupp's teams asserted their dominance. In 1946 the Wildcats won the National Invitation Tournament, which was then as prestigious an event as the NCAAs; two years later UK had become so good that the star and leading scorer of that '46 team, Jack Parkinson, was no longer starting. By the end of the decade the basketball budget had hit $200,000, and the school had built, at a cost of $4 million, a state-of-the-art arena, a monument to the passion and following for Wildcat basketball that existed even then. Memorial Coliseum went up on the fringe of campus, on a site where Rupp, on his first visit to town, had been appalled to find fifty-five dilapidated Negro shacks.

Between 1945 and 1950 a parade of great players came through Lexington: Ralph Beard, the gum-chewing little guard. Alex Groza, the splendid forward from the gritty Ohio town of Martins Ferry. The irrepressible Wallace (Wah Wah) Jones. The seven-foot Georgian, Bill Spivey. The 'Cats won 155 of 170 games during this span. But their winning percentage against the point spread was suspiciously lower. A few years earlier, Phog Allen himself had warned of the possibility of a massive point-shaving scandal. His remarks earned him an upbraidment from the college coaches' association for exhibiting a "deplorable lack of faith in American youth and a meager confidence in the integrity of coaches."

But Allen's caveat soon proved to be tragically on the mark. In 1951, scandals came to light first in New York City, at City College and Seton Hall; and then in the Midwest, at Bradley. Most of the players implicated had fallen in with the fixers over the summer. *In the summer, everybody's on vacation. That's the time to rob the house.*

In the Borscht Belt of the Catskill Mountains, a couple of hours north of New York, scores of college kids found jobs as waiters, bellhops, and busboys on the staffs of resort hotels. Indeed, athletic departments around the country steered ball players there. The pay was good—you could expect to make $300 in a summer, plenty for that era—and the tips ample. Most important, there was a summer league in which teams representing the hotels competed against one another. The college kids could keep their skills sharp. The guests found the games, played outdoors at twilight on the resorts' grounds, diverting entertainment. And gamblers, who flocked to the Jewish Alps, found they could scare up plenty of action.

Even as evidence emerged of point-shaving by players at Bradley, a school in the bellwether middle-American city of Peoria, the scandals looked like an East Coast, big-city problem. Certainly Rupp thought so. The fixers, he said, "couldn't touch our boys with a ten-foot pole."

In fact, mobsters had gotten in with Rupp's players late in 1948. In virtually every game during their 1948–49 NCAA championship season, Beard, Groza, and a third Wildcat, Dale Barnstable, had controlled the point spread. To shave points wasn't the same as throwing a game; all it took was a bad pass here, or a defensive stumble there, to please the bookmakers and please the fans—in short, to win twice. But in the first round of the NIT that year, against Loyola of Chicago, Kentucky lost startlingly, 67–56. "We were flat," Rupp said. "Awfully flat. That's all there was to it."

There was more to it, of course. For a total of $1,500, a measly $500 apiece, Beard, Groza, and Barnstable had fixed things so well that they forgot to win.

The state of Kentucky had no law against the bribing of amateur athletes, so those involved in the scandals of '51 were brought to justice in New York City. As the Manhattan district attorney's office moved its investigation forward, two more Kentucky players, Jim Line and Walt Hirsch, confessed to shaving points during the 1949–50 season. They in turn implicated Spivey, who maintained his innocence and was never convicted,

In his Manhattan chambers, Judge Saul Streit, the man who sentenced Beard, Groza, and Barnstable, conducted a one-man vetting of the Wildcat program. He issued a philippic whose themes would recur again and again over four decades. Streit called Kentucky's basketball program "the acme of commercialism and overemphasis. . . . I found undeniable evidence of covert subsidization of players, ruthless exploitation of athletes, cribbing on examinations, illegal recruiting, a reckless disregard for the players' physical welfare, matriculation of unqualified students, demoralization of the athletes by the coaches, the alumni, and the townspeople."

Rupp, he added, "aided and abetted in the immoral subsidization of the players. With his knowledge, the charges in his care were openly exploited, their physical welfare was neglected, and he utterly failed to build their character or instill morals—indeed if he did not impair them."

As Kentucky's punishment for paying players and playing them when they were ineligible, the NCAA recommended that member institutions not schedule the 'Cats for the 1952–53 season. Before schools could respond to that call, UK president Herman Donovan canceled the team's season. The gamblers who couldn't get at Rupp's kids with a ten-foot pole had pulled the whole program offstage with a gaffing hook.

Faced with the damning conclusions of the NCAA and Judge Streit, Rupp admitted to socializing with a Lexington bookie named Ed Curd, a man with ties to the mob. But he retreated into a warren of explanation and rationalization. "How could I suspect my boys were working with gamblers

101

when we were beating every damn team in the nation?" he said. And: "The Chicago Black Sox threw games. These kids only shaved points."

Rupp would never fully put to rest questions about his own knowledge of scandal within the program. Barnstable testified that after one game, Rupp chewed him out for missing a late shot. The miss, Barnstable said Rupp told him, had cost Burgess Carey, a friend of Rupp's, $500. And a Lexington attorney named J. A. Edge sued Rupp for $500,000, alleging that the coach had conspired with Curd and Frank Costello, the notorious New York gambler, to fix games. A local district court judge dismissed the suit, ruling that it had been filed solely to gain "notoriety"; for his impertinence Edge was suspended from practicing law for a year.

Rupp owned up to doling out anywhere from $10 to $50 per player after victories, depending on the performance. Yet the university wasn't about to let him go. President Donovan pronounced Rupp "an honorable man who did not knowingly violate athletic rules." The school's board of trustees absolved him of any involvement in the point-shaving.

And so the Baron's imperial reign continued. The Wildcats, chafing from that year-long hiatus, went 25–0 in 1953–54, their first season back, and would go on to win another NCAA title in 1958. Nor did Rupp's views on race moderate, even after Kentucky lost the 1966 NCAA championship game to Texas Western, a team with an all-black starting five, in what has been called the *Brown v. Board of Education* of college basketball. Columnist Jimmy Breslin remembers working on the sports desk of the New York *Journal-American* during the early sixties, and taking a call from Rupp himself, who wanted to know whether this Hawkins fellow—Connie Hawkins, a high-schooler from Brooklyn who was scoring all these points—was white or "colored." Breslin told him. The Baron thanked him for his

help, and asked whether the *Post* might in the future tag
with asterisks the names of Negro players in its box scores,
so he would know where to bother sending his scouts.

Rupp was quite happy to play *against* blacks, for it gave
him a chance to confirm his notions of white supremacy.
Twice Kentucky went to the NCAA tournament despite
finishing second in the SEC, because first-place finisher
Mississippi State refused to play in an integrated field. But
he wouldn't suit up his first black player until 1970, a
couple of years before his retirement. Seven-foot-two Tom
Payne played only one season before being imprisoned for
eleven years on a rape conviction, and to this day there are
Kentuckians who believe the Baron specifically picked out
Payne as a pioneer so the coach could say, "I told you so."

As Hall prepared to ascend, Rupp maintained his cur-
mudgeonly defiance in the face of any change. Occasionally
he indulged in a favorite pastime, fox hunting. "It's the best
sport for a man my age," he once said. "You turn the dogs
loose and sit down and listen to them with some sand-
wiches and a fifth of bourbon. The fox holes up and doesn't
get caught. The dogs have a happy time running about.
Nobody wins and nobody loses. And the alumni don't write
letters."

Kentucky is a land of breathtaking diversity and paradox.
It may be the only place in the world where a county called
Bourbon could be half dry. Three distinct cultural and
geographic entities stretch from the fastness of the Appalachians in the East, through the moneyed and gracious world
of the Bluegrass, all the way to the Bible-believing counties
in the West. Lexington society, centered around the Thoroughbred industry and the genteel millionaires belonging
to the exclusive Idle Hour Country Club, is one extreme of
life in the commonwealth; the other is stark poverty. But for
rich and poor alike, University of Kentucky basketball has
always been the state's one great love object.

"It was heaven," remembers Scott Courts, a Coloradan who played on the Wildcats' 1978 national championship team. "Everything's easy there for a basketball player. Easy friends, easy money, easy grades. I never had a date in high school and I had nine gorgeous women ask me out at registration. Everyone was saying, 'You're one of the new freshmen.'

"It was a beautiful place, of course. Friendly people. We lived with the country-club, horse-race set. We never really experienced reality. I guess that's both the great part of it, and also the problem. I come from a well-to-do family and I could see how this whole money- and hero-worship thing was a false scene.

"The biggest adjustment of my life was coming down from the Kentucky high. We were coming back from Dayton [where the 'Cats had won the Mideast Regional en route to the Final Four], and the whole thoroughfare was lined with people with signs welcoming us home. I used to hang my sneakers out the window to dry—you know, after practice. One morning there were just the laces blowing in the wind. I got a ransom call from some women who wanted a date if I was going to get them back."

Kentuckians grew up in intimate touch with the ten-foot culture. If you tour the state's byways and remote county roads, you'll still find hoops on the sides of humble shacks and horse barns, tire rims tacked to tree trunks. And every school could field a basketball team, since it took only five guys. Once you had your team, there was no telling what you could do with it, because Kentucky had a magical, free-for-all state tournament to which the champions of the state's sixteen regions advanced, with no regard to enrollment.

Jock Sutherland quit high-school coaching in 1979, right after winning the state tournament with his Lexington Lafayette team, to become a radio commentator. His first trip to the state tourney, however, had been twenty years earlier, when he took Gallatin County High, which represented a little patch of land on the Ohio River between Cincinnati and Louisville, to the big show. "I remember checking into the Phoenix Hotel in Lexington," Sutherland says. "And to this day, outside of the birth of my two children, that means more to me, more even than winning the state championship. My team was there. I was given an envelope with all the player badges, and I dumped them all out on a table and ran my hands over them. I couldn't have been any happier if I'd won the lottery. We played the very first game. Got beat by the team that eventually won it. And none of us gave a damn."

If a local high-school star got it going up at the state—if he shot the lights out and caught the eye of Coach Rupp—he just might get an offer of a scholarship, and the town he came from would be bound even closer to the Big Blue. In 1987 a chunky, mustachioed little guard named Richie Farmer, from the eastern coal-belt town of Manchester, willed and shot Clay County High to victories over the big-city schools and a state title. The next year Farmer nearly did it again, scoring fifty-one points in a loss in the finals to Ballard High of Louisville.

Joe Hall and Eddie Sutton operated in a different era than Rupp. If they had only lifted up their eyes unto the hills for their help, they wouldn't have won many games. But it's a measure of how little Sutton understood the politics of basketball in Kentucky that he had to succumb to public pressure before offering Farmer a scholarship.

Bret Bearup was a little too smart, a bit too aware, a little too fun-loving and immature to be the ideal Wildcat, a mindless cog in the Big Blue machine. A power forward with a soft touch, he had been a high-school All-America at Harborfields High on Long Island during the late seventies. But unlike most precocious, highly sought-after young ball players, he was a shameless fan too. The recruiting maelstrom thrilled him. Soon he would be receiving hundreds of letters from colleges interested in his services, and in time he would become as jaded as the next guy. But he still remembers the day that first envelope came, with its smart letterhead and crisp postmark, from a Maryland assistant coach named Joe Harrington. Bearup was so excited he wrote back.

As a high-school sophomore, he had followed Joe Hall's first championship, the 1978 "season without celebration." He had read all the accounts of the Wildcats' karate defense, how they had no fun, how they grimly stalked the title for which they were consensus favorites. He knew, too, about the exuberance of the Duke players, how the Blue Devils held hands on the court and engaged in funky handshakes and "elbow sex" and the like. In Bearup's mind, that of a young fan, it was no contest. He pulled for Duke in the Monday-night final.

But later, when they vied with Kentucky to sign him to a letter of intent, the Blue Devils didn't have a chance. "If you were wanted by Kentucky, *you were the best*," Bearup says. "I still remember how they came to my house. They brought in films of Rick Robey and explained how I would be playing his position. And they had this slide show. The very last slide was of Coach Hall standing with the NCAA trophy in one hand, and a jersey with my name on it in the other. And that just blows you away.

"When he was recruiting me, I could not imagine Joe Hall yelling. When I got to school I told my new teammates that. Freddie Cowan, Dirk Minniefield, Sam Bowie—boy, did they laugh. By the time the season started I'd heard so many stories, I'd been steeled.

"Joe Hall knew the level of adoration the people of the commonwealth had for the players. He thought his mission was to cut us down to size, or else we wouldn't work. Especially someone as immature as I was coming out of high school. I wanted to have fun."

If you played basketball at Kentucky, there was no room for fun, at least not officially. In many ways Hall, a former catsup salesman, was even better suited than Rupp to run the Big Blue machine. He had learned under Rupp what Eddie Sutton found out the hard way: that the program was now so big that a coach was just a steward of something belonging to several million other people, none of whom wanted to watch you X and O. Hall's problem wasn't an outsized ego, or a need to take his players' accomplishments as his own; it was that he took their failures personally. In 1983, when they wilted in the face of the Louisville press in the overtime of the first "dream game," Hall spent a crucial time-out just foaming at the mouth. He had fought bitter battles at the highest level of state politics to keep from having to play Louisville, a school he thought to be UK's inferior, and here his players were embarrassing him.

A year later, as Georgetown harassed the 'Cats into a 3-for-33 second-half shooting performance at the Final Four in Seattle, the coach's sphincter muscles contracted accordingly. The line on Hall after UK's ignominious performance that day was that you couldn't have driven a nail up his ass with a sledgehammer. Indeed, after Hall's retirement he took a job with a Lexington bank, and the joke around town had a masked man making off with a handsome sum "because Joe B. wouldn't let the guards shoot."

But then the entire mood of the program was one of tight control. The only lassitude was in Hall's policy toward boosters, the moneyed men from around the state whose largesse funded the program. Hall felt he could indulge them. After all, at a cost of $500,000 they had built the Joe B. Hall Wildcat Lodge, a basketball dormitory so opulent that the NCAA forced the university to stop the cooked-to-order breakfasts and remove some of the $200,000 in furnishings, to bring the place more in line with the facilities in which the typical undergraduate lived.

And so Hall was less a head coach than a finicky sheriff.

The boosters were his deputies. Once every fall the heaviest hitters gathered in Lexington, and one by one posed for a picture with Hall's team. A print of "me with the 'Cats" would hang prominently in the offices of the state's most favored horsemen, doctors, bankers, tobacco growers, and coal operators, to be pointed to with pride over and over during the season to come. "The seriousness those guys attached to basketball was so superficial, but it's so easy to get into," remembers one former Wildcat. "It was an ego thing for them. They wanted to be seen around Lexington with you, for their kids, and to show off for each other."

Boosters visited the locker room at halftime; the press couldn't even enter it after games. Hall never fully trusted the media, with justification. His thin skin made him their ready foil. He drilled his players to conduct themselves in interviews just so, to spout the innocuous bromide and sidestep the sharp question. Each 'Cat was videotaped in mock television interviews, then critiqued in how he held his head, how he made eye contact, how many times crutches—"you knows" and "uhhhs"—crept into his answers. Then he would be put through the process again to measure his improvement.

Over one Christmas break, Hall even took his team to a Lexington hotel for instruction in etiquette. Everyone, including the blubbery Melvin Turpin, whose eating habits would torture Hall for four years, sat down to a twelve-course meal. Their hostess, a sort of manners instructor, guided them through the various servings, explaining the purpose of each piece of silverware and the social niceties attending to every course. Early in the exercise, as the players worked on the proper ingestion of beef vegetable soup—*Like little ships that go to sea/I push my spoon away from me*—a reserve forward named Tom Heitz dredged up an unusually large piece of beef, one that appeared quite capable of flummoxing even the best-intentioned diner.

Rather than muddle through like a slob, Heitz shot his hand up.

"Excuse me, ma'am. What do you do when you get a *whole cow*, like this?"

Bret Bearup, sitting across from Heitz, was in midswallow. The gulp never got down. As Bearup dissolved in hysterics, Hall glowered at him.

"Bearup, git your ass out of here," he said. "This is for people with *manners*."

Bearup, young and impertinent, would never get along with Hall. One night, a Wildcat had too much to drink and bashed in one of the many half basketballs, each with the name of one of the boosters who helped build the place, that grace the doorways to bedrooms in the Wildcat Lodge. Hall immediately took it to be Bearup's work, and held him responsible until the other player 'fessed up. Yet Bearup was always the first player Hall would send out into the state for speaking engagements. Hall knew the whimsical innocence that drove him nuts worked a spell on the faithful.

When the 'Cat worshippers came by the lodge, most of the players would shrink from their prying eyes. Not Bearup. He loved giving tours, bantering with the proud adults, imagining the thrill the kids were getting. Young Bret had once asked Sidney Wicks for his autograph after an NBA game, and Wicks had blown him off. The circumstances of that slight were still seared into his memory, the sting like yesterday's. If he wandered into the lodge while Bearup was around, a youngster could expect a tour not to forget.

Bearup would take them up where the players lived. He showed them the TV room downstairs, with its majestic coal fireplace, a sort of altar to the legions of well-to-do coal barons. And he would always be sure to point out the tiny hideaway door under the stairs, the one leading to the basement. "And that's Dicky Beal's room," he'd say, referring to the popular little UK guard. The tourists lapped it up.

Once, at halftime of a 1984 game at Vanderbilt, Hall came into the locker room brandishing the stat sheet. The Commodores' star, Jeff Turner, had three fouls. Time to plot strategy. "Who's Turner guarding?" Hall wanted to know.

The players sat silently.

"Who's Turner guarding?!" Hall bellowed again.

For a few beats no one moved. The players exchanged glances. Then Bearup spoke up.

"Coach," he said. "They're in a zone." Bearup turned to someone sitting behind him. "What game has he been watching?" he whispered. "They've been in a zone the whole first half. They've been playing zone ever since [Vandy coach] C. M. Newton came to Nashville."

Bearup was too smart for his own good. "It got so at the end of my career I wouldn't talk around Joe Hall for fear of being rebuked," he says. Nor did he ever blossom into the Rick Robey of his era. He became a good player over five seasons, including one redshirt year. But the promise of Kentucky, the apotheosis of big-time college basketball, always eluded him. One night during Bearup's junior season, a visitor had holed up in Bret's hotel room to shoot the breeze. He shared with Bearup something Indiana coach Bobby Knight had confided in him.

"If we had that Bearup kid who's wasting away down at Kentucky," Knight had said, "we'd win the Big Ten."

It was a compliment, the visitor thought. It would make Bret feel good. But within a few seconds a tear was running down Bret Bearup's cheek.

Notwithstanding his differences with the occasional Wildcat, Joe Hall moved Kentucky basketball adroitly through the college game's boom years. He did it by taking the suffocating attention of the people of the state and turning it to his advantage. There wasn't an item on a high-school prospect's checklist that Kentucky couldn't offer. The luxurious lodge. Rupp Arena, whose 23,000 seats made it the largest in the country when it was built in 1976. Summer jobs at horse farms, which many of the current players held, and which recruits could properly assume would be theirs. To turn down Kentucky, it seemed, was to spurn the embrace of an entire state.

Fans wrote letters by the sackful to everyone on the shortlist of prospects that Hall and his recruiting coordinator, Leonard Hamilton, drew up. Town and gown alike would get gussied up for a recruit's official visit. One night during his visit to campus in 1982, Barry Sumpter, the seven-foot son of God-fearing parents, was half scared to death to find a naked woman walk into his room. That was how much Kentucky was prepared to love you.

And of course there were the fans at the top end, the boosters, whose ubiquity and proximity to the program seemed to assure a prosperous life after one's basketball career, if not during it. Before 1987, when NCAA legislation barred boosters from any contacts with prospects, Hall would make recruiting visits with a retinue of high rollers in tow. They would fly into a town for a high-school game, usually in a private plane a member of the traveling party had supplied gratis. There, recalls Bob Hill, who recruited against the Wildcats while an assistant at Kansas, "They would dominate everyone so no one could get to the key people. The pilot, friends of the program—two or three of them would grab the mother, some guys would grab the father, someone else grabbed the girlfriend, and then Coach Hall would go back and get the head coach. They would tie everyone up. They were ahead of their time. They didn't miss a trick. It got to the point where if you were fighting them without the forces they had, you would go recruit someone else."

That was the idea, of course. And many schools did bail out as soon as the Big Blue showed up. With its six-figure recruiting budget, Kentucky was a bully swaggering into the school yard. Even UNLV's Jerry Tarkanian, who has plenty of influential boosters surrounding his own team, tells how demoralizing it was to recruit against the Wildcats. Every time Tarkanian checked into the main hotel in Sam Bowie's hometown of Lebanon, Pennsylvania, UK assistant Leonard Hamilton was registered. But Hamilton often wasn't in his room, and wouldn't be for days at a time. And then it dawned on Tarkanian: Kentucky had taken out a room for the entire season. Just to recruit one kid.

But then the Wildcats didn't recruit, or even select. They anointed. "Joe would look at the top five guards in the country, all about the same in ability, and sit us all down and ask, 'Which one do we want?'" remembers Jim Hatfield, who preceded Hamilton as the Wildcats' chief recruiter. "We wanted the guy who would represent UK the best and get the most out of it, who could take the praise and not become big-headed."

The Thoroughbred Classic—for years it was called the Hillbrook Classic, after the horse farm owned by Cap Hershey, a crony of Hall's and a UK booster—was as potent as any recruiting tool. A high-school tournament played in December, usually in conjunction with the Wildcats' invitational holiday tournament, it took place just as a new recruiting season was getting under way. The university would stage a clinic, at which the high schools' coaches would speak, usually for a generous fee. But the event existed primarily to bring to town the finest talent in the land, most of which the Wildcats were pursuing. Through the eighties the visitors included Danny Ferry, Terry Mills, Jimmy Jackson, Richard Madison, and Eric Manuel. It was as if Hamilton and his successor, Dwane Casey, had chosen the participating teams.

With every conceivable advantage within the rules, and so much to lose if caught breaking them, why would Kentucky risk crossing the line? The answers might be found in the state's tradition of political chicanery; in two of sport's most corruptive influences, wealth and wagering, both of which pervade the Bluegrass; and in the implicit message the head coach sent by taking scores of sports-crazed Babbitts to his bosom. And there's a hubris that develops with something so big and insular and successful. It can foster a recklessness not unlike that of the Wildcat point-shavers in the 1949 NIT loss to Loyola: It's so easy. Just this once. They won't catch us.

Where the money came from has been a lively topic of speculation among people around the game. There was once a story that a small fortune sat in an account in some Kentucky bank, and might well sit there forever, because the NCAA was somehow monitoring it and it couldn't be touched. And tales of a booster-maintained slush fund have circulated since before the days of Hall and Sutton. Indeed, former Hawaii coach Bruce O'Neil says that Rupp himself once described to him an arrangement by which several hundred boosters kicked $1,000 each into a fund used for recruiting and rewarding players.

With the lantern jaw of a television anchor, John Carroll looks as if he stumbled into the wrong branch of the news business. His pedigree, however, is entirely that of the stouthearted newspaperman. He spent much of his child-hood in the North Carolina Piedmont, where his father was an editor at the Winston-Salem *Journal*. Classical refer-ences, dropped occasionally into the columns he writes today, betray a liberal arts education from Haverford Col-lege. In 1973, after doing tours in Vietnam, the Middle East, and on the White House beat for the Baltimore *Sun*, he hooked on with the Philadelphia *Inquirer*, one of the primary links in the Knight-Ridder chain. Knight-Ridder sent Carroll to Lexington six years later, as editor-in-chief of the morning *Herald* and afternoon *Leader*.

Until Knight-Ridder bought them in 1973, the newspapers had always been courtly broadsheets, locally owned and reflective of the prevailing values and prominent interests of central Kentucky. But Carroll had been involved in three Pulitzer Prize–winning series as an editor with the *Inquirer*, and soon made clear that his notion of good journalism didn't include blindly boosting the Bluegrass status quo. The University of Kentucky, with its sprawling campus just blocks from the paper's offices at Main and Midland, was a logical subject for scrutiny.

In 1982 Carroll's ace investigator, Gary Cohn, detailed abuses at the university's black-lung clinic, where coal miners from around the state would go to be certified for medical benefits. A short time later Cohn outlined waste and mismanagement in UK's Tobacco & Health Research Institute, which operates in a state with omnipotent tobacco interests. As far as Carroll was concerned, improprieties in the Kentucky basketball program would be like any other public malfeasance, ripe for exposure.

"We knew for a long time that things were going on," Carroll says. "The atmosphere just surrounded the program. Business people would sort of nudge each other, and say things like, 'You can't have a team without paying for it.' I imagine some of those people weren't actually paying players, but merely acting as if they did to be among the in crowd. To be on the inside was a feather in one's cap. But it was constantly being discussed obliquely. I remember my first year we talked about what we'd do if we actually caught them, because we knew there'd be hell to pay."

Soon enough, Cohn was on to something. A former Notre Dame forward named Dave Batton described improper inducements offered him during his recruitment out of high school near Philadelphia. Batton has said that Seth Hancock, owner of Claiborne Farm and a UK booster, offered him spending money as he needed it, and work at Claiborne over the four summers he would be a Wildcat. Upon graduation, Batton would collect $20,000—$5,000 per summer—or could credit it toward a share in a racehorse. "Kentucky was illegal from day one," Batton says. Hancock has denied Batton's account.

But Carroll chose not to run the story. For one, it was old. And, Carroll says, "I told Gary that if we were going to do the UK story, we weren't going to pin it on one person, a Dave Batton. One person couldn't take the pressure. We would be hanging him out to dry."

The *Herald*, now merged into the *Leader*, regrouped. The paper would end up backing into its UK story unexpectedly. Over the 1984–85 season, reports surfaced that Hall had been selling some of his personal allotment of 323 season tickets, with a face value of $24,000, for upward of $1,000 apiece. Twice UK investigated how Hall disposed of his tickets, and neither time announced any finding of wrongdoing. But Hall suddenly stepped down as coach the day the season ended. While poking around in the Hall ticket situation, Jeffrey Marx and Michael York began to turn up the material that would constitute the Pulitzer Prize–winning series.

Marx was in his early twenties, fresh out of Northwestern's Medill School of Journalism. He had been an intern at the paper while an undergraduate, and came to know a number of former Wildcats while working on a "where are they now" piece about the 1977–78 NCAA championship team. York, a thirty-two-year-old graduate of UK's law school, gained the trust of a number of other players, who in turn suggested a few more who might talk. "We'd get one or two off the record, then three or four on," Carroll says. "A few players would actually help round people up. We'd bring them in in bunches."

The reporters put their tape recorders on the table when they interviewed people in person. Over the phone they tape-recorded conversations in accordance with Kentucky's single-party consent law, telling a subject he was being taped only if he asked. A dislike for Hall motivated some ex-players to speak; others felt the NCAA rules they broke were ridiculous, and thought they could effect change by coming clean. From one interview Marx and York might get a piece of information, albeit something short of a nailed-down fact. Then they'd present it to another player, always phrasing questions so they couldn't be answered with a summary "yes" or "no," and the second party would wind up confirming it. It was shrewd, ruthless investigative reporting—in short, the only way the story was going to get told. Soon a critical mass of current and former Wildcats formed. No one would be hung out to dry.

As the leaves turned during the weeks leading up to publication, Lexington was aflame with rumors of the *Herald-Leader*'s project. "It was like covering the South Vietnamese legislature," says Carroll. "A new rumor every day." Carroll's fiancée was accosted in the supermarket by Lexingtonians wanting to know when "that friend of yours" was going to do in their beloved 'Cats. The university's general counsel, John Darsie, asked the newspaper to turn over its material so the school could get a head start on its investigation. Carroll declined.

As the paper readied the series, lawyers vetted each sentence for libel. Editors excised any controversial quote that wasn't on tape. City editor Dave Green listened to every cassette, balancing the quoted extracts with what came before and after to make sure nothing was used out of context. Carroll put the building's security guards on notice, and arranged for extra people to man the phones. "We knew we were doing something that would antagonize the community," Carroll says. "We knew it wouldn't be fun. But we had no way of knowing how bad it would be."

The Sunday *Herald-Leader*, with its headline PLAYING ABOVE THE RULES, must have left people in shock, for the wrath of the state didn't really come down until Monday. In its way, Lexington is a small town, the kind of community where Carroll's daughter could soon start dating Eddie

Sutton's son, Scott. Nearly a third of its residents come from eastern Kentucky, where the Appalachian values of loyalty and clan hold sway. "This is a fairly gentle place," Carroll says. "People are polite to each other. But there were a lot of unpleasant things said. The hardest thing was, nearly all our employees had a friend or acquaintance get right in their face and express rage. This was not something you could view from a distance. It divided families."

One of the newspaper's production workers canceled his free subscription. A *Herald-Leader* paperboy was run off by a man with an ax handle. A local club staged a "hate the *Herald-Leader* rally," at which someone sold subscriptions to the Louisville *Courier-Journal*. A bomb threat forced evacuation of the paper's offices. Meanwhile, the electronic media, in Carroll's words, "did all they could" to discredit the story. One man called to cancel his subscription; when told he wasn't a subscriber, he demanded to cancel anyway.

The fury didn't come only from hotheaded yahoos. It cut across all social classes. The following spring, *Herald-Leader* publisher Creed Black came upon Mrs. Waddell Hancock, the mother of Seth Hancock and a doyenne of Bluegrass society, at a party. A Claiborne horse had recently raced well, and Black approached her to offer his congratulations.

"Nice day," he began.

"It *was* a nice day," Mrs. Hancock said, her words bitten off with venom, "until I was required to be nice to *you*."

The paper was under siege. "I probably should have responded more vigorously," Carroll says. "But I was responsible for keeping morale up in the newsroom. And there were people working here who doubted that this was ever going to let up. In fact, it probably never will. It's left a scar on our relationship with the community that won't heal in our lifetime. Even those who believe we were right—and most realize we told the truth—don't look at us as kindly, sympathetic people anymore."

Carroll isn't a Kentuckian, a fact he has been reminded of many times since the story appeared. But his understanding of what, for better or for worse, Kentucky basketball means to the citizens of the commonwealth is now sharp and profound. Of the many letters he received, one sticks with him to this day. It was signed "Blue Bleeder." Its last line read, "It's all we got."

At his very first press conference, even before offering the obligatory remarks about how he was following a legend, Joe Hall had made a point of saying he was going to recruit the black athlete. He wanted to send signals to Jack Givens and James Lee, a couple of local high-school stars, that they needn't leave town. It would prove to be a point absolutely worth making, for Givens, the 1978 Final Four MVP, and Lee helped give Hall his only championship.

But there was much more bridge-building to be done, particularly after the abortive Tom Payne experiment and decades of Ruppism, if UK basketball were going to establish credibility with black prospects and their families. Hall soon hired Leonard Hamilton, a black Tennessean and former assistant at Austin Peay, as his recruiting coordinator. At first Hall and Hamilton were careful to bring in blacks they were sure would thrive at Kentucky. LaVon Williams, Reggie Warford, Dwane Casey, Givens, and Lee— all were from in-state, either from small towns or immediately around Lexington, and each adjusted well.

Hamilton would soon look beyond UK's traditional recruiting grounds of Kentucky, Ohio, Indiana, and Illinois for the black athlete. Yet the neofeudal way of life in the Bluegrass, coupled with the attitudes ingrained in so many of the program's followers, made UK a potentially inhospitable place. Where Louisville has a prosperous and coherent black middle class, Lexington has none to speak of. Even today, newspapers around the state regularly receive calls from fans curious to know the race of players UK is recruiting. Longtime Kentucky sports columnist Billy Reed may have understated things when he wrote, during the search in 1985 to find Hall's successor, that "there'll be a Martian in the White House" before Kentucky hires a black coach.

In 1988, former governor and commissioner of baseball A. B. (Happy) Chandler touched off a controversy with a remark made before a subcommittee of the university's board of trustees. On the question of whether the school should divest itself of holdings in companies doing business in South Africa, Chandler argued against. "Look at Zimbabwe," Chandler said, pronouncing the name as if it were "Sam Bowie," and perhaps revealing how deep the UK basketball psychosis really runs. "It's all nigger now."

Chandler is an octogenarian beloved throughout the state, and most parties to the controversy were willing to cut him some slack. But he only offended further when he bumblingly tried to apologize. In the small Kentucky town where he grew up, Chandler said, black folk didn't mind being called "niggers." Multiracial efforts of students and Kentuckians to force Chandler from the board, including an extraordinary threatened boycott of spring practice by the Wildcats' football team, were unavailing, and black Kentuckians had to suffer their offense without redress. Very simply, either too few sensibilities had been offended, or the ones that had been hurt didn't count.

At Kentucky, a black ball player was likely to encounter more than just a clash of cultures. Hall's tight rein was at odds with the unfettered style of basketball popular in the inner cities. In one of his very first UK practices, James Blackmon, a raw black freshman from Marion, an industrial town in northern Indiana, slalomed through a press and flipped in a clean, backhand-to-the-rim layup.

"Goddammit, Blackmon!" It was Hall, yelling from the sideline. "We don't *do* finger rolls at Kentucky!"

If you wanted to run free, you went to Louisville and played for Denny Crum. To be young, gifted, black, and Blue took its toll psychologically and emotionally. After UK lost a shocking 50–44 first-round game to Middle Tennessee State in the 1982 NCAA tournament, one black Wildcat shook his head dolefully. "I just want to get away from these motherfucking horse people," he said, "and go back to being a nigger again."

One thing could help take some of the sting out of Rupp's racist legacy, and that was to be found in the deep pockets of the boosters. The very best black players might have money and inducements offered up front, during the re-cruiting process, usually to a family member. But unless the player went on to show he had the grace to move unthreateningly through Bluegrass social circles, he could expect little after his playing days were over. The white players, by and large, were expected to make do with the adulation and the lifetime embrace it seemed to promise. The occasional booster shot of pocket change, the sinecure summer job, the proceeds from scalped com-plimentary tickets, and honoraria from speaking engage-ments were expected to be enough to get a white player through.

The double standard took root, and some of the whites on the team came to resent it. "It wouldn't have bothered me so much if the black players weren't flaunting it," says one former 'Cat. "But they were waving hundred-dollar bills in our faces, and here we're calling home for money."

Black and white played together at UK, but they weren't as one. And then, just as Sutton replaced Hall, out of the northwest part of the state came a startling crossover figure, a player so gifted, so full of an unbridled joy that Big Blue basketball had never known before, that he blurred race and prior rules. In Latin his first name meant "ruler." They called him the Boy King.

* * *

Fans who didn't know any better expected Rex Chapman to be another Great White Hope, a precise and anal-retentive ball player in the tradition of Kyle Macy. Only better, of course, because he was theirs. Macy was a small-town Indiana boy, with a mechanical jump shot and textbook game. But Rex was from the river city of Owensboro, the son of a former Western Kentucky star and ABA player. And oh, how he played basketball.

Wayne Chapman was now the head coach at Kentucky Wesleyan, a Division II power, and he raised a precocious and freethinking son. Rex had grown up not just around the game, but around an integrated version of it. He hung out at Kendall-Perkins Park on the predominantly black, west side of town, running in the Dust Bowl league games there. At Apollo High he felt just as comfortable among blacks as whites, and dated a member of the girls' track team, a young black woman named Shawn Higgs. When he walked into the athletes' cafeteria in Donovan Hall on the UK campus his freshman year, his neck hung with gold, a Wildcat football player would remark, "Here comes Rex in his Mr. T starter's kit."

Chapman's game had the same racial ambiguity. He never lost a slam-dunk contest, and his every step bespoke the beat of the music he enjoyed listening to—black music. "Rex is as close to being a black player as a white player is ever going to get," says Jock Sutherland. "He jumps, he's free in his movements, he has a style all his own. The typical UK fan thinks Rex should be throwing a bounce pass and going over and getting the ball back behind a screen. But the only guy who'd enjoy him doing that would be the guy trying to guard him."

Coming out of high school, Chapman's instinct was to choose Louisville, with its freewheeling style and easygoing coach. But Kentucky basketball will always hold an in-state youngster in its thrall. And Eddie Sutton had that reputation for turning out great guards.

121

5

The Coaches' Code

AS NIGHT FELL over the Sangre de Cristo Mountains, Gary Colson sat in his office trying to sort things out. It was the autumn of 1980. He was about to embark on his first season as head coach at New Mexico. Several years earlier the university had been torn apart by the Lobogate scandal, a series of abuses that disgraced coach Norm Ellenberger and his staff and profoundly shamed the school. Given the recent ordeal, these Lobos were bound to conducting themselves honorably. Yet soon after arriving on campus Colson took an informal opinion poll. "Can I win at New Mexico without cheating?" he asked a number of fans and sportswriters. Nearly all of them told him he couldn't. "And if you do cheat," one local scribe added, "I'll be the first to expose you."

Still, Colson wondered, If I had to cheat, how would I do it? There in his office, as the twilight gathered, he hatched a plan.

On his official visit to the UNM campus, soon after

checking into his hotel, a prospect would receive a phone call. The caller would introduce herself as "Mrs. Williams," a wealthy widow whose late husband was a loyal supporter of the Lobo program. Only this would really be Colson, his voice slipped into an upper register and creaky tone.

In the privacy of his office, with no one around, he practiced it. "I know Coach Colson would disapprove of this," she would squeak. "But I want to honor Enselmo's memory and help the team myself. If you go by the front desk you'll find an envelope in your name with five hundred dollars in it. When you sign, you'll get an envelope with five thousand dollars in it. The first day you show up in September you'll get another nice envelope. You won't have to worry about a thing for four years. But if I ever hear you're creating any problems for Coach Colson, or if you ever betray this trust we have, everything shuts down. I just want to see this program survive. You're the key."

It was perfect, Colson thought. She just delivers. And if the NCAA finds out about her, they'll never actually *find* her. She doesn't exist. When Colson saw Dustin Hoffman in *Tootsie*, he thought again of his Lobo in woman's clothing.

Nothing happened as a result of that reverie; "Mrs. Williams" never went beyond the bounds of the coach's imagination. But then Colson hardly thought she needed to. The doomsayers of his informal opinion poll were wrong. He did win at New Mexico—within the rules, so far as anyone knows. He put together an enviable program, a team that played running basketball and drew well. Though they never could seem to beat out Brigham Young or Texas–El Paso in the Western Athletic Conference's postseason tournament, the Lobos did average eighteen wins a year over his eight seasons, and three times broke twenty. Win twenty, Colson had come up believing, and you could declare yourself successful.

Even so, at the end of each of those seasons the NCAA tournament committee passed New Mexico over for a bid.

The NIT, the bittersweet consolation prize, didn't sit well with the good burghers of Albuquerque, who filled the 17,126-seat Pit for virtually every home game. It didn't please New Mexico's athletic director, John Koenig, who watched the six-figure minimum paid out to those schools qualifying for the NCAAs leap upward every year. Hell, it didn't sit well with Gary Colson.

He had done all he could. He had recruited well—few great players, to be sure, but an abundance of good ones. He had tried scheduling nonconference teams with high power ratings, the sorts of opponents that would impress the NCAA elders who doled out those bids. But few schools were foolhardy enough to agree to play in the din and thin air of the Pit. And the last thing Colson's bosses wanted was to see the Lobos hit the road to play intersectional games, however glamorous the opponent, when they could pack their own place against Tumbleweed Tech and bag a tidy gate.

By the end of the 1987–88 season, Colson's bosses had him pegged as someone incapable of taking the New Mexico program to "the next level." It didn't matter that his players graduated and involved themselves in the community, or that the NCAA's enforcement people hadn't heard so much as a peep from Albuquerque. The sportswriter who had told him he couldn't win without cheating—and promised to expose him if he did cheat—was the first to crucify him for not winning enough. He was fired in April.

"Oh, people came to me and said, 'We've got the money. Just tell us when,'" Colson says now. "I told them thanks, but no thanks. The thing is, I'm an example of why there's cheating. There's so much pressure to get into the tournament. We missed getting in by a bucket one year. One basket. You talk to the A.D.'s, a lot of them expect that tournament money. They have it budgeted in already.

"A friend of mine called me recently, a coach. He said, 'Gary, you're gonna hear rumors that I'm cheating. And I want you to know they're true. I've got a wife and kids. The league I'm in, it's the only way I can survive.'

"I screwed up," Colson says, referring wistfully back to his wealthy widow. "I didn't do it."

Over the past few years, Colson and a number of other coaches—Bill Foster, George Raveling, Stetson's Glenn Wilkes, and Virginia Commonwealth's Sonny Smith among them—have gathered together over a long summer weekend to sit around and talk candidly. They'll broach anything, from their philosophies of life to their favorite out-of-bounds plays, from the state of their marriages to the state of the game that has them in its employ. Eavesdrop on one of these bull sessions, listen in on the fears and frailties of some of these men, and you'd have a hard time concluding that any of them is evil people, whether or not he might put a "Mrs. Williams" up to paying his players.

Basketball coaches are like anyone else, only more competitive. Just as the professors on their campuses do, they work with young people. But unlike their tenured counterparts, they're held to much starker standards. Exams are games, passing is winning, and the teacher is held accountable for every flunked test. It makes for an insecure lot. In 1986 the National Association of Basketball Coaches, under its president at the time, Eddie Sutton, passed a resolution calling on television analysts to refrain from criticizing coaches over the air.

The typical head coach—not the men like Dean Smith, Bob Knight, and John Thompson, who lord over small fiefdoms, but the tradesmen like Gary Colson—knows he'll be fired eventually. His assistants work on year-to-year arrangements they know won't be renewed unless talent continues to flow into the program. Should a coach be blamed for rearranging his values to accommodate the exigencies that crop up when he's lucky enough to have a job? For violating the spirit, if not the letter, of rules? Many coaches pose these very questions to themselves, and answer them no—because they perceive the demands on them as unreasonable, because they have families to feed, because it seems everyone else is doing these things and getting away with them. "You know Dwane Casey?" Colson says. "Great guy. Oh, great guy. There are a lot of great guys across the tracks. But it's not Johnny Coach. It's the administration, the A.D., the president, the board of regents —they want wins, money, prestige, and TV time. They get the coach backed up against the wall. What's he gonna do?"

He trusts in the security of overnight delivery services. And hopes no one breaks the Code.

Among coaches, the Code is simple: even if you aren't breaking any rules yourself—and many coaches find the *NCAA Manual* so baffling that they're probably violating something without knowing it—you never point a finger at someone who is. "I grew up in an Italian neighborhood in Ohio," Jerry Tarkanian says. "I was raised that you could do anything you wanted and everybody would be behind you, except squeal on somebody."

Oh, they'll gesture toward a general area. "The Southeastern Conference," says one veteran coach. "This is big-time bucks, big-time cheating. The most blatant cheating conference in the country. No other conference comes close. The big joke among the coaches is they have a salary cap in the SEC. One coach in that conference will come right out and tell you: 'I'm not about to go to seventy-five thousand for that kid. He's only worth sixty thou.' The word is he signed some kid from Florida a few years ago for nothing, no cheating. Then he had to rush an assistant down to pay the kid anyway because they were worried he'd come to campus and find out how much his teammates were making and feel out of place."

And coaches are willing to outline the problem without naming names. One coach has been ensconced comfortably at a school. He has been enormously successful there, and his school's way of recruiting—swoop in just before signing day and make an offer that can't be refused—would figure to make him a few enemies. But the Code still holds. "Why doesn't he get mentioned, much less nailed?" asks another coach. "Because everybody likes him. He's easygoing, never criticizes anybody else. Keeps that low profile. Never gets obnoxious." And obeys the Code.

Like honor among thieves, the Code prohibits specific charges against specific schools. No one "dimes" on anyone else. To get a sense of how much force the Code has, one need only look at what happens when someone breaks it, as Notre Dame coach Digger Phelps once did. At the 1982 Final Four in New Orleans, he charged that the going rate for blue-chip high-school stars had hit five figures per year. (It has since spiraled well beyond that, of course.) The money, he said, came from slush funds set up by boosters and winked at by coaches and athletic directors. Phelps stopped short of naming names, but said he knew of at least seven schools that were doing it, two of which—the Code be damned—he had reported to the NCAA. Those close to the game suspected at least one program Phelps had in mind: Southern Cal, which had signed Ken Johnson and Wayne Carlander, big men Phelps had wanted.

Notre Dame isn't known to buy its basketball team. Thus, many of his colleagues concluded, Digger wasn't just speaking out of school; he was whining, trying to commandeer the stage during the sport's showcase event. His comments soon passed, but his role as pariah didn't. After Arkansas–Little Rock upset Notre Dame in a first-round NCAA tournament game in 1986, UALR coach Mike Newell could hardly get through the lobby of the Loews Anatole Hotel in Dallas, where the coaches' association met a short time later, for all the congratulations offered by his peers. Thanks, they all more or less said, for beating that sanctimonious jerk.

Digger Phelps has weathered good seasons and bad over

his two decades at Notre Dame. He'll clearly have the Irish coaching job as long as he wants it. But most of his colleagues operate in a different world. The business of procuring, and winning with, young basketball players—to say nothing of educating them—is understood to be so daunting an undertaking that you do what you must to make it more bearable. "The letter of the rules isn't violated all that much," says Duke coach Mike Krzyzewski, who comes as close to doing things by the book as anyone at the elite level. "But the intent of those rules is hammered to hell. In order to make money and get exposure, we're always looking at ways to use rules, to use players. I grew up in Chicago, and Richard Daley ran that city through graft. It was a beautifully run city."

Coaches are even more loath to turn one another in because so many doubt the NCAA's commitment to evenhandedness. Tarkanian is as cynical as any of them. He spent a dozen years fighting the NCAA, claiming his constitutional rights were violated when that organization ordered him suspended from coaching in 1977 after violations were found in the UNLV program. That Tarkanian lost in the Supreme Court strengthened the NCAA's power, and only redoubled many coaches' perception of the governing body of college athletics as an omnipotent bully.

Another doubter is former Bradley coach Dick Versace. The NCAA put the Braves on probation in 1986, forcing Versace to flee to the pros, where he's now coach of the Indiana Pacers. "I blasted them nationally in 'eighty-two because they didn't select us for the tournament, even though we were outright champions of the Missouri Valley. I'd plotted for four years to build that team. [Tournament selection committee chairman] Dave Gavitt was head of the Big East, and he wanted to get a lot of his teams in to make money for his conference. So they choose Boston College over us. They're eight and six in the league, with wins over Stonehenge [sic], Bentley, Merrimack, and St. Anselm.

And people told me, 'You can say this. You're right. But you're making them look bad, and down the road they're going to get you.' And they did."

Tarkanian will say much the same thing. He has been on the lam for so long now that he settles naturally into the role of the game's guilty conscience. "If an alumnus gives a player one hundred dollars after a game, that may be an isolated incident," he says. "There's no way a coach is going to know about that. But if a kid's getting paid to go to school, there's no way a coach is *not* going to know." Notwithstanding the lesson of the Italian neighborhood of his youth, he'll let slip a skeptical aside if he thinks a school is being hypocritical. He likes to say he prefers transfers "because their cars are already paid for," and that he once lost a player to another school because "we got vanned." Don't try to tell Tarkanian that money doesn't drive the sport.

Before shoe companies turned college coaches into well-heeled human billboards, coaching was an adequately remunerated profession, but no one expected to get rich doing it. For all his success, John Wooden never made more than $35,000 a year before retiring from UCLA in 1975. But then the game boomed. As Nike, Converse, and Reebok jockeyed to sign coaches to endorsement deals, their bidding pushed the numbers higher. TV and radio shows assured another chunk of change. If a coach had a name and a shtick, he could sign up with an agency that booked him into after-dinner speaking gigs or motivational lectures at $5,000 or $10,000 a pop. Come the summer, he ran his basketball camp, renting the gym from his school at little cost and turning a tidy profit.

As coaching became a year-round cottage industry, coaches learned to keep their hands out. And just as they became accustomed to profiting from their position, there developed a problem, exactly the pickle that led to Gary Colson's undoing at New Mexico. Midmajor and lesser

Division I teams found it harder and harder to persuade a high-profile school to play them. And without a strong enough schedule, all the wins in the world won't get you an at-large bid to the NCAAs. If the powers wouldn't schedule you, what could you do?

A handful of schools figured out what you could do. You could make it worth the coach's while to schedule you.

The practice first came to light in the case of former Memphis State coach Dana Kirk, who served a jail term for income tax evasion and obstruction of justice. Among the income Kirk didn't declare was $10,000 paid him in 1983 by organizers of the Winston Tire Classic, in exchange for Kirk delivering his team to that Christmas tournament in Los Angeles. Payoffs like this are usually arranged quietly, by a desperate athletic director or tournament director, through one of several brokers who matchmake games. The baksheesh is paid the visiting coach on the pretext of his giving a clinic or a speech.

It's difficult to document such payoffs, unless the Internal Revenue Service intervenes, as it did in Kirk's case. But everyone in the sport knows they're made, and the figure Kirk received is the going rate. "I've been offered that much to take a team somewhere to play," says Miami's Foster. Almost all the athletic directors responding to a 1986 NCAA questionnaire on the practice urged that it be banned. Yet among coaches, an astonishing forty-four percent objected to any legislation prohibiting it. Perhaps channeling so much money into the hands of eighteen-year-olds has dulled their sense of propriety.

Coaches don't profit personally from another scheme, but it, too, is a way of selling players down the river. In a profession with small margins for error, it's an expedient that buys a coach breathing room. It's called "overbooking," and colleges notorious for its practice are called "airline schools." A coach normally pilots his "aircraft" into each season with fifteen "seats." That's the NCAA-mandated scholarship limit. Yet many coaches sign several high-school seniors in the fall, stock up on a few more in the spring, perhaps add a junior-college transfer or three for good measure, until they have on their hands more passengers than room. Somebody has to get bumped.

Some coaches insist that natural selection pares a roster judiciously down to size. But those coaches are, however briefly, pitting themselves against their players. They're hoping implicitly that one or more won't make it academically, will get hurt, or will just up and leave. "If you're hoping for that," says Krzyzewski, "then you're orchestrating that, consciously or subconsciously."

Here's an arithmetic lesson, Kentucky-style. In the fall of 1986 the Wildcats landed six recruits during the early-signing period. At the time, nine of the 'Cats who would play during the 1986–87 season were expected back the following year. Two more UK players were sitting out the '86–'87 season (one with an injury and one for academic reasons), giving Eddie Sutton a projected seventeen players for fifteen '87–'88 positions.

But logjams break easily when the timber is virgin and a burly, big-time program wears the plaid flannel shirt. A reserve named Todd Ziegler quit over Christmas—not, he said, without encouragement to do so. Down to sixteen, Sutton signed yet another player in April '87, pushing his roster back up to two over. Only when Irving Thomas, a senior-to-be, transferred out in May, and recruit John Pittman was suddenly denied admission for academic reasons several weeks later, did Kentucky meet the limit. Sutton's stance on all this: "I'll bring in a whole new team each year if I want to."

Sutton was far from alone in harboring that attitude. If high-schoolers were husbands, North Carolina State's Jim Valvano would make Zsa Zsa Gabor look like Mother Teresa. Larry Brown, despite all his maudlin references to "my kids" while coach at Kansas, brought youngsters in and chased them off. One college scout who monitors such things counted twenty names on the Jayhawks' roster at one point over the summer of 1986. Before Bob Wade resigned as coach at Maryland in 1989, he tried revoking the scholarship of Phil Nevin, a fine student and exemplary benchwarmer who happened not to have blossomed into much of a player. Nevin fought Wade and won reinstatement, only to leave the Terps the following season.

In 1982, Oklahoma got the signature of junior-college guard Nelson Peterson on a conference letter of intent, but never sent it into the Big 8 office. Neither Peterson nor his coach found out until the spring, when OU was booked solid with high-school players, all with four years of eligibility. Peterson was left to scramble to find a spot with Idaho State. Sooners coach Billy Tubbs says he soured on Peterson because Peterson had gotten married, and he and his staff were worried about a spouse having a disruptive effect on the team. But once more, before he could learn about Darwin from his bio professor or rejection from the homecoming queen, a youngster got a dose of both from a college coach.

Almost to a man, coaches concede that running a youngster off is an unpleasant business. But most point out that scholarships are renewable each year, and claim overbooking as their prerogative, as much an entitlement as the right to hire and fire staff. Wherein lies yet another trick: the high-school coach–high-school player "package deal."

LSU coach Dale Brown has brought more people in by twos than anyone since Noah. When Rudy Macklin came to Baton Rouge in the late seventies, Macklin's high-school coach, Ron Abernathy, came with him—as an LSU assistant. When Howard Carter joined the Bayou Bengals, so did his high-school coach, Rick Huckabay, also as an assistant.

Care to guess where Jim Childers, LSU star Stanley Roberts's coach at Lower Richland High in South Carolina, is working now?

Some high-school coaches see a blue-chipper as their meal ticket out of the boondocks, a way to get out of teaching driver's ed. twice a week and having to monitor the cafeteria. "A high-school coach [with a blue-chip star] who entertains hundreds of college coaches, his main objective is getting a college job," says one college coach. "It's very obvious. And all the colleges cater to him even if they know what he really wants." Once a two-fer deal has been struck, the standard explanation goes something like, "Oh, we got to know Coach Beauregard real well during the recruiting process, and thought he'd make a fine addition to our staff." Of course none of the other schools that got to know Coach Beauregard real well during the recruiting process—but happened not to land his prize protégé—see fit to hire him as an assistant coach.

A popular variation on this tactic is to forgo romancing the coach and simply hire the young man's father. Kansas's Danny Manning would likely have been a North Carolina Tar Heel if Larry Brown hadn't hired Danny's father Ed, a truck driver at the time, as an assistant coach while Danny was still in high school. The family moved from Greensboro to Lawrence, and the rest is history. Southern Cal's George Raveling, by contrast, miscalculated. He hired LeRoy Ellis, father of L.A. high-school star LeRon Ellis, not knowing that LeRon was closer to his mother, Lucille, who was then separated from LeRoy. LeRon went to Kentucky, and LeRoy quietly left USC after two seasons there.

None of the aforementioned tricks of the trade—the acceptance of favors for scheduling a game, or overbooking, or the coach-player–father-son "package deal"—can be considered good for the game. But none is against NCAA rules either. (The membership did try to get a handle on outside income in 1987, passing legislation requiring coaches to report all of it to their superiors. But that only assured that scheduling payoffs, which were mostly under the table anyway, will stay underground.) Of course, colleges engage in an array of other activities that do contravene the rules. Foremost among them is the disbursement of cash.

At the time Frank McGuire retired in 1980, South Carolina had in place a strangely principled system of under-the-table payments. They were the Gamecocks' Christmas bonuses. Come the holidays, according to one former South Carolina player, an interested player could pass through the basketball office to pick his up. The bonuses were never mentioned in recruiting, just as they were never to be disclosed to anyone outside the Gamecock family. And there was a meritocracy to them. The amounts—roughly $800, $1,000, $1,500, and $2,000 at the end of the McGuire era—were set strictly according to a player's class, not his ability or performance. The money was supposed to last through the spring.

That we know about the Christmas bonuses today suggests how McGuire lost control over some of his younger players as he neared the end of his career. Dan Doyle, a former college coach, remembers running into an old friend who had played for McGuire back in the early seventies. When Doyle brought the subject up, the ex-player was astonished.

"How did you . . . ?"

Doyle explained.

"Those young guys," the player said, shaking his head.

When asked about the unofficial Christmas bonus program, McGuire says, "It's a hell of a plan, but that's completely erroneous, unless they're talking about some generous alumnus I don't know about."

More than ever, cash money—scratch, bread, juice—is the means to the end of victory. "It's all cash these days," says one head coach. "With the new rules and limits on alumni involvement in recruiting, everybody deals in cash. You won't see a lot of new cars, fancy clothes, furniture, housing all of a sudden. I'm always surprised the IRS never gets involved when these recruiting stories break out."

If a school is actually going to make a player work for his stipend, an entirely different set of rules must be skirted. The NCAA won't let a ball player earn more than the prevailing wage from a summer job. So a booster who owns, say, an insurance business says, "Fine. The NCAA wants me to pay an athlete the going rate. But that's assuming I pay my employees a salary. Here at the Go Team agency, we work on commission." The youngster gets hired as a "summer sales associate." All sorts of business are mysteriously channeled his way. Come the fall, he has a nest egg to take him through the season in style.

A payment may come in kind instead of cash. One school in the West is notorious for its condo lease-option deals. A player moves into a condominium his freshman year. Depending on how he performs, by the time his eligibility is up he can either assume title to the property, buy it at a reduced rate or—if he was a washout—pay the full price.

For years, players drove cars thanks to the ingenuity of the "balloon note," a financing arrangement that requires no payments for the first three months. Installments are supposed to increase in three-month intervals thereafter, but sympathetic car dealers would simply renew the note after the first quarter, and renew it again. The athlete paid nothing but a small renewal fee each time. After nine months the dealer sold the car, with the proceeds going toward the player's plane fare home. When Southwestern Louisiana was nailed for the practice back in the seventies, coaches had to retool their thinking. Now cars are purchased with up-front money, by the family itself, using school-supplied cash. The purchase of brand-new sets of wheels is frowned upon as being unnecessarily provocative, and the registration is usualy put in the name of a family member or girlfriend to throw the dogs off the scent.

The NCAA's passage of Proposition 48 has spawned an entirely new field of fraud. Because it forces an athlete to sit out a season, Prop 48 has become a stigma, a scarlet letter so onerous that some schools have figured out they can use a guarantee of eligibility—a precious thing to a young ball player—as an inducement. Don't worry, they tell a youngster, you'll play as a freshman. We'll see to it that you'll play as a freshman.

No less a student of the game than Jerry Tarkanian considers "pinch hitting" on standardized tests the brave new world of rule-breaking. But coaches are still figuring out the best way to do this dirty deed. One popular solution: a player takes the test himself, but is told not to answer questions he's not sure about. Later, a paid-off proctor sees to it that the unanswered questions get answered.

The forging of ID cards is another popular way of getting a pinch hitter up to the plate. In Detroit, for instance, there are no strict internal controls on issuing ID cards. Lose one, and another is issued. The IDs themselves are flimsy, with plastic covers that can be easily pried off. A pinch hitter's picture replaces the athlete's picture, but the star's name stays on the ID, and no one's the wiser.

Or a player might simply be given the answers to the test before he takes it. They're written out on a small crib sheet he can slip under his answer sheet. "It's the perfect way," one Detroit high-school coach says. "And I've seen it done."

With all these methods at their disposal, a college should never get caught for abetting test fraud—particularly with more and more test proctors, who are usually high-school counselors and teachers, willing to collude with coaches on behalf of athletes. "Why don't these schools figure it out?" says one college coach. "The best way to have someone take the test for your recruits is the junior year, the year before.

Then there's no suspicion. The kid's eligible for every school."

Within the trade, coaches take great pains to distinguish between two types of cheaters. Front-end cheaters are inducers, schools that lay out in advance for a player what he'll get in exchange for his signature on a letter of intent. That's cheating in anyone's book. But many coaches look more kindly on back-end cheaters, schools that don't lure players to campus improperly, but "take care" of them once they arrive. They make a distinction between the crass appeal of a fat wad on the one hand, and the sophistication of a no-show summer job on the other. Back-enders can always claim they're just trying to help a youngster cope, that their intentions are better than those of the cold-hearted NCAA. When Rick Huckabay quit as coach at Marshall in 1989 after widespread abuse was revealed in his program, he uttered what could be considered the back-end cheater's credo. "There's a fine line," he said, "between being in the NCAA and being a Christian person." David LeuLuai seemed to be treading that fine line when he talked about the circumstances under which he would accept charity.

Back-end or front-end, coaches are careful to maintain plausible deniability. This leads right back to the Code. If anything untoward comes to light, complicity never gets revealed any further up the chain of command. If you're an assistant coach, it's understood you'll be the stoic soldier. As British enlisted men fighting in France during World War I liked to say, "Generals always die in bed."

The Code is so taken for granted, so much a part of the landscape, that for years even the press was a faithful party to it. In 1961, St. John's coach Joe Lapchick mentioned at a basketball writers' luncheon in Manhattan that a school in the Midwest had offered one of his players, Donnie Burks, $10,000 to transfer. No one in the room that day saw fit to write it. Lapchick had to threaten never to speak to the

Chris Mills, in one of his first games as a Wildcat, looks for an opening against Western Carolina. (David Coyle)

Sean Higgins plays a mercurial game of daring swoops and sallies to the hoop. (Bob Kalmbach)

Claud Mills outside the apartment building on South Orange Grove in Los Angeles, where both Chris Mills and Sean Higgins grew up. (David Crane/Los Angeles *Daily News*)

When Richie Farmer announced he would attend Kentucky, at a press conference in the Clay County High School gym, an entire state gave him its ear. (David Coyle)

A familiar scene at Rupp Arena: Bret Bearup gets a piece of Joe B. Hall's mind. (G. Alen Malott)

Through the entire ordeal, Eddie Sutton *(right)* and Dwane Casey never said a public unkindness about each other. (David Coyle)

Eric Manuel throws one down against Alabama during his freshman season. (David Coyle)

Underneath a portrait of his predecessor, University of Kentucky President David (little mathematician) Roselle fielded questions about Sutton's resignation. (David Coyle)

Sonny Vaccaro (he's the one in casual clothes, second from right) with a few of the horses in his Nike stable *(from left)*: Creighton's Tony Barone; Bob Wade, formerly at Maryland; California's Lou Campanelli; North Carolina State's Jim Valvano; St. John's Lou Carnesecca; and UNLV's Jerry Tarkanian.

American Roundball Corporation CEO Rich Goldberg has hoops ambitions that go beyond the driveway of his San Fernando Valley home. (Tom Jagoe/Los Angeles *Daily News*)

Summer action, like this at Lexington's Dirt Bowl, is a backdrop for recruiters' shaking and baking. (Chuck Wielgus)

Super recruiter Kevin O'Neill with two of the players he lured to Arizona, guards Matt Othick and Harvey Mason. (Scott Borden)

Former New Mexico Coach Gary Colson gets in a snit in The Pit. (David M. Benyak)

Rex Chapman *(right)* **joined Chris Mills at a Wildcats'
football game during Chris's official visit to campus in fall
1987. But they would never play together.** (Jay Fuller)

**Sutton and Rex Chapman, the Boy King, after Kentucky's
astonishing home loss to Auburn in January 1988. Their
troubles had already begun.** (David Coyle)

In the clannish world of Chicago high-school basketball, Martin Luther King Coach Landon (Sonny) Cox reigns supreme. (Don Bierman/Chicago *Sun-Times*)

Al Ross toasts Carl Eller, the former Minnesota Vikings defensive lineman who began the flow of great black athletes into the Ross stable during the early seventies. (Julian Wasser)

After announcing Rick Pitino's hiring as Kentucky's new coach, Athletic Director C. M. Newton sticks a University of Kentucky pin on Pitino's label. (David Coyle)

group again before the New York press finally broke the story.

"Everybody in the business knows who's cheating," says Georgetown's John Thompson. "But like drug dealers in the neighborhood, it's a question of proving it."

The NCAA requires a more exacting standard of proof, but here's an armchair guide to cracking the Code:

• When there's never any turnover among assistant coaches, particularly in the position of Ace Recruiter, it's because someone knows too much.

• If a school always seems to have stars from poor backgrounds who stay four years, they aren't jumping early to the NBA for big money either because they're already getting big money, or because their getting it is contingent on serving a four-year hitch.

• If a prominent local automobile dealer, haberdasher, or purveyor of any good or service that might be of interest to a nineteen-year-old male sits behind the bench or hobnobs in the locker room, it's not because he moonlights as team chaplain.

• When a roster is peppered with poor, inner-city kids from far beyond a school's pale, the players' families aren't paying for those round trips to and from campus.

• If a recruit has narrowed his choice to a handful of schools which have been, or are about to go, on probation, there's a bidding war going on.

• If a school graduates players at a shameful rate, but still attracts great ones, players are getting something, even if it isn't a degree. Kids aren't fools.

Sometimes the fate of adults can rest on the whims of one eighteen-year-old, and the story behind the downfall of UCLA coach Walt Hazzard illustrates just how. To be sure, Hazzard had made things hard on himself over his four seasons in Westwood. He had a proud streak that sometimes alienated the press and fans, and became restless behind a desk, spending long stretches out of his office. UCLA athletic director Peter Dalis, a precise and methodical man, knew better than to expect from Hazzard the midwestern humility that John Wooden had brought to the position. But he nonetheless wished his coach would at least make the effort to live up to the UCLA image.

Hazzard had grown up tough in Philadelphia, and an attitude was part of the baggage he brought west with him. That edge made him a great defensive guard during his playing days. The defensiveness didn't retire when he did. But in spite of Hazzard's brusque front, those closest to him knew him to be a softie, the son of a minister, a man whose stubbornness also accounted for deep convictions and abiding loyalty.

The travails of the UCLA program since Wooden's retirement weren't the most flattering conditions under which to judge anyone, and the Bruins continued to struggle after Hazzard replaced Larry Farmer in 1984. Hazzard had come to UCLA from Chapman College, a tiny school insulated from the realities of big-time college basketball. One of those realities is the preeminence of recruiting. Just weeks after Hazzard took the job, John Williams announced for LSU. Through his connections in L.A.'s black community, Hazzard had heard the stories of what went down. The Williams fiasco augured ominous things for the task ahead. As the media told him he would be expected to keep the best local players at home, the streets were telling him what it would cost.

Yet Hazzard was hostage to his pride. He wasn't going to kowtow to teenagers, just as he wouldn't put up with Sonny Vaccaro telling him to "pay your dues." Only there's no room for pride in recruiting. It's an activity that requires cloying accommodation. Hazzard knew in his head the importance of landing players, for he had been on UCLA's 1964 national title team, Wooden's first. "Even John Wooden, he didn't start winning until he got the horses," says one former Bruin star. "You can't win with claimers in a Thoroughbred race. Just give 'em the horses."

On his terms, Hazzard tried to rustle them up. And he had Sean Higgins, until—*whack!*—came the baseball bat. When Chris Mills spurned the Bruins for Kentucky, that hurt even more, for Chris had actually lived in the Hazzard home for nearly two years. Yet Hazzard refused to set up Derick Mills with a job, a favor Claud had asked for during the Bruins' home visit.

So it was that as Don MacLean prepared to make his college choice in spring 1988, Hazzard was deep in the count. He didn't just need the next great local talent; he needed MacLean, a 6-foot-10-inch senior from Simi Valley with a soft shooting stroke. Hazzard had to silence the malevolent whispers that he was an out-of-touch militant who couldn't sign a great local white kid. If the UCLA staff couldn't get around on this one, it would be strike three.

But MacLean had learned early the rules of the game, and he wasn't averse to playing it. He was another high-school All-America, from a single parent home and modest circumstances, who had come up through the L.A. summer leagues. He took his first basketball trip to Vegas as a sixth-grader, and within a few years ARC and Slam-N-Jam were fighting over him, pulling him, says his mother, Pat Coyne, "in ten different directions. Finally I had to say, 'This is one kid. He's only got one body.'"

MacLean had seen Williams, Lewis, Higgins, and Mills before him, and knew which buttons to push. He made his campus visits—to Kentucky, Pittsburgh, UNLV, UCLA, and Georgia Tech—with his hand out, says one of Hazzard's former assistants. "He knew everybody wanted him, and he wanted a piece of the pie. He would say, 'I'm getting this and that from them, Coach. I need spending money, money for my car, to take out my girl, to eat.' It wasn't big-time money. But he was playing the game, heavy-duty."

The fans in Rupp Arena had chanted "We want MacLean!" during his visit to Lexington, and he came back to California with tales of promises of cash and clothes. UNLV, he told people, set him up with women. He liked Pitt and Tech, too, but he had been coming to watch UCLA play since junior high, and Bruin recruiters had returned the favor many times, showing up at his games since ninth grade. When MacLean refused to sign early, several members of the UCLA staff felt it was because they hadn't come through with an inducement. The Bruins would back-end him; they told MacLean so. But there would be nothing at the front end, not so long as Proud Walt was in charge.

There was another, more daunting problem for UCLA. MacLean saw plenty of Hazzard's assistants, but the head man wasn't going to pander to anyone. Meanwhile, MacLean hadn't really cottoned to Hazzard. He didn't think he could coach, and during his senior season said so publicly, to the mortification of Hazzard and his staff. "You work with a kid for three years to recruit him, and then he bad-mouths Hazzard," says one ex–UCLA assistant. "He was an eighteen-year-old punk dictating the situation." MacLean's comment brought to a head all the issues that had already made Hazzard's position so tenuous within the athletic department. On March 30, the very day the Emery package left Lexington for L.A., UCLA swept its basketball staff out of office.

With Hazzard's firing, UCLA shot suddenly to the top of MacLean's list, dead even with Georgia Tech. And several weeks later, on the day before the Monday signing date, in the midst of the forty-eight-hour, pre-signing date "dead" period during which one of the most elementary of NCAA rules bars all face-to-face contacts with recruits, new

UCLA coach Jim Harrick left a weekend clinic in Lake Tahoe and went by the MacLean home.

Harrick's knock on their door caught Pat Coyne and her son by surprise. The visit, which lasted about fifteen minutes, wasn't just improper; it was probably unnecessary. MacLean was as likely as ever to sign with the Bruins on Monday morning, for the only real impediment to his signing, Hazzard, was now gone. But the same day Harrick came to his doorstep, MacLean went ahead and signed a letter of intent with UCLA.

Don's mother would innocently let slip to Georgia Tech coach Bobby Cremins in a phone conversation that Harrick had been in their home that day. "I called Jim about it," says Cremins, who had made scores of trips to the Coast in pursuit of MacLean, even flying out one Christmas Eve just to watch Don practice. "It's a real pet peeve of mine, coaches being out during dead periods. But if that had been the reason Don chose UCLA, I'd have been more upset. That wasn't the reason. The reason was the distance [between L.A. and Atlanta], and the coaching change. After the change, I was dead meat. It was over."

When questioned about the improper visit, Harrick denies he was in the home. "That's a lie," he says. "No way, no way." The Pac-10 investigated and was unable to substantiate a charge made anonymously to its office.

Don MacLean didn't cause Walt Hazzard's downfall. He only precipitated it. But Hazzard wasn't politically or ethically malleable enough to survive at UCLA. Rules—not so much the NCAA's, but his own—kept Hazzard from doing the things he needed to do to land the youngster who could keep him a head coach. To sign the recruit who had reversed UCLA's local recruiting fortunes, Hazzard's successor allegedly broke a basic one.

Hazzard had tried in vain to keep boosters away from the program, and the wealthy denizens of West L.A. didn't

143

appreciate it. His failure to win or recruit to their taste did nothing more to endear him to them. "In an institution you become institutionalized," says a former member of the UCLA staff now coaching elsewhere. "It's like a prison. You protect. Our response to the NCAA [on the Higgins investigation] must have weighed twenty pounds. The way we manipulated everything to make it seem like all was kosher nearly drove [Hazzard] to kill himself.

"Even if [a program]'s not corrupt, you have to take care of the kids. Do you know what a date costs in Westwood? Dinner and a movie runs fifty dollars. Now, where are they going to get that money from? You know they're being paid. It's like everybody gets his sugar daddy. Every school has theirs. They couldn't survive without them.

"Let me give you an example, one stupid instance in a thousand. [UCLA forward] Kevin Walker comes from Orange County, a white, predominantly wealthy neighborhood. But he just happens not to be that well off. His first year we required players to wear a suit and tie when we traveled. He's not allowed to work during the season and this is October. He says he needs a couple of suits to travel on. We asked him how much it would cost. Now, this kid was seven feet and two-sixty pounds, so it's gonna take six hundred dollars to make him feel comfortable. He says, 'Well, where am I gonna get six hundred dollars from?'

"We play the game and say we don't know.

"He says, 'Well, where do all my summer-league friends from other schools, where do they get their suits and ties?'

"What are you supposed to do? The first trip he came on the plane in jeans and a T-shirt. He's embarrassed. What do you do at this point?

"*What do you do?*"

From where he sits, which on this July afternoon is in the stands at the Nike/ABCD Camp in Princeton, New Jersey, Marquette coach Kevin O'Neill seems impervious to any of the disillusionment that besieged the Hazzard regime during its final weeks. O'Neill will grant you that cheating goes on. But he thinks cheating is overstated, that too many recruiters use it as an alibi when they were simply outworked. And O'Neill makes sure no one, anywhere, outworks him.

Except for a blunt manner of which he's aware and faintly proud, there's nothing on the surface that would distinguish O'Neill from a generation of lookalike young bankers and lawyers. Glib and driven, he spent three and a half seasons as a recruiter for Lute Olson at Arizona, developing a reputation as such a precocious coaching property that in spring 1989, at the age of thirty-two, he was hired to direct the Marquette program. "When I got to Tucson I wanted to become known as the best recruiter in the country," he says. "When I walked into the gym, I wanted everybody to say, 'That asshole's here.'"

His peers didn't exactly say that, but they did vote him the game's best recruiter in an informal poll by the Seattle *Post-Intelligencer* during the 1989 Final Four. While O'Neill was with them, the Wildcats rarely missed out on the players they really wanted. He and another Arizona assistant, Ricky Byrdsong, homed in on several prospects a year and worked the bejeezus out of them. They perfected a good-cop–bad-cop routine: O'Neill, the hyperintense and short-fused Irish-American, would make the pitch and turn the screws; Byrdsong, black and easygoing, smoothed things over. They always wanted to have the last crack at a prospect, for they trusted the chemistry of their disparate personalities. And they would try anything to make an impression. A couple of recruits visited campus over Halloween one year, and O'Neill met them at the Tucson airport in a gorilla suit. Byrdsong once ducked into a video arcade with a prospect, only to emerge after three hours of Pac-Man with a willing signee. Together, they were brutally efficient. Thirteen kids made visits during O'Neill's tenure in Tucson, and ten wound up signing. "Ten for thirteen," O'Neill says, "is pretty damn good."

He's a head coach now, but O'Neill still thinks like an assistant. For twenty-one unbroken days in July 1989 he traversed the country, working the summer circuit, without once alighting back in Milwaukee. Through his first season he concluded practice at five o'clock, then drove an hour or two to catch a high-school game. He discouraged his two assistants from attending Marquette games, like the Warriors' upset of Notre Dame, their first victory over the Irish in ages, so they could be on the road, rustling up the program's future. "I still wake up at five every morning, thinking about recruiting. How can I get an edge? It's like game day every day. I send out little notes. Address the envelopes late at night. Write and send them out in the morning. Stick a little piece of gum in the envelope so they remember you, so you stick out from the crowd.

"Recruiting is the single most important thing in college basketball. Dean Smith is a great coach and Lute's a great coach. But you give me their talent, and give them Bemidji State's talent, and I kick their ass. Ninety-five percent of recruiting is knowing who you can and can't recruit, identifying them and going and getting them. I know I can't get Ed O'Bannon. But after a couple of months I'll know the ten or twelve guys I'm going to go after, and I'll sign three or four."

"Again, it's ego. So some guy can say, 'Hey, I was in Ed O'Bannon's home,' he goes after him. Big shit if you're in Ed O'Bannon's home. So are all of Ed's friends. Or, 'Hey, we were third on him.' Well, whoop-de-do. That's not gonna put ten extra points on the scoreboard for your first game.

"Every kid looks to somebody for advice, a parent or a friend, somebody who's gonna help him make his decision. Now, the guys who position themselves for influence, the street agents, those guys are scumbags. At Arizona we were on a solo mission to recruit the kids themselves, and if we had to deal with street agents, we just didn't recruit those kids. Hey, some kids just didn't have an interest in us. Sean Higgins didn't. Chris Mills didn't coming out of high school. Don MacLean said we weren't big-time enough for him, and that was the year we went to the Final Four.

"Bob Hawking, Don MacLean's high-school coach, told us we couldn't talk to Don, that nothing could be sent to his home. Fine. We didn't send anything to the home. We sent everything to the coach. Over three years we probably sent, no exaggeration, nine hundred pieces of mail, maybe a thousand. All of them handwritten. All of them to Don at the school, care of the coach. In the fall between his junior and senior years we finally get the okay to talk to the kid, to give him a call once a week. I said, 'Don, I'll bet no one's sent you more mail than we did.'

"Don said, 'Coach, I've never gotten a piece of mail from Arizona.'

"And where's Bob Hawking now? He's involved in college basketball, at Pepperdine as an assistant coach. Where did Don MacLean go to school? UCLA. Who's the coach at UCLA? Jim Harrick. Where did Jim Harrick come from? Pepperdine. Who got the job at Pepperdine? Tom Asbury, Jim Harrick's old assistant. Who hired Bob Hawking. You tell me who the street agent is."

[O'Neill doesn't know the entire story behind how Hawking came to be hired at Pepperdine. Hawking originally thought he would join Harrick's staff at UCLA, and exactly a week before MacLean signed with the Bruins, Harrick actually offered Hawking a $40,000 assistant's position. But on the same Sunday that Harrick is said to have made his improper visit to the MacLean home, he also went by Hawking's house to tell MacLean's coach there might be a hitch in his plan to hire him. Image-conscious UCLA would balk at the appearance of Hawking and MacLean coming aboard as a package deal. Harrick regretted leaving Hawking, who had already quit his job at Simi

Valley High, hanging. But there wasn't much he could do. "The hardest thing Jim has had to do so far was come over that Sunday night and talk to you and Bob," Harrick's wife, Sally, would write Jeannie Hawking. "He has felt terrible about it. . . . Jim feels very confident that Bob will get into the college ranks. It may not help, but patience is a virtue. Believe me, we are proof of that."

But patience wasn't going to help Hawking, who was out of a job. He found out—from Bobby Cremins and Don himself—about Harrick's improper contact. On Friday the thirteenth of May, when Harrick told Hawking once and for all that he wouldn't be able to hire him, Hawking let Harrick know how angry he was—and that he had the leverage to do something about it.

"Yes, you can blow me up," Harrick told Hawking. "But who will that help? I can help you, but not right now."

Hawking hooked on with Pepperdine soon thereafter.]

"All along I thought we were in great shape. I was naive enough to think [Hawking] was really straight up with us. I used to stop by the school when I was in L.A. Ask Bob, 'Is Don getting all our mail?' 'Sure, sure.' Don never got a fucking piece of it. To me, that's a federal offense. The coach was controlling the recruiting. And I guarantee you he was letting certain people call and certain people write, and not letting others.

"In my opinion, Wayne Merino's doing that. Don't tell me Ed O'Bannon's living in a vacuum, with no one talking to him. Somebody is. My feeling about high-school coaches is simple. If they're not for you, they're against you. Any high-school coach around a kid who says he doesn't have a favorite is a liar. 'Oh, you're one of twenty,' they'll say. What the fuck is one of twenty? *What are we?* Are we in it?

"I'd much rather deal with an Issy Washington or a Rich Goldberg than a high-school coach who has that kind of shit on his mind. That's unfair to me, unfair to my school, and unfair to the kid. In retrospect, Bob was unfair to himself. He sold himself over a goddamn eighteen-year-old.

"You have to get to the kid. You have to make him trust you. If a kid trusts you, you have a good chance. In the case of [UCLA guard and Los Angeles native] Darrick Martin, we had trust. It came down to our [Arizona's] argument versus theirs. Their argument was you can stay home. Be the point guard. A year from now when Pooh Richardson graduates you can be the man and carry on the UCLA tradition. That's pret-ty damn attractive. Our deal was we're on top, for the next ten years we're gonna be what they used to be. And then you've got to say, 'Hey, Darrick, what the hell you gonna do? Comin' to my place or not?'

"See, kids aren't honest with you. They'll tell you what they think you want to hear. Every kid. That's where closing comes in. Closing is turning their positives into negatives, and your negatives into positives. Say a kid from L.A. says to me, 'I want to stay close to home.' I'll ask him what he wants to stay home for. 'Don't you want to get out, meet new people, see new places?' If I get a kid from Wisconsin, someone like Milwaukee's Damon Key, I'm saying, 'Damon, there's a great advantage to staying home.' That's the close. It's lawyering, the prosecution versus the defense."

O'Neill and Byrdsong pulled off one of the most inspired closes ever when they landed Sean Rooks, a 6-foot-11-inch junior-college star who had narrowed his choices to Arizona and Washington. Rooks had just visited Washington, and he and his mother were on their way to Tucson for an official visit on a Friday afternoon. But a story had appeared in the Seattle paper the evening before, quoting sources saying Rooks had told the Huskies staff he was signing with Washington, and was going through with his visit to Arizona only as a courtesy. An Arizona booster living in Seattle saw the story, and faxed it to the Wildcat basketball office even as Rooks and his mother were winging their way down.

"So here we are," O'Neill says. "Sean and his mom are on

their way, but they haven't seen the story. So we have it blown up, and send a manager out to the airport to meet them. When he and his mom come into the office, we jump them. Tell them we can't believe they did this, how ridiculous this was. That we had two plane tickets right there, and they could take them and go on home. It was an act, of course. Within two hours he'd changed his mind. Said he was coming to Arizona. By the time he left on Sunday, he'd called Washington and told them the same thing. That's a close. We turned their positive into a negative.

"Recruiters forget these kids are seventeen or eighteen years old. They forget what turns them on. What, they're gonna be impressed when someone calls and tells them they're a great player? Everybody tells them that. But when you call and say, 'Hey, did you get any last night?'—*that* turns them on.

"They say excess kills. Maybe it does and maybe it doesn't. But I just love to compete. I'm always looking for an edge. When I'm writing postcards to players at night, I'm thinking there's some son of a bitch out drinking or in bed, and here I am, awake and working. Sometimes I work just for the sake of working.

"And if I know a kid's gonna be cheated for—and you do know—and I don't wanna cheat, I don't recruit that kid. Hey, if there's five cheaters going after one kid who wants to be cheated for, somewhere along the line even one of the cheaters is going to do a better job and outwork the others. That's why I'm not sold on this whole bullshit line, 'Oh, he cheated.' That's your fault if you were cheated on and you didn't want to cheat."

Matt Maloney, a precise, 6-foot-3-inch guard from New Jersey, is sinking jumper after jumper down on the floor. O'Neill can't stop watching him. "Now, Matt Maloney—I would crawl across burning sand to hear him piss in a can on the radio. I swear I would. 'Cause that son of a bitch is a winner.

"I know some coaches who recruit a kid because he wants to come to his school. Fuck that. I want the kid I want. I have to watch a kid go up and down the floor only five or six times to know if I want him. If you have to go back to see a kid more than once, you don't want him.

"You need so much energy in this business, why waste it playing games? Let's get right to the heart of it. I want that kid, and I'm gonna try to get him. When he gets home tonight there'll be three overnight packages waiting on him, and he'll know I want him."

If you were to chart Kevin O'Neill's ascent in the coaching profession—plotting jobs against time—you would draw a steep upward line. High school, junior college, then NAIA head coach. Small-time Division I assistant, midmajor Division I assistant, then big-time assistant. O'Neill never spent more than a few years in each way station before getting his major-college head job. Ricky Byrdsong got his break in 1989, too, taking over as coach at the University of Detroit. But for many more black coaches, careers move in fits and starts. As an assistant he's usually pigeonholed as a recruiter, and won't be the first to be asked to run practice or break down film. And as a black recruiter, he's expected to deliver the black athlete.

Basketball is already calcified in the minds of many Americans as an inner-city game, and black coaches as procurers of talent. There are no more crooked black coaches than white ones; indeed, there will always be more outlaw whites than outlaw blacks until blacks are hired to coach the game in proportions better reflecting the number of blacks who play it. But cynics perceive recruiting as a matter of black recruiters cutting deals for black kids. And in many cases, that's exactly what recruiting is.

The mores reflected by NCAA legislation are a luxury that simply doesn't hold truck in much of the black community. Benny Dees, the Wyoming coach, tells a story that points up how little bearing one of those rules—the one preventing a school from paying a player's airfare to and from campus—has on reality. "I've got some kids from the Houston ghetto, and they struggle. Hell, Laramie—you have to send up a flare from Denver just to find it. And Reggie Fox [a Cowboys guard], he comes by the office asking whether he's got any mail. Turns out he's expecting money from his mother so he can fly home. The secretary tells him no, and Reggie says, 'I bet she sent it to Wisconsin. She tells all the neighbors I go to school in Wisconsin.'"

Allen Sack, a sociologist at the University of New Haven, canvassed 644 college basketball players, both men and women, between 1983 and 1985 to determine their attitudes toward NCAA rules prohibiting improper payments. When asked whether it was wrong to accept them, more men than women, more lower-class ball players than upper-class ones, more Division I athletes than Division IIs or IIIs, and more scholarship holders than walk-ons, said no. But the biggest gap was by race. Some sixty-one percent of the black players queried saw nothing wrong with accepting improper payments, versus thirty-four percent of the whites. "Many athletes, blacks among them, may view amateurism as an exploitative ideology whose primary function is to keep labor costs at a minimum," says Sack. "Amateurism may be as alien a concept to them as Prohibition was to the Italians, Poles, Irish, and other immigrant groups to whom alcohol was a perfectly acceptable part of everyday life."

That leaves the cops on the beat, the NCAA, with no moral authority in the very places where the seeds of big-time college basketball are planted. No one is thought less of in the inner city than someone who drops a dime. And if anyone sees firsthand the inequities of enforced amateurism, it's the inner-city parent, street agent, coach, and recruiter. The black recruiter becomes a sort of Robin Hood to David Berst's Sheriff of Nottingham. The rich are the colleges and their surrogates, the boosters, all fairly oozing money; the poor are the kids who, even if they play college ball, have only the slimmest of chances at the big payoff of a pro career. Thus the black coach is indoctrinated into a subcode of the Code. Says Nick Moore, an assistant at the University of Buffalo and a member of the board of the Black Coaches Association, "I would never turn a school in. Never."

In the blunt argot of the city, the parent who lets a son play for free is a fool. The collegian who lets himself play for free is a tool. That the best are put up for bid "is a way of life in the black community," says another black assistant coach. "I may be helping mankind by speaking out against it. But I wouldn't be worth a damn as a recruiter."

And so it is that virtually no one, black or white, will stand up and point out and decry what is going on. Not after what happened to Tates Locke.

You can be a cadet at the U.S. Military Academy at West Point, pledged never to lie or cheat or steal. You can be a professor there, committed to educating cadets to better honor the spirit of that exacting creed. But a coach at West Point, charged with leading young men into friendly strife, is beholden to standards that implicitly surpass even the lofty ones the academy sets for those who teach and study there. Tates Locke began his coaching career at Army in 1963. With his blue eyes and scrupulous devotion to the game, he cut an imposing figure, a presence that eclipsed even that of the brash young assistant he hired, a former Ohio State reserve named Bobby Knight.

What happened to Locke after his two seasons at West Point is an odyssey of sin and redemption. He wended his way to Miami of Ohio and then to Clemson, where he went 9–17 in his first season, 1970–71. It stung, stung badly, to lose nearly twice as often as he won. There in the crucible of the Atlantic Coast Conference, Locke became a different person. Soon an assistant coach's daughter was taking a correspondence course for a player to make him eligible. He and members of his staff put together what they euphemistically called "programs"—packages of money and benefits to attract high-school stars, particularly poor black ones. They even invented a phony Afro-American fraternity on the predominantly white, backwoods campus to hoodwink visiting black recruits into thinking a social life awaited them at Clemson. The "program" Locke put on Tree Rollins and his mother, Wilma Robinson, was lavish enough to keep the 7-foot center from going to Kentucky, and it turned the Clemson program around.

The turnaround, however, occurred just a bit too suddenly. The NCAA showed up, and Locke's fall was quickened by personal problems, including a yen for diet pills and Scotch. None of this would have been particularly noteworthy in the rancid scheme of things in college basketball, except that Locke wrote a book about it. *Caught in the Net*, published in 1981, was a catharsis for Locke, whose West Point past had only heightened his sense of fall and pricked his conscience. But he also hoped, naively he now admits, to lay bare the way the college game worked and change it. Instead, his book, with its blend of finger-pointing and mea culpa, assured his alienation from the community of coaches, and made him a casualty of the Code he flouted.

Locke is in the business again only because of his former assistant. With his reputation for integrity, Knight was able first to purify him, by adding him to his staff; and then bring influence to bear, in the state that he owns, to get him the job at Indiana State in the spring of 1989.

A Division I head coach once more, Locke sits in the stands at the Las Vegas Invitational, trying to get a fix on how the game works today. There's so much to acquaint himself with: the hectic summers and "pimp camps" like this one, where the bantam-rooster AAU coaches strut in, dwarfed by their kids; the breathtaking multimillion-dollar stakes at play each season; the moneyed celebrity the top coaches now enjoy. He says the temptations that did him in at Clemson will bypass Terre Haute. There's too much balance in the Missouri Valley Conference. Expectations are depressed among followers of the Sycamores, who went 4–24 the season before. Nor will Indiana State be involved with the blue-chip youngsters, the ones that cost. Every recruit will get a copy of *Caught in the Net*, and its author's disclaimer: "This is where I've been."

It will just be Locke and basketball, and sometime during his first winter the two will make their peace. "For what I did to the game, I thought I'd never forgive myself," Locke says, the blue eyes misting over. "And I thought the book would have more of an impact. But all the words in the world aren't going to change this. They haven't affected those guys against the wall." He gestures at the coaches standing back of the baseline, checking out the talent. "The same shit's going on.

"Do I regret writing the book? For what it did for me professionally, yes. For what it did for me personally, no. There's not a lie in it. But you can't take a stand if you want to stay in the business. Or there are very few guys who can. It's better to stay quiet. Better to stay in a total-denial position."

6

Bluegrass Blues

FROM THE moment he arrived at the University of Kentucky in the summer of 1987, David Roselle made clear that his would not be an imperial presidency. His home number went into the phone book. He refused to sit for an inauguration, believing the cost—estimates for a full-blown inaugural approached $50,000—to be a profligacy the school could ill afford. After much cajoling he agreed to let Honors Day, an occasion already on the academic calendar to recognize outstanding faculty, students, and staff, include his austere "investiture" as the university's ninth president.

Honors Day fell on April 15, a day things traditionally come due, some nine and a half months after Roselle had moved into the Administration Building on Euclid Avenue. In spite of the minimal pomp, these were maximally difficult circumstances. The Los Angeles *Daily News* had carried the tale of the misbegotten Emery envelope the day before, and the morning papers throughout the state were filled with the story. Earlier that month trustee Happy Chandler had made his racial slur about Zimbabwe being "all nigger now." Most ominously, Roselle had already taken a hit in the state's political arena. Over the previous winter the legislature, at the direction of Governor Wallace Wilkinson, had voted UK a budget increase so inadequate that some administrators believed it would bring the university to a standstill. Roselle didn't flinch. To make up the shortfall he took an unprecedented step, ordering the Athletics Association, a nominally independent scholarship and fund-raising group, to sign over up to $4 million of its money for the school's general fund. Veteran UK watchers say athletics director Cliff Hagan's hand was all but shaking when he signed the first check.

One of the honorees on the Honors Day dais, marketing professor Thomas Ingram, was on crutches for a foot injury suffered playing tennis. "Tom," Roselle told the gathered crowd, "helped at our recent legislative session." It was vintage Roselle: light acknowledgment of a grave problem. Yet now the basketball program was dumping another crisis on his desk.

When the ceremonies wound down, Roselle took off his cap and gown and the presidential medallion just given him by his predecessor, Otis Singletary. He went straight to a press conference to announce that he was entrusting the investigation to a highly respected Lexington attorney and former judge named James Park. It had been an extraordinary day of ambivalent emotions for those who loved the school, a commingling of pride and humility. After the last question had been answered, a sympathetic woman approached the president.

"It's a shame all this had to happen today," she said.

At that, Roselle gave the first hint that he had a reformer's agenda. "Maybe," he replied softly, "it's not such a bad thing."

* * *

157

To Kentuckians who still consider David Roselle an egghead with little interest in sports, news that he played high-school basketball would come as a surprise. But he did, in Apollo, Pennsylvania, a town just outside Pittsburgh, before entering the University of Pittsburgh as a night student on scholarship. He found a niche in the world of theorems and problems, and went on to earn his doctorate in mathematics from Duke. He taught at Maryland and LSU before taking a professorship at Virginia Tech in 1974, where he rose to become provost, the second-ranking administrative position. Roselle hadn't been the UK search committee's first choice as a new president. But he immediately distinguished himself, if only in contrast to the man he succeeded.

Singletary is a historian by training, with the humanist's knack for reading social settings. Roselle is a hard scientist, accustomed to gathering empirical data and applying to it rigorous principles. Roselle enjoys golf as much as the next man, but unlike his predecessor wouldn't become a member of the exclusive Idle Hour Country Club, that epicenter of Bluegrass power. Tall and silver-haired, Singletary was "Dr. Jock." Roselle refers to himself as "the little mathematician," and believes his kind have a vocational aptitude for administration. "We're used to a climate of problem-solving," he says. "Mathematicians actually look for problems."

As different as Roselle and Singletary are, Wallace Wilkinson makes Singletary look like Roselle's fraternal twin. The governor is symptomatic of the superficial "personality politics" that have long influenced gubernatorial races in the commonwealth. A self-made man with no college degree, he came from two percent in the polls in 1985 to win the Democratic primary and then the general election, running on little else but the promise of a statewide lottery. In the short time they had presided over their respective entities, Wilkinson and Roselle had already butted heads. Roselle and the other seven presidents of the state's institutions of higher learning, meeting in the governor's mansion for the first time to make their plea for public funds, had to listen to Wilkinson call them "a bunch of crybabies."

Wilkinson and Big Blue basketball share the same constituency. It's the rural and small-town folk of the state, people with basic schooling and simple passions. Many of them were more troubled by having to drive to Ohio or West Virginia to buy their lottery tickets than by the state's sorry national ranking in education. These are the people whose phone calls are patched through to the nightly sports talk shows, where Roselle's determination to conduct a real investigation became a favorite target.

The president took to calling some of these diehards the "ready, fire, aim!" people. But much more was at stake, for their patron was Wilkinson. The governor had several more appointments to make to the UK board of trustees, the panel at whose pleasure Roselle serves. And in the luncheonettes and barber shops from the Appalachians to the Mississippi, people questioned Roselle's willingness to "defend the program."

Without seeing any documentation from the ongoing investigation, Wilkinson wet his index finger, stuck it in the air, and intimated that he would throw his support to Sutton. One night a woman in a bar reached Roselle at home to share her thoughts with him, and said she would call every ten minutes for the remainder of the evening. ("She seemed quite capable of doing that," remembers Roselle, who for the only time during the ordeal unplugged the phone.) In *The Cats' Pause*, Oscar Combs wondered editorially if it weren't time for someone to take the new president up into the mountains and have explained to him the importance of UK basketball. You could almost hear the first plucked banjo notes of the theme from *Deliverance*.

If Roselle was affected by any of this, his actions belied it.

His plan for navigating the riptides and eddies of state politics, which have so often tossed the hull of the university, was full speed ahead. While Judge Park pursued the truth, the "little mathematician" took over the PR job. More than one hundred times over that summer and into the ensuing basketball season Roselle made forays out into the state. He spoke at every kind of civic club, at breakfast meetings and Rotary luncheons and alumni club banquets, from the hollows of the east to the river towns in the west. In one village in northern Kentucky the room was so small and the interest so large that the people filed in and out, in shifts.

Roselle and the members of his small retinue soon discerned a pattern. Time after time their hosts would greet them warmly, only to warn of angry postprandial questions. Then Roselle would launch into his remarks. From make-shift daises in places like Horse Cave and Fulton, to shimmering head tables in hotel banquet halls in Bowling Green and Louisville, he limned his vision of the university. In boilerplate, Roselle's speech was a paean to the value of higher education, All-America stuff that even the most prejudicially hostile listener couldn't take issue with. Only at the end did he turn to basketball and the NCAA probe.

He spoke of the UK athletic department of the future. Roselle wanted three things from his coaches. One, that they be fair to every student in their charge. There would be no more "overbooking." Two, that they comply with the rules. "I can handle T-shirts," he would say. "But don't give me a thousand dollars in an envelope or academic fraud." Three, that they be competitive. In that order.

"There are two sides to that street," Roselle says. "It's one thing to say these things, and then to dump a guy because he had a bad season." As collateral on his good faith, Roselle took to mentioning Jerry Claiborne, the Wildcats' football coach. Before stepping down suddenly in December 1989, Claiborne would go through four straight five-win seasons, yet receive a four-year contract extension because of his performance on counts one and two.

The president also took pains to explain that the NCAA isn't an adversary, but a sort of club, chartered to act in accordance with the will of its membership. "It's like a regulatory commission," Roselle said. "When they call you in, you go in hat in hand." The school's defense of the basketball program would be the investigation, its thoroughness and integrity. Defendant and prosecutor were one and the same.

By the end of Roselle's speech, it wasn't uncommon for audiences to stand and applaud. There was the occasional sharp question from an unmoved ready-fire-aimer, but most interrogatories were underhand lobs.

Possible political repercussions simply were not relevant. "To tell you the truth, I didn't care," Roselle says now. "The question was how the university was going to live up to its obligations."

As 1988 wore on, issue of the Emery package continued to be about as open and shut as the unsealed envelope itself. To hopeful 'Cat fans, the events of that March morning at LAX seemed altogether too extraordinary to have been anything but a setup, an attempt by UCLA or UNLV to exact revenge for losing Chris Mills. Emery employees either made up the story or, at the very least, made off with the cash.

To others, here was the ultimate test of the NCAA, which for so long had been accused of considering Kentucky its most sacred of cash cows, and barely a month earlier concluded its follow-up of the *Herald-Leader* series with no sanctions. "The NCAA's so mad at Kentucky," Jerry Tarkanian said, "they'll probably slap another three years' probation on Cleveland State."

Tarkanian's cynicism is long-standing. The UNLV coach believes his troubles with the NCAA can be traced back to

1973, when he was coach at Long Beach State. He wrote a newspaper column calling it "a crime" that Western Kentucky was being placed on probation, while Kentucky "isn't even investigated"—in spite of evidence that Tom Payne was subsidized while a Wildcat. "The University of Kentucky basketball program breaks more rules in a day than Western Kentucky does in a year," he added. "The NCAA just doesn't want to take on the big boys." Since then others had taken up the cry of selective enforcement, and the charges stung the NCAA's top cop, Berst, a former small-college ball player who has the bearing of a church deacon. Walter Byers, the longtime, low-profile executive director, was an intimate of Singletary's. David Cawood, one of the organization's top executives, counts Cawood Ledford, the Wildcats' beloved broadcaster, as distant kin. A Lexington firm called Host Communications has for years controlled a number of lucrative publishing and broadcast contracts for NCAA championships. However far-fetched their charges might be, conspiracy theorists have noted these connections over the years as the 'Cats, who seemed indeed to have nine lives, again and again dodged major penalties.

But what if UK had been set up? Kentucky's best defense was Dwane Casey himself. "It's like saying Mother Teresa committed a crime," one former teammate said. Added Georgia coach Hugh Durham, "Now, I don't want to sound like I know what I'm talking about. But Dwane wouldn't do it. And he's an intelligent enough person so if he did do it, he'd find another way to do it."

Soon everyone near the case, even a secretary in the basketball office, had an attorney. Casey's counsel, Joe Bill Campbell of Bowling Green, who had just been named the state's Lawyer of the Year, was particularly aggressive. He would sue the university in an instant, he said, if Casey were somehow made a scapegoat for the NCAA not having been able to get the goods on UK in previous investigations.

And Campbell did file a $6.9 million suit against Emery and the employees quoted in the *Daily News* account, claiming they had violated Casey's privacy, defamed his character, and caused him "severe and grievous mental and emotional suffering."

Meanwhile, Sutton was convening long, closed-door meetings in his office and tossing an Emery envelope about to see whether it could possibly come open. It took Sutton five days to muster a statement of support for his beleaguered assistant. While drafting it, he emerged from his office in search of a dictionary. "I need to know the meaning of the word *absolve*," he said.

The statement Sutton produced said the coach was "hopeful" Casey would be absolved. Not certain or confident; "hopeful."

The Emery affair quickly turned out to be only the hem of a much larger garment. The NCAA and UK, finally working jointly, began a shakedown of the basketball program. Berst, sick of the "selective enforcement" mantra, detached ten investigators to work on the case, and one even phoned Tarkanian for leads. The list of alleged violations grew and grew until it hit eighteen.

Several charges involved Shawn Kemp, the 6-foot-10-inch, 230-pound manchild who had signed with UK the same day Chris Mills did. Kemp was a buddy of Chris's from the high-school All-America circuit, and one of the ringers Rich Goldberg had flown in for his ARC Mid-Valley All-Stars. But Kemp had failed to meet Prop 48 requirements, and was sitting out his first season on campus. Questions soon arose about a trip his mother, Barbara Brown, had made to Lexington several days before the signing date, during which she met with academic advisers. She paid cash for her plane ticket and hotel room shortly after receiving an Emery envelope from Dwane Casey. If the Wildcats had paid her way and put her up, they would have violated NCAA rules. Brown says she paid her travel costs out of her own pocket, and says the Emery package she received contained only literature about academic life at UK.

About a month after that visit—and a few weeks after he signed with Kentucky—Kemp began driving a slightly used, $11,000 Z24 Chevy Cavalier. Barbara Brown says she made a $1,000 down payment to buy the car, over the objections of Kemp's high-school coach, who told Kemp and his mother that people were going to talk.

Investigators took Kemp and his mother at their word— that she had paid her own way to Lexington, and bought the car as a gift for her son—and the allegations were eventually dropped. But improprieties involving cars and cash are virtually impossible to document. It took something else to undo Kemp.

That fall UK guard Sean Sutton, Eddie Sutton's son, reported that two gold chains worth $700, bought for him by his mother, Patsy, during a trip to Japan, were missing. Police soon got in touch with the Suttons with word that a pawn-shop detail had found Sean's jewelry and a suspect in the theft. But before Sean and Patsy Sutton saw the recovered chains, police showed them a photograph, taken according to Kentucky law, of the suspect pawning the jewelry at the Johnson Diamond Exchange on East Main Street. The picture was of Shawn Kemp. The Suttons declined to press charges, and within a week Kemp had left school for Trinity Valley, a junior college in Texas, where he wouldn't play a game before signing a two-million-dollar, six-year deal with the NBA's Seattle SuperSonics.

Life in Lexington was indeed getting curiouser and curiouser. In early September Bob Hensley, a reporter for WTVQ-TV, received a tip from a well-placed source. Campus police had just towed an illegally parked, late-model Mazda RX7 from the parking lot of the Wildcat Lodge. The car, with Kentucky plates reading MILLS, had been claimed, the tipster told Hensley, by "a tall black person wearing lots of gold." Hensley ran a check with the state Department of Motor Vehicles, and found the car was registered to Virgil Mills, a UK booster and resident of the eastern Kentucky town of Inez. Martin County, of which Inez is the county seat, has one black among its 9,000 residents.

Hensley phoned Claud Mills in L.A. No, Claud told him; Chris didn't take to campus the Datsun 300ZX Claud had bought him. It was in the driveway right then.

Hensley called the UK basketball office. Dwane Casey said he knew nothing about the car, but didn't rule out that Chris Mills might have driven it. He allowed that Virgil Mills's son, then enrolled at UK, and Chris might be good friends, and that perhaps Chris was doing a fellow Mills a favor by fetching the car. Eddie Sutton soon reached Hensley to tell him much the same thing.

An hour or so later Hensley called a source who would have been familiar with the RX7's impoundment. "This person confirmed the make, model, and year I'd been told earlier," Hensley says. "But whoever claimed it had suddenly shrunk in size and changed races and lost all his gold."

Hensley never went with the story because it was within the realm of possibility that Chris was doing Virgil Mills's son a favor. But he couldn't help wonder how, after three days of school, a youngster from Martin County had gotten to know a black freshman from L.A.—let alone become such fast friends with him that one would be claiming the other's impounded RX7.

The Mills-Mazda episode, if there was anything to it, was quashed before any damage could be done. But with each successive incident, publicized or not, Kentucky's normally guarded basketball program became even more secretive. The team turned into itself. Sutton restricted access to his players, and spoke ritualistically about the cohesive effects of adversity.

The investigation continued apace, subsuming Lexington

in speculation and gossip. "You couldn't walk down the street without someone giving you their opinion," says attorney Larry Forgy, a UK trustee. "You'd see a milk-truck driver, and he knew as much about it as you did." Over the summer, soon after Wilkinson sided with Sutton and the coach became more bold in his personal protestations of innocence, Roselle had briefly lost control of the board. A faction of trustees became restive, wondering whether the decision to cooperate with the NCAA meant the program was cutting its own throat.

Then, in late August, one more allegation came to light. It was far more alarming than cars or cash, for it struck right at the core of the university. The mere possibility of its truth strengthened Roselle's reformist hand. Sophomore Eric Manuel, the cornerstone of UK's 1987 recruiting class, stood charged of cheating on his college entrance exam.

It may seem odd that Eric Manuel was even in Lexington in June 1987, for he wasn't yet enrolled at the University of Kentucky. He's a Georgian, from Macon, one of several children Mary Manuel raised by herself in a public housing project. Eric found a father figure in Don (Duck) Richardson, the coach at Southwest High, whose hugely successful program had turned out such NBA All-Star guards as Norm Nixon and Jeff Malone. Quiet and diligent, Manuel wasn't a bright student, but he was responsible and did what he was told. He even worked an after-school job at a local McDonald's. As one of the nation's top five prospects in the class of 1987, the 6-foot-6 Manuel seemed destined to become the next in that line of great Southwest guards.

After committing to Kentucky in the fall of 1986, he came to Lexington to take a job with the Wildcat Cab Company over the summer before his matriculation, as NCAA rules permit. Having failed to score at least 700 on his first two cracks at the SAT, Manuel signed up to take the ACT being offered at Lafayette High School on the morning of June 13.

It would be one last chance to meet the test-score requirements of Prop 48.

Sean Sutton drove by the Wildcat Lodge that morning to give Eric a lift to the test site. While he waited for Eric, another would-be chauffeur showed up: Don Harville, the Lafayette basketball coach. Harville runs the Thoroughbred Classic, in which Don Richardson's Macon Southwest team had recently played, so he already knew Eric and his coach. He wound up taking both Sean and Eric in his car.

From its location on a tree-lined, dead-end street in a residential section of town, Lafayette High has the look of an aging southern courthouse. Across the hall from the gym sits the cafeteria, where Eric took a seat near the front, at the middle of one of one hundred or so Formica-topped tables. On either side of him was an empty chair, and to his left sat a Lafayette senior-to-be named Chris Shearer, a onetime Lafayette basketball player and the son of a Lexington car salesman. In the early afternoon, after finishing up the four-hour, four-part test, Eric and Sean went out to get something to eat and play some ball.

Weeks later, when Manuel found out he had "passed" and would be eligible as a freshman, he phoned his mother in Macon, ecstatic. But about a year after that, as they began exercising the mandate given them, UK investigators combed through the academic records of every basketball player. There they came upon something that had either escaped the attention, or hadn't raised the concern, of Bob Bradley, the athletics official in charge of academic affairs: Manuel, who had gotten the ACT equivalent of a three the first time he took the college boards and the equivalent of a seven the second time, had scored a twenty-three that morning at Lafayette High.

In the ACT-SAT conversion table, a fifteen translates roughly into the Prop 48 minimum of 700. An increase like Manuel's was highly improbable statistically. Upon further checking, the university found that Manuel answered exactly the same number of questions as Chris Shearer, the neighbor to his left. Of those 219 answers, 211—right *and* wrong—matched identically. Seven of the eight unmatching answers were said to be in the same column. The chances of all this happening without fraud, ACT officials in Iowa City said, were two in a million.

What really happened in the Lafayette cafeteria that Saturday morning?

Manuel has said over and over again, to anyone who has asked, that he didn't cheat.

Shearer has told various people probing the case that, among other things, Manuel could have cheated from him, but he wasn't aware of him doing so; and that he looked over one time and noticed that he and Manuel had similar answers.

Harville has said he didn't do anything other than drive Manuel and Sutton to the test site.

Terri Guion, a counselor who supervises the administering of testing at Lafayette and was once romantically involved with Harville, trolled through the cafeteria with four other proctors. She was stationed in the front of the room and says she noticed nothing unusual. "As far as what I know, nothing," she says. "As far as what I saw, nothing." Guion also says that another proctor hoped to get Manuel's autograph for her son. Not wanting anyone to distract Eric, Guion took Eric's completed answer sheet and photocopied it in the high-school guidance office the following Monday, before she sent the originals to Iowa City. The proctor who wanted the autograph kept the facsimile of Eric's signature, and the rest of the photocopy was discarded.

Sean Sutton has said he was taking the ACT that morning —even though he had already met Prop 48 requirements— "because my mother wanted me to [take it again]. For the pride of having a higher score." And he has said he falsely told investigators that he and Manuel didn't drive over to the school with Harville because he believed the ride violated NCAA rules, and he was scared. By misleading an NCAA investigator, Sutton won a place in one of the eighteen allegations.

The easiest way to approach all this conflicting information is to eliminate possibilities. One thing seems far-fetched: that Manuel copied answer for answer from an unknowing Shearer. To see the little black pencil marks made by the right-handed Shearer, Manuel would have had to have done several hours of neck-craning toward an answer sheet four feet to his left, and over an intervening empty seat and Shearer's right arm. Further, he would have had to have done all this in front of several students squarely facing him, and in full view of five proctors—none of whom told investigators they noticed anything suspicious, and all of whom knew he was the 'Cats' highly touted signee. "It's so obvious if they look at someone's paper," says Guion. "I discount that completely, because we are just studying them."

Yet the answer sheet on file in Iowa City testifies overwhelmingly to some sort of fraud. Perhaps Manuel knew about things that were done on his behalf; maybe he didn't. But whether he was aware of what went on, or was just an innocent third man, what happened with Eric Manuel's college entrance exam that morning in Lexington in all likelihood involved the complicity of others.

The man turns off the ignition of his sky-blue Chevy S-10 pickup, then reaches into the glove compartment and pulls a red coupon from a stack. "Eric may have done it," he says. "But Eric was not the one who came in and said, 'I'm gonna cheat off of this kid right here.' The thing is, the adults who screwed him are the ones who should be burning, and not Eric. But you see, that's not the way the NCAA thinks."

He allows himself a thin smile, then says, "This is a hell of a job, you know."

With that, the man makes his way to the door of a

dilapidated house on Locust Street, in the shadow of the Lexington skyline. He's in his mid-thirties, with blue eyes, and brown hair worn boyishly. He knocks. "Understand you're a little short on food today," he says cheerfully, handing over the coupon as he walks inside.

By politics and vocation, Ed Dove embodies his surname. He's a public defender, the last hope for the poor and helpless whom troubles always seem to stalk. For much of the day, whether he's delivering emergency food coupons, or making a court appearance to file a motion on behalf of a destitute defendant, his office is this pickup. Legal briefs are strewn across the front seat. Styrofoam fast-food flotsam litters the floor of the cab. A faded Dukakis-Bentsen sticker graces the rear bumper. He deals typically with a workaday blur of domestic disputes, tenant-landlord squabbles, and custody fights. Or such was Dove's life until the day in June 1988 when Dwane Casey and Eric Manuel walked into the downtown office of Lexington Legal Services. There was a question about Eric's standardized test scores, Casey said, and no private attorney was willing to take the case pro bono.

Dove took the case, took it to his bosom, and hasn't let go since. Chip away at him, and Dove concedes that Manuel may have cheated. But he doesn't believe it. Every time Dove asked, Eric looked him in the eye and told him he didn't cheat. One night Dove sat in a Macon hotel room with Eric and Mary Manuel, laying out the possible consequences, pleading for the truth. "Eric, if you go in and tell the truth and they hammer you, at least you'll feel good that you told the truth," he said. "But go in there and lie, Eric, and they're just gonna hammer you."

Dove left to get a cup of coffee, and returned a half-hour later. Manuel again said he didn't cheat—said so in front of his mother, whom he worships—and Dove bought in. "That's why," he says, "I kind of believe the kid didn't cheat."

Dove's heart would advise Manuel to proclaim his innocence to the heavens. But the lawyer in him counseled a much more practical course when he first saw the stark figures summarizing the similarities between Manuel's and Chris Shearer's test sheets. Dove was stunned. He knew the numbers would leak to members of the press, who would scream their indictment. He told Manuel to cut his losses. Leave UK and go back to Macon, he advised him. Regroup. Find an NAIA school. Manuel told Dove he wanted to talk things over with his mother.

The very next day Dove received a phone call summoning him to the Lexington offices of Greenebaum, Doll & McDonald, a big law firm. Manuel was already there, driven over, Dove would discover, by Dwane Casey. A couple of people would be added to the legal team, Dove was told. "Because we weren't powerful enough," Dove says. "But I think the true reason is they didn't like my advice to get out [of Kentucky]. Sutton's whole thing was fight this, you're gonna make it, they can't prove anything."

Dove thought that was a suicide mission, a reckless course that set Manuel up as a fall guy. "So over there [at Greenebaum, Doll & McDonald] I lay it out. I say it doesn't look real good. I think he needs to leave. 'Oh, no, no, no, he's not going anywhere.' Robbie Stilz"—a Greenebaum attorney and active UK booster—"is saying this."

This was no longer Ed Dove's lonely crusade. Things were hot now, and suddenly private counsel had an interest in the case. No matter how grim the odds, Eric would stay in the womb of the program, fighting on under strict supervision.

Even with Greenebaum pitching in—and one of the new members of the legal team, a talented young attorney named Danny Reeves, donated hundreds of hours and good faith to the cause—the Manuel defense was handicapped. There was little money for the discovery process, nothing to pay a handwriting analyst, for instance, to determine whether the signature on Manuel's answer sheet had been forged.

Efforts to question people who might help Manuel's defense were met with hostility. Shearer never granted permission to have his answer sheet examined for any physical evidence that a second sheet might have been placed underneath it. When Dove tried to find the duplicated copy of Manuel's signature, all parties clammed up. Dove says he approached Shearer's father early on, only to be told, "Listen, you son of a bitch, you're not coming around my kid."

All these frustrations only strengthened Dove's belief in Manuel. "Supposedly at the beginning of the school year Shearer is going around telling everybody he helped Eric Manuel get into school," Dove says. "All his buddies at school. Go over and ask anybody at Lafayette. Ask Guion if he wasn't saying that."

[Guion confirms that after the investigation into Manuel's score had begun, several Lafayette students told her that Shearer had made such claims. "If in fact the rumors are true and (Chris) told these kids (what they) keep talking about," Guion says, "then the only people who know anything are Chris and Eric."]

"If Eric would talk, [the NCAA] would let him off," Dove says. "But here's a nineteen-year-old, his coaches are telling him to keep his mouth shut, the NCAA is saying talk—it's hard for the poor kid to put it in perspective. Everybody was saying Eric was getting the wrong advice. But how do you break a bond between a coach and a kid? And that's what we would have had to do.

"You have these damn test papers. They're real damaging. And you don't have the link, the little piece of twine that shows conspiracy or whatever. I mean, we could have shown motivation. But where's the string to bring them all together, to show he's the innocent victim of all this?"

Manuel never took a lie detector test to help resolve the

matter. Nor would he take the ACT again. The authors of this book commissioned an expert handwriting analyst who has worked for more than ten years in the questioned-documents division of a major metropolitan police lab to compare the signature on a photocopy of Manuel's answer sheet with contemporaneous samples. After examining nine characteristics, including such things as slant and pressure, he concluded that it's "highly probable" the signature is indeed Eric's.

Still, Dove doesn't want to believe that Manuel cheated. And he simply won't believe that if he did cheat, he acted on his own. Devote a year of your life to a case like this and it can turn you into a rampart of faith. Like everyone in Lexington, Dove has a theory. His involves two answer sheets. "It's like the Kennedy assassination," he says. "Two bullets, three bullets . . ." It goes something like this:

An answer sheet is already on the table in the Lafayette cafeteria when Eric arrives. He signs it before the test begins, then gets up to visit with Sean Sutton, who has taken a spot in another part of the room. When he comes back, he finds another answer sheet at his place. He signs that one, too, and takes the test. The first answer sheet has already been given to another party to fill out. Or it's withheld, to be filled out later. The second sheet, on which Manuel takes the test honestly, is never sent to Iowa City; hence Eric's protestations of innocence. "If you want to believe Eric is guilty or minimally guilty, he signed the test and slid it over and Shearer filled out the rest," Dove says. "But none of the proctors saw him doing that." (Eric, according to Mary Manuel and Don Richardson, says he signed his name twice that day—once on an answer sheet, and once after the test, when someone asked him for an autograph.)

Dove contends that the NCAA had only a limited interest in pursuing whether anyone collaborated with Manuel, because neither of the people closest to him that day—

Harville and Shearer—is employed by the university and under NCAA jurisdiction. "They found the test and that was it," Dove says. "They focused in on the smoking gun. All the proctors say he didn't cheat. 'Tough. We've got the smoking gun.'"

Berst says his office "couldn't get any further than the prospect, because the prospect wouldn't help."

One of the most persistent unanswered questions has to do with Harville and Shearer. Did they speak to each other before the test, and if so, what did they say? They alone among the principals in the affair refused to be interviewed for this book, despite repeated requests. "Let's face it," says Richardson, who has vowed never again to send a Macon Southwest star to Kentucky. "Grown-up people aren't going to mess themselves up to save Eric Manuel. Maybe ten or twenty years from now, someone will say, 'I did it,' when he feels safe and secure."

Even a member of the UK team that investigated the affair worries that Manuel was made a scapegoat. "[Sutton and Casey] were trying to protect their asses like crazy," he says. "You can certainly ask whether they were protecting Eric or themselves. For whatever reason, he stuck by his story and, sadly, paid the price."

But another question nags, even if it, too, was outside the purview of official inquiries. Why would Eric, or his supposed benefactors, or both, cheat given the extraordinary risks?

A couple of answers suggest themselves. One is the instant-eligibility-as-an-inducement theory: that a school promises a prospect he'll play as a freshman to get him to sign, and then has to make good on the promise by fixing a test.

The other is Manuel himself. Like Chris Mills, he was a playmaker and defender skilled beyond his years, a freshman who could contribute right away. Soon after taking the UK job, Sutton had said he would be content with only the occasional high-school All-America. The less-heralded player was more coachable, he said, and Lord knows Sutton believed in his ability to coach. But after a couple of seasons Sutton went back on his vow to settle for players of lesser ability. "You don't win the Kentucky Derby with jackasses," he said. And soon enough UK was back to its old ways, hoarding studhorses as ever: first Manuel and LeRon Ellis; then Mills and Shawn Kemp. Sutton had figured out that there isn't any margin for error when you're judged by the big-stakes race.

"Who has the most to gain out of the situation?" It's Dove speaking again. "If Eric doesn't pass the test, the worst that could happen is he's Prop 48. He plays the next year. Speculate with me. If he passes, you've got a chance at the national championship with Eric. *That* year.

"The kid was screwed. And it doesn't sit well."

The Boy King soon found out what it's like to rule a state at eighteen, and Rex Chapman didn't much like it. "I never saw Rex go out in two years," a former teammate says. "He couldn't go to a movie. He couldn't go to the mall. If he went out to dinner, the fans wouldn't let him eat. Rex as a freshman could do no wrong. He was by far the most popular person in the state."

Only one man stood to be threatened by that popularity. When Eddie Sutton told Chapman to stop being seen in public with Shawn Higgs, Chapman told his coach it was nobody's business who he spent his time with.

Sutton and Chapman clashed on other counts. Sutton delegated extraordinary power to James Dickey, the baby-faced assistant who had come with him from Arkansas, and a fiercely loyal favorite of Patsy Sutton's. Even when Sutton wasn't off on one of many speaking engagements, Dickey ran practice. And Chapman came to resent taking orders from this surrogate Eddie.

But more than anything, Chapman resented his image.

His sophomore year he asked ESPN's Dick Vitale to tone down the complimentary hyperbole. He knew it pandered to the adoring Kentucky fans, whose affection only nurtured jealousies among his teammates, particularly those who were the very things Rex wasn't: veteran, black, from out of state. And his teammates' acceptance of him was more important than being some home-grown, unreal idol.

As if to prove this, around the team he was desperately normal. He would romp through the Wildcat Lodge in his underwear after curfew. Once he took gobs of green skin lubricant in his hands and pretended to sneeze through it, gucking up everyone near him. In the sanctum of the lodge, Chapman became what he really was—like anyone else.

Rick Bozich, a columnist with the *Courier-Journal*, tells a revealing tale from Chapman's stay in Louisville over the summer of 1987, where the Pan Am team trained. The year before, at the Olympic Festival, Bozich had written up a story told him by Bill Foster, the Northwestern coach who was in charge of Chapman's team there. Chapman, Foster told Bozich, had come by his room after one of the games at the Olympic Festival, and apologized to him for playing poorly.

But here in Louisville, Chapman made a point of finding Bozich and mentioning the anecdote. "I just want you to know it's not true," he said.

Bozich apologized, and explained who his source had been. "There's only one thing I don't understand, Rex," he added. "It made you look good."

"People already have this image of me that I'm goody-goody," Chapman said.

Wow, Bozich thought to himself. A year later, and that's still on his mind.

By his sophomore season, Chapman had logged a summer with the Pan Am team. He had seen life outside UK, and participated in the United States's sobering loss to Brazil. When he came back to campus in the fall, he was more mature, but more guarded. He wasn't going to let the program devour him. Chapman put his emotions off limits.

All business, the 'Cats got off to a fast start. They were unbeaten and ranked No. 1 coming out of December, this despite nearly losing at home to North Carolina–Charlotte in a holiday tournament. But on January 9, UK lost by a point to a weak Auburn team in Rupp Arena, and the fragile bonds of team chemistry started to dissolve.

Sutton harped on his star's shot selection. He instituted a rule, clearly aimed at Chapman, requiring his players to make at least seven passes on each possession before letting fly. Chapman took it personally. "Eddie and Rex would fight through the newspaper," one 'Cat says. "It caused the team to self-destruct. And if you know Rex, a seven-pass rule wasn't going to stop him from shooting."

No UK player had ever left school early for the NBA, least of all one who had the best grade point average on the team. "Why go pro," the cynics always said, "when you'll have to take a pay cut?" But as if to accentuate just how exceptional he was, the Boy King in the spring of 1988 made plans to abdicate. He fled the glare and the pettiness and declared for the NBA draft. Chapman was so fed up with life under Sutton that he and his father asked pro teams interested in an honest appraisal of his abilities to bypass the Kentucky coaching staff and instead get in touch with Louisville's Denny Crum, who had coached the Pan Am team, and his assistant, Jerry Jones.

Chapman didn't go pro primarily to cash in, or to dodge the Wildcats' impending NCAA sanctions, or really even to escape the intrusive adulation of the people of the commonwealth—all theories advanced at the time. He went because the coaching staff made his life miserable. "Rex didn't want to go through another year taking orders from James Dickey," a teammate says. "Why stay in college and put up with that bullshit? I felt sorry for him."

The day Rex said he was leaving, little boys and girls across the state cried themselves to sleep.

Eddie Sutton's last team, the 1988–89 edition they called the Young and the Rexless, prepared for the season in a gathering gloom. In late September Sutton said he accepted much of the responsibility for violations in the program. Indeed, his contract allowed the university to fire him if any NCAA rules were broken on his watch. But before the traditional "midnight madness" practice—it's a hoary UK ritual to invite the public for the first workout of the basketball season, at 12:01 A.M. on October 15, the earliest mustering permissible under the rules—Sutton sounded like a man who had reconsidered. "I know I'm innocent," he said. "Let's hope the program is."

That fall he made more remarks seeming to distance himself from the quickening troubles. "I don't think anyone who is head of an organization, whether president of an institution or a company or a head basketball coach, can be fully responsible for everything," he said. Nor did he "want to be the recipient of past sins"—a clear reference to the NCAA having been unable to substantiate and mete out punishment for the charges outlined in the *Herald-Leader* in 1985. Joe B. Hall, commandant of the Big Blue legion of thousands, must have blanched when he read that.

A few days before practice started, the university announced that Eric Manuel had voluntarily left the team until the completion of the investigation into his test scores. If the charges of academic fraud held up, and UK used an ineligible player, the Wildcats would forfeit any victories and tournament income. Chris Mills, on the other hand, could play without prejudice until the Committee on Infractions passed judgment on his case, and the team's record and revenues wouldn't be jeopardized.

A thumping by Duke in the Tip-Off Classic augured the tough year to come. But the Wildcats' desperation wasn't laid bare until a weekend in early February, when they were to play at Georgia. The day before, news leaked out that the university, in its findings forwarded to the NCAA, would concede that Manuel cheated on his ACT test. In addition, the university would grant that $1,000 was indeed in the Emery envelope when it left Lexington, even if it couldn't be concluded with certainty that Dwane Casey put it there. When word of this reached Chris Mills in Athens, he was inconsolable. The Wildcats' loss to Georgia that day left them 11–11. They finished 13–19.

Sutton held up admirably through it all, only occasionally backsliding into the bouts with the bottle that had afflicted him during the 1986–87 season. Back then, as UK went 18–11 and suffered an abject 76–41 loss to LSU at home, Sutton's drinking had so alarmed a number of colleagues and rival coaches that they offered him their help and sympathy. He sought treatment in the fall of 1987 at the Betty Ford Center in Rancho Mirage, California, and seemed to return to campus rejuvenated for the next season, the one in which he warred with Chapman.

Yet Kentucky's first losing season since the pre-Rupp era had been torture, like being put out on a rack and stretched for thirty-two games. Oh, for the days of the last scandal, the days before David Roselle. Back then it had been so simple, so manageable. A few newspaper articles, a little uneasiness, ultimately a wrist slap from the NCAA so mild that the basketball program considered itself vindicated. Why, Sutton had described the *Herald-Leader*'s Pulitzer Prize as "tainted" because no sanctions were handed down.

If you were going to get in trouble, that was the way to do it. "The article exploded, '*Boom!*'" is the way one former Wildcat put it. "Then they rebuilt Hiroshima."

That the *Herald-Leader*'s two reporters, Jeffrey Marx and Michael York, got people to talk about rules violations in college basketball wasn't in itself that remarkable. But to induce people to talk about Kentucky in Kentucky—where loyalty to the program extends to every corner of the commonwealth and carries virtually statutory force— merited journalism's highest honor.

Not surprisingly, some of the most damaging material in the newspaper's series came from a former Wildcat who now lived and worked in Denver, presumably far from the reach of the coaches and moneymen who might keep him in line. Scott Courts described how, on the first day of school in 1977, Joe Hall introduced him to Lexington developer Donald Webb. Hall said, as Courts recalled, "This is going to be your best friend on the campus."

Later, Courts was quoted as saying, Assistant Coach Leonard Hamilton clarified Webb's role: "If you ever have money problems or anything, well, Don Webb might be able to take care of you."

Courts went to Webb "a couple of times" for cash thereafter, he said, receiving as much as $500 in one visit.

Neither Hall, who had resigned as the Wildcats' coach the spring before the article appeared, nor Hamilton nor Webb agreed to be interviewed for the newspaper's series. But in April 1986, six months after the stories appeared, Webb said he had a signed letter in which Courts disavowed the statements attributed to him.

Soon after Webb revealed the existence of that letter— and at the very time the NCAA was conducting its investigation of the *Herald-Leader*'s charges—the newspaper published excerpts from taped telephone interviews of Courts by Marx. The exchanges took place on October 27, 1985, just hours after the article containing Courts's disclosures hit the newsstand. Courts told Marx that Hamilton, Webb, and Dudley Webb, Donald's brother and business partner, were pressuring him to retract his statements. Hamilton and Donald Webb had awakened him in the middle of the night with a phone call, Courts said. The interview went on:

COURTS: Leonard Hamilton called me first, okay? And he

flat out asked me, you know, to completely lie about it to save his career. Then he connected me to Don Webb.

MARX: They were together?

COURTS: I guess it was a party call.

Later in the conversation Marx asked Courts whether Hamilton had disputed the substance of what Courts had been quoted as saying. Courts told Marx that Hamilton hadn't.

MARX: He was just saying, "Why did you say it?"

COURTS: Yeah. That's right. "Why couldn't you have just said, 'No comment'?"

In another call, later that day, Courts told Marx that "[Dudley Webb] is going to come out [to Denver]. He wants me to sign a letter that says none of it is true."

These exchanges were published five months after the original stories appeared. Even though they suggested an orchestrated cover-up of some of the very improprieties the NCAA's enforcement office was then investigating, Berst has no recollection of them ever being brought to the NCAA's attention.

For a booster like Donald Webb, whose Webb Brothers construction firm had developed the hotel space that helped land for that city the 1985 Final Four, the few sentences Courts told the *Herald-Leader* could have severed for good all ties to his beloved Big Blue. Dudley Webb has acknowledged that he did fly to Denver right after the *Herald-Leader* story appeared, in a private plane, and met with Courts— but not to coerce him into changing his story. He was only showing Courts a copy of the article and getting his reaction to it, he says. Several months later Don Webb said on *Your Government*, a Lexington public affairs television show, that Courts had sent him a letter of retraction, a copy of which Webb had forwarded to the NCAA.

For the record, Courts still stands by his letter to Don Webb. But he also says, "Those alums are a bunch of J.R. Ewings. . . . They're heavy hitters, those guys. They came out and asked me to write the letter and sign it. There are some powerful boys there. When you've got billionaires breathing down your throat, they can do some powerful things."

Courts never heard from the NCAA, probably because the original incidents fell outside the four-year statute of limitations. The NCAA wasn't going to lodge and pursue a new round of charges alleging a cover-up. But Berst has recently said, "There were forces at work that caused us not to get the full story."

Leonard Hamilton's career survived its brush with Scott Courts's conscience. To many schools, a basketball coach with an unblemished reputation is of little use. Hiring someone with a past sends a signal to boosters that inconveniences like NCAA legislation won't be permitted to interfere with winning. Before introducing Hamilton as Oklahoma State's new coach in the spring of 1986, OSU athletic director Myron Roderick noted that the NCAA had cleared Hamilton of any wrongdoing in connection with the recent unpleasantness at Kentucky.

In fact, Berst's staff was still investigating the case. Berst says that no one would have cleared Hamilton or anyone else before the probe was finished. And even if Berst was unaware of it, the story of Hamilton's after-hours phone call to Scott Courts was on the record, waiting for Oklahoma State to discover.

Could it have been that the Cowboys, whose football program was about to go on probation for a raft of violations, didn't want to?

Bret Bearup was a happy man as he walked into the Kentucky locker room in Rupp Arena on a December afternoon in 1985. The night before, the Wildcats had beaten Indiana, the one team he always seemed to wear out. Bearup had come back from playing ball in Europe and was preparing to enter UK Law School the following fall, but most of these 'Cats were still friends, erstwhile teammates, guys he had shared wind sprints and road trips with. A little vicarious thrill-copping was in order. Bearup lingered for an hour or so, sharing the good feeling of whupping Bobby Knight with the players as they got taped for practice. The room was emptying out when Bill Keightley, the florid old basketball equipment manager, told him he had a phone call.

Keightley handed him the receiver on the locker room extension. Eddie Sutton was on the line, calling from his office in Memorial Coliseum.

"Bret, in light of the *Herald-Leader* article, I think it would be best if you stayed away from the players. I don't want to see you in the locker room, the basketball office, or the Wildcat Lodge anymore."

Bearup was speechless. He had talked to the *Herald-Leader*, but then so had more than a score of others. Then it began to dawn on him. Virtually everyone else had recanted what they said, claiming suddenly that they were "misquoted," or their comments were "taken out of context." Bearup hadn't done that. He had simply refused further comment. For having told the truth and not taken it back, he was now persona non grata.

At first, Bearup had no idea how thorough and troublesome this banishment would be. UK seniors and recent graduates traditionally barnstorm after each season. It's great fun and good money—a few thousand bucks that Bearup, with law school approaching, could use—plus a chance to see the state and once again hear the hosannas of the faithful. Bearup had counted on barnstorming in the spring of '86. Sutton wouldn't let him.

And there was the matter of Rob Lock, the starting center on the current Wildcat team. Bearup had been Lock's player host on his campus visit, and in spite of the four years' age difference between them, the two had hit it off. To Lock, Bearup was a sort of mentor and guide. To Bearup, Lock was a protégé, a comparative innocent whom Bearup hoped would get through the Big Blue jungle more deftly than he had. To Sutton, their friendship was trouble.

"Why do you hang around him?" James Dickey asked Lock. "What kind of person plays at the University of Kentucky for four years, and then goes and talks? Bret Bearup is finished in Kentucky. What are your future employers going to think if they see you with him?"

Dickey and Sutton told Lock that for his own good, Bearup was off limits. Yet Bearup and Lock kept sneaking around together, hanging out at Two Keys tavern and shooting the bull. Lock would walk the block from the lodge to the McDonald's on South Limestone, where Bearup would pick him up. One Friday night during Lock's junior year they went to a Stevie Wonder concert in Rupp Arena together, and as the lights came up at intermission, found themselves locking eyes with Dickey and Sutton, who were entertaining a number of recruits in town on a visit. "Rob," Sutton said, "I want to see you in my office first thing Monday morning."

The next week Lock did his penance. He was up at five A.M., running five miles. If he were seen with Bearup again, the coaches made clear, he would lose his starting job.

"After that, Lock and I couldn't be seen in public together," Bearup says today. Sitting in his office at Greenebaum, Doll & McDonald's Louisville headquarters, where he's an associate, Bearup is clearly not finished in Kentucky. "I was really disappointed in Eddie. After the *Herald-Leader* story came out, nearly everybody in some way or form denied what they'd said. If it came down to lying or saying nothing at all, I chose nothing at all. Chuck Verderber chose nothing at all. He's gone on to be a dentist. I'm going on to be a lawyer. And we got chastised. Castigated. And I told the newspaper I sold Troy McKinley's tickets once for fifty dollars. Big deal.

"I couldn't help but think, 'Oh, this is what five years gets me. They really support their players.' Chuck didn't want to stay in Kentucky. He's practicing in Vermont. But I love Kentucky. I've made it my home."

Bearup, remember, grew up a fan. He was always hostage to that lingering bit of wide-eyed wonder. And UK was the city on the hill. No one representing the school had hinted at the slightest impropriety in its pursuit of him. "If you're looking for something under the table," Joe Hall had intoned in the Bearup living room, "look elsewhere." Bearup had bought it.

The disillusionment that washed over him when he came to Lexington and saw that things were otherwise stings to this day. "Kentucky doesn't need to cheat to recruit," he says. "With its fans and facilities, it's second to none. When I first discovered that shenanigans went on, it broke my heart. I asked myself, 'What am I doing here?'"

The revelation might have curdled his idealism into cynicism, but it didn't because of the state and its people. And that's what pains Bearup the most. He was making something of himself after basketball, and adopted Kentucky as his own. The program should have pointed to him with pride. And Sutton's message was loyalty all, integrity nothing. It seemed so petty, so small.

For having the fortitude not to run from the truth, Bearup was an outcast. Meanwhile, the Webb brothers became Sutton's intimates, as involved with the program as ever.

The overarching premises of the NCAA's enforcement arm are hopeful ones: that the interests of school and governing body are the same; that all parties are committed to "compliance"; that the enormous amounts of money liable to be lost as a result of sanctions won't deter a school from turning itself in. A brushfire breaks out on some campus, and the NCAA conducts an investigation. It also expects the school to investigate vigorously on its own, so the NCAA's Committee on Infractions can consider evidence from two independent probes of the same case. But it soon became clear to the committee that under Singletary and the university's chief counsel, John Darsie, UK's in-house investigation of the *Herald-Leader* findings would be "inadequate."

The efforts to get Scott Courts to recant were the most brazen part of a much broader effort. The university knew the series was coming. Darsie called players in before it was published to find out what to expect. At three A.M. on that Sunday morning, Glenn Rutherford, a Louisville *Courier-Journal* columnist, got a call from Leonard Hamilton, who had his boiler-room operation up and running. Hamilton told Rutherford he had talked to many of the players named in the story, and all said they were misquoted to one degree or another. Before the *Herald-Leader* had even hit the doorsteps of Kentuckians, Hamilton was asking the *Courier-Journal* to discredit the story. "I did call those players," says Rutherford, who now works as a *Herald-Leader* correspondent. "The unsettling thing was everybody had pretty much the same answer. Leonard was playing fireman."

Damage control was quick and brutally effective. The school would contact thirty-six current and former players during its investigation. Eight refused to cooperate. Of thirteen boosters contacted, five wouldn't talk. And virtually no one who did talk confirmed anything. "Some players would publicly slam us," says Marx, "and then call me to basically apologize. They said they had to do what they had to do, but they hoped it wouldn't affect our relationship. What could you say? I understood. But I have more respect for the guys who no-commented than the ones who lied their asses off to protect themselves."

As UK's probe proceeded, Darsie persuaded the NCAA to permit the school to report its initial findings orally. Presumably Darsie wanted to frustrate any requests from the press under the state's open-records law to see written progress of an inquiry. Darsie is the man who, after the 1976

NCAA investigation that led to a mild probation, successfully persuaded a judge to keep secret the identities of twelve boosters implicated in improprieties. He cited the civil liberties and "personal privacy" of boosters. That public exposure is the only way to meaningfully deter their excesses didn't seem to count.

If you were quoted in the *Herald-Leader*, UK investigators presented to you the option of saying you weren't going to play ball. Blanket denials weren't followed up with pointed questions. If a quoted charge were denied by the party to whom it was attributed, the school didn't pursue sources not named in the newspaper series who might corroborate it. Investigators, as Berst would ultimately put it, "seemed to suggest that refusal to talk would be satisfactory."

Among the players who did talk, all but one disavowed what was attributed to them, or confirmed improprieties up to the four-year statute of limitations and no further. The *Herald-Leader* refused on principle to release tape recordings of its interviews. That left the NCAA with no case.

But the reprimand of the university for not cooperating, as laconic and low key as it was, all but screamed, "We know you did it, and you'd better keep your nose clean." That's why Joe Bill Campbell, Casey's lawyer, was so worried three years later that his client would be made a scapegoat. "From what I understand," Campbell said, "the NCAA gave them such a tongue-lashing, they had some UK administrators near tears."

Yet the NCAA never got a handle on the stories behind the story—exactly why the players' accounts changed. "Everybody knew the *Herald-Leader* series was true," one of those quoted players says now. "Everybody said everything on tape, and then when it all came out, we all had to take it back. I was threatened within an inch of my life: 'You're gonna take it back and I'm gonna make damned sure you do.' But if my name ever came out that I said this to you, I'd have to take that back too."

Of the thirty-three current and former Wildcats interviewed for the *Herald-Leader* series, only two were smart enough never to say anything they might ever have to take back. Unique among the thirty-three, they denied participating in or being aware of any wrongdoing while at Kentucky. Each happened to be a major-college recruiter at the time, subject to the Code.

One was Dwane Casey. "If that makes me look like an oddball," Casey, then an assistant at Western Kentucky, told the newspaper, "I guess it has to."

The other was an ex-teammate of Casey's who had gone on to become an assistant at Pittsburgh. His name was Reggie Warford.

7

Cry "Uncle"

LEAVE RUPP ARENA and downtown Lexington, follow Georgetown Road north as far as Booker T's Drive-In Liquor Store, and you'll come upon an oasis in a blighted neighborhood, a swatch of green called Douglass Park.

Folks throughout central Kentucky call the summer basketball league here the Dirt Bowl, after the earthen tennis courts on which it began in 1967. The place has come a long way since.

Now, great concrete basket supports arch primevally out of painted macadam, like the necks of dinosaurs. Current and former Wildcats play in the league, and in the get-down pickup games that push into the early hours of summer mornings. But high-school kids run here too, as do sundry dreamers and pretenders eager to try out a double pump or flying lay-up against the city's best. With lights and bleachers, the only thing missing is a roof, a shortcoming that locals coyly acknowledge by calling the site the Skydome, "'cause the only roof is the sky."

Every July, Lexington's black community sets one Sunday aside for a festive basketball blowout in Douglass Park. Here is the flip side of elite Bluegrass society. Ladies young and old step out in their finery. A flamboyant creature in gaudy spectacles always makes his entrance in a late-model limousine. Nearby tents dispense baby-back barbecue and revivalist religion as the basketball rages into the gloaming. For years the first shot couldn't go up until a youngster from the community, a grade-schooler named Randall (Toot Toot) McAfee, took the mike in his hands. Dressed in Sunday whites, his hair newly processed and shoes glistening from a fresh shine, he looked like Little Stevie Wonder about to belt out "Fingertips," only it was the national anthem he screeched. Or something vaguely similar; Toot Toot, the man on the P.A. system always said, is the only person alive who can do "The Star-Spangled Banner" "in twelve different languages at the same time."

Super Sunday is proof that hoop in this town is a game for all seasons, as raucous at the Skydome in July as at Rupp in December. Both Dwane Casey and Reggie Warford had come by the Dirt Bowl during the late seventies while at UK, and each knew the league's tradition and menagerie of regulars, characters who went by names like Cheese and Pretty Pie and Stickman. But over the summer of 1983 these two former Wildcats showed up at Douglass Park in a different, more businesslike capacity. Casey, on behalf of Western Kentucky, and Warford, representing Pittsburgh, were both stalking the same player, a Lexington high-school star named Steve Miller.

Warford had grown up in Drakesboro, a little town near Bowling Green. As UK's second black scholarship player, he was everything Tom Payne wasn't and nothing that Payne was. Mentally tough, a little defensive, but enough of a leader to be named co-captain of Joe Hall's 1976 NIT champions, he graduated in four years before going on to

Iowa State. There he joined the staff of Lynn Nance, who had been a UK assistant, and in 1980 he hooked up with Roy Chipman, the head coach at Pitt. Warford was something of a swashbuckler, an effusive sort who wasn't above belting out a song in a prospect's home. That fall, during one of many trips through Lexington in pursuit of Steve Miller, he would rescue an elderly couple from their burning house, and be honored for his heroism with the governor's Medal of Valor.

In 1976, the same season Warford was named the Wildcats' senior scholar-athlete, Casey joined the team. He didn't play much, but nonetheless won UK's freshman leadership award. Casey, too, was from a small town in the western end of the state, but he was more engaging and socially adroit than Warford, with fewer rough edges. Ordinary UK students, with nothing more to their credit than a love for Big Blue basketball, found Casey to be that rarest subspecies of Wildcat, the kind who talked to them as if they were equals. That unaffected manner served him well as he tried to lure talent to Western.

By the summer both Warford and Casey were feeling pressure. Pittsburgh had recently moved from the Eastern 8 to the big-time crucible of the Big East. Only a few months earlier, right after Pitt's first-round loss to Villanova in the Big East tournament, Chipman had called Warford into the head coach's New York City hotel room and told him he was sorry, but he was going to have to let him go. All of the recruits Warford pursued that season had either signed elsewhere or said they weren't interested in Pitt. He was disorganized, Chipman told Warford. He didn't recruit hard enough. And all the time he spent in Kentucky wasn't justified by the results it was yielding.

Warford was crushed at this, so much so that Chipman drew back. The Pitt coach asked himself whether he was being fair, whether he wasn't just reacting rashly to the disappointment of an early postseason loss. Before Warford left the room, Chipman told him he would take a few more days to think things over.

And Chipman did reconsider. He took Warford back on the condition that he use his time more productively and become more aggressive. "Just get out there and bird-dog," he told him. Chipman had come to Pittsburgh from small-time Lafayette, and to get a better sense of corporate college basketball he spent several days at UK studying the Hall machine. Leonard Hamilton, Chipman told Warford—now, there was a guy to emulate.

Meanwhile, Casey had rejoined the Western Kentucky staff just as the Hilltoppers made a move of their own—from the sleepy Ohio Valley Conference to the more competitive, TV-conscious Sun Belt. Dwane and Reggie, the two black ex-Wildcats who had made the same journey from little western Kentucky towns to the big show, talked frequently; at one point, Chipman recalls Warford saying, Dwane confided that he was under the gun at Western, that he felt pressure to recruit and "do some things." Indeed, the NCAA publicly reprimanded Western for violations, some of them Casey's, in the recruitment of Tellis Frank and Kannard Johnson, two high-profile signees in the class of '83. Kevin McCormick, the NCAA investigator in charge of that case, believes there was much more to it than he uncovered. "In my opinion, Dwane wasn't a very honest character," says McCormick. "I would ask him things I already knew the answer to. For example, Dwane said he hadn't been to Kannard Johnson's house but one time. Kannard had said Dwane had been there five times. It's only my opinion, but I think he was as crooked as the day is long."

Twice—while pursuing Chip Watkins of Louisville, and Brian Mitchell of Lexington—Casey and Warford had competed against each other, and Reggie edged out Dwane each time. But the Watkins and Mitchell chases had been innocent, just friendly jousts, for neither turned out to be much of a catch. Steve Miller was different.

Miller was solidly built, a 6-foot-6-inch, 220-pound senior-to-be at Henry Clay High with excellent grades. To sign him would be a coup for any recruiter. His parents were split, and his natural father now lived in Massachusetts. But Steve's mother, Jean, had remarried, and Steve lived with her and his white stepfather, Bob Trahan. Though both worked, the Trahans were vigilant parents. They had invited a family friend named Jimmy Gay, who had coached Steve in the Dirt Bowl, to help guide them through the recruiting process—to answer questions, sit in on home visits, and see that things stayed on the up and up.

Miller would be named Kentucky's "Mr. Basketball" in 1984, and first dibs on Mr. Basketballs normally went to the University of Kentucky. Indeed, if he were white and from one of the state's small towns, a great public clamor would have arisen for the Wildcats to offer him a scholarship, à la Richie Farmer. But Miller was a black Lexingtonian, the best of a middling crop that year, and didn't really figure in UK's plans. Certainly if they could sign Richard Madison, a muscular rebounder from Memphis known as the Master Blaster, the Wildcats wouldn't need Miller. From the looks of things, Leonard Hamilton was going to pass, and let his protégés, Warford and Casey, fight over the spoils.

Casey doped out the situation quickly and shrewdly. He worked the women, Jean Trahan and Miller's girlfriend, Dana Allen. He discovered early on that Steve liked Western Kentucky coach Clem Haskins, whom he considered to be the black father figure absent much of his life. By September, Steve had assured Dwane that he would sign with the Hilltoppers, and that he had no interest in Pitt. As long as Leonard didn't change his mind, Dwane knew, Steve was his.

Warford, meanwhile, never really got the message. In a signed statement given to an NCAA investigator, Miller

193

describes how Pittsburgh recruited him. One evening in September, shortly before Kansas coach Larry Brown was to appear for a scheduled home visit, Warford came by the Trahans' house unannounced to pitch Pitt. Five or six times over the next several weeks he telephoned. And one afternoon he tracked Steve down in the gym at Henry Clay High.

Warford said he couldn't understand why Miller had no interest in going to Pitt. Was anyone offering him anything?

Miller wanted to know why Warford wanted to know.

"Not to report anyone," Warford replied. "But if anyone's offered you anything, we could, you know, match it."

Several days later Warford phoned the Trahan home again. He asked Steve if he needed a job. As a matter of fact, Steve said, he did—but with school in session and the basketball season coming up, he could work only odd hours. Not to worry, Warford told him. He'd take care of it.

Soon a Dirt Bowl character, a convicted ticket scalper named Irvin Stewart, came by the high school.

"How much money you have in your pocket?" Stewart asked Miller.

"Oh, four or five dollars," Miller said.

Stewart shook his head. "When I was your age, I always had money. And you're an All-American basketball player, man. You should have three or four hundred in your pocket at all times. I mean, you need money?"

"Everybody can use some."

"I can make a telephone call and put three or four hundred dollars, cold cash, in your pocket by afternoon. You need some wheels?"

Stewart went on to tell Miller that he could get him a used car too. Reggie Warford had made him a deputy in the recruiting process, he said. Stewart said he could set up a visit to Pittsburgh—get the airline tickets, make all the necessary arrangements.

Miller soon heard from Stewart again. The job Reggie got you, he was told, won't pay $50 a week, but $300 to $400.

The money, Miller says Warford told him later, was to be funneled through a Pitt booster.

Sometime in October, Steve let slip to Jimmy Gay, the Trahans' friend, that Reggie had gotten him a job. Gay was upset. He knew Irvin Stewart from the Dirt Bowl, and knew that Stewart had been taking Miller around town and out to dinner. Now Gay went by the Trahans' to tell them about the job, about Irv Stewart—that all of this could jeopardize Steve's eligibility.

But no sooner did Gay reach the Trahans' than Irv Stewart pulled up. And right there in the yard, in front of the Trahans' house, Gay and Stewart got into it.

"The boy is going with me, going to dinner, and Steve's going with me to Pitt," Stewart told Gay.

"I'm not gonna take none of your shit," Gay shot back.

"I'm gonna whip your ass," Stewart yelled.

The shouting escalated, and the two nearly exchanged blows. Finally Gay turned to Miller. "The only thing I'm here for is to try to make sure things are done right. But Steve, hey, if you want to go to dinner, you're a grown man, go on to dinner." Miller and Stewart roared off.

The scene on their front stoop disgusted the Trahans. Jean Trahan had been upset with Warford for inviting himself over weeks earlier, and furious at Pitt for getting in touch with Steve's natural father, whom she felt had abandoned the family. Now she called Chipman to tell him about the fracas at their doorstep, and that Irv Stewart was unwelcome around her son.

For Miller, it had been fun while it lasted. Stewart had bought lobster dinners for him and a friend, Henry Clay teammate Jeff Blandon, always telling them not to worry where the money came from. Miller and Blandon looked forward to a trip to Pittsburgh, particularly the way Irv billed it—catch a Steelers game, do some shopping, scope out some girls, meet up with Steve's dad. The trip never came off because Jean Trahan put her foot down, and Steve didn't work more than a week at the job Warford lined up for him. But Miller and Blandon knew exactly what was going on. From the beginning they gave Dwane Casey a play by play of each blundering step Reggie and Irv made, until November, when Steve signed with Western Kentucky.

Warford denies he did anything improper in recruiting Miller. He says Stewart was just a friend, someone he pulled aside at Super Sunday and asked to feed him information. (In his expense vouchers, Warford lists Irvin Stewart as a "recruiting aide." Chipman would later characterize Stewart as Pitt's "pimp.") Yet most of Miller's account is from information gathered by the NCAA for Operation Intercept —the NCAA's annual debriefing of each year's most heavily recruited high-school seniors. Because prospects are interviewed while the recruiting process is still fresh in their minds, and before they have settled into the see-no-evil, say-no-evil cocoon of college basketball and become versed in the Code, the NCAA considers information gathered through Operation Intercept to be unusually credible.

With the help of a middleman, Pitt had enticed a youngster with meals and a job, and offers of a weekend junket, money, and a used car, all in violation of the rules. But in spite of it all, the Panthers had failed to get their man.

The Steve Miller case didn't turn into yet another sorry story of a young man being wooed and won over by a street agent. Miller and Jeff Blandon were too smart, the Trahans and Jimmy Gay too vigilant, and Irvin Stewart simply too inept for that to happen. But more and more, a middleman —a.k.a. bag man, flesh peddler, broker, third party, street agent, confidant, guardian, family friend, recruiting aide, pimp, or "uncle"—is playing a role in where a high-school ball player will go.

A third party is most likely to surface alongside an inner-city youngster from a single parent home. Far from being avuncular do-gooders, many are after a piece of the action, a ticket to the big time or an all-expenses-paid ego trip. As much as coaches decry their proliferation, middlemen make recruiting easier. Because an "uncle" is neither a parent nor a legal guardian, the NCAA permits coaches to have an unlimited number of contacts with him. It's the middleman's contacts with a prospect that can get a school into hot water, if the emissary can be identified as "a representative of the school's athletic interests," as Irvin Stewart was.

Since 1987 such representatives haven't been allowed to contact recruits, even by phone or mail. But if a middleman has no real ties to the college, recruiters can approach him during so-called dead periods, when coaches' contacts with prospects are prohibited. Third parties have a sense for the lay of the land, an expertise that recruiters can tap into to gauge many of the subjective factors that go into a youngster's decision. And where "the old one-two combo" is absent, an "uncle" can be a catalyst in getting an indecisive youth to make up his mind.

Middlemen have been around for years, and the New York City of the fifties produced the most colorful ones. Aldo (The Waiter) Leone, who used to work at Mamma Leone's restaurant, kept Miami in talent. Uncle Harry Gotkin, a retired manufacturer of baby bonnets, looked after North Carolina's needs. Howard Garfinkel and Walter November were AAU coaches who doubled as matchmakers; Garf fed players to North Carolina State, and November —his surname has a particular felicity today, given when the early-signing date falls—delivered the core of Loyola's 1963 national championship team.

But none rivaled the spectral presence of the Spook. Fred (Spook) Stegman was so frail it's a wonder he didn't disappear down some sidewalk grate. Out-of-fashion clothes barely clung to him, and his hair looked as if it had been tamed with motor oil. He lived in a tiny apartment in Queens with no phone. Coaches trying to reach him—and there were many—knew to try him during "office hours." They would call a pay phone next to the orange-drink machine at the Nedick's by the old Madison Square Garden. A Chinese man ran the place, so if someone answered in rapid Mandarin, the coach knew enough to say, "Spook," whereupon the receiver was passed and business duly conducted.

"I've got a player that's great for you," Spook might tell a coach in his asthmatic wheeze. Then he'd go tell the player, "I've got a situation that's great for you."

Once the two parties agreed, Stegman would collect from the school what he called "carfare"—a few hundred dollars, tops—so the youngster could get to campus. Then he'd turn around and ask the player's family for the same. "Nickel-and-dime stuff," Spook calls it today.

The world in which players are now offered up and procured retains little of the Runyonesque charm of the Spook's day. "Those guys did a lot of good back before integration," says Georgetown coach John Thompson. "They were a necessity. There were only a few places [black] kids could go—out west, for instance, or to New England. [Elgin Baylor and Bill Russell went to Seattle and San Francisco, respectively; Thompson himself went to Providence.] No one would go into the [black] community. It's like those Tarzan movies. If bwana's gonna go into the jungle, he's got to call on someone to take him there. Kids had no contacts, no way of being seen.

"But after integration demand got so great, his role changed. 'Hey, man, we can market this.' Just like anything else. Today you have organizations that serve as street agents. They claim to be community groups, but they try to serve as clearinghouses. Some of them have good motives. But a lot of them don't. 'My kids' is the byword now. You get a lot of that."

"My kids" is only one of the middleman's buzz phrases. Listen to the language of the flesh-peddling game, and from its very imagery you can tell the Machiavellian subtext. A surgeon is a negative recruiter, a bad-mouther who tries to improve his school's position by swooping in and "cutting up" another college. To get juiced is to be paid off, something most middlemen are hoping to be. A boat or ride is a scholarship, all a school can offer a prospect (along with books, room, and board) under NCAA rules; but in street argot both words are synonyms for cars, which often get offered anyway.

The free-lance uncle of today has a simple m.o. He gets to the player early, building up trust by spending time with him—but also by spending money, on clothing, dinners, movies, or tickets to ball games. When the colleges come calling, around the high-schooler's sophomore year, the middleman invokes another school that's supposedly hot for his protégé. "School A really likes him," he tells the recruiter. "I'd like to see him at your school, but his mother needs help, his sister needs help." Then he "camouflages" the deal, interesting a school or two with clean reputations —an Indiana or a Duke—so as not to arouse suspicion. (John Williams's handlers neglected to do this, and the bidding got out of hand.)

If the broker wants to represent the youngster when it's time to turn pro, he asks the college coach to steer him back after three or four years. More often, the broker will look for an immediate payoff. He may ask for a flat finder's fee. Terry Kirkpatrick says a broker once asked him for biweekly $1,000 payments. But an uncle won't necessarily want money. He may want a car. If he has a summer-league or AAU team, he may want equipment or shoes or free tuition for "his kids" at the school's basketball camp. If he styles himself a real coach, he may want a college job. Or the motivation may be in simple ego gratification.

The college recruiter can hardly ignore him. "They don't come to you," says Seton Hall assistant Rod Baker. "You go to them. You have to seek them out. What you really want from them is information. Where are they going to be? What's the kid thinking? Who else is in the hunt? What do we have to do to either keep our position or move up?

"Now, is that right or wrong? All I can tell you is it's part of it. Because I'm on a mission, and if he's in my way I have to deal with him, one way or another. I can't act like he's not there."

Just as some kids play pickup ball according to "losers' out," and others play "make it, take it," there's an indigenous profile to the way players, "uncles," and schools get paired off. It all depends on local custom and patterns of power. In Los Angeles the high-school coach doesn't usually get involved, but everyone else does. In Chicago and the sleepy towns across the Deep South, it's just the reverse: the kid's coach gets the right of first refusal. Detroit belongs to freelancers, a handful of street agents who not only feed high-schoolers to colleges, but determine which high schools the middle-school kids will attend in the first place. And New York City is every man for himself.

"It's control, man, all about control," says Rudy Washington, the Iowa assistant coach. "It's an investment. Like any other investment, there are risks. Sometimes it doesn't work out. But generally the broker says, 'I'll take care of [the player]. I'll make sure he's got new shoes, food, and spending money. You protect my investment. Give me access to the kid, allow the relationship to continue.' The coach doesn't have to do anything; the kid can't go anywhere else. It's a done deal.

"How tough is it to buy an inner-city kid? Buy him some shoes, take him to dinner, get him some nice clothes, maybe a car. You become his best friend, and he gets hooked, like a junkie. Then you control the product. The secret is controlling the product early. It's just like slavery. Modern-day slavery is what it is. They're just doing it in advance now, that's all.

"And you know the saddest part? The kids don't even know. It's like a pervert offering a kid some candy to get in his car."

High-school games in Detroit tip off in the afternoon, right after school, to forestall nighttime violence and fan rowdiness. It's tough for a college coach to make a 3:30 P.M. starting time; he usually has his own practice to run. Yet there's one place in town where every recruiter in the country knows he can find a first-rate game at just about any hour, "a super skill game," as Gary Mazza, a longtime coach in the Motor City, calls it, "all reflexes and reaction —wide open, like a punt return. Where you either have it or you don't."

A wrought iron railing vainly shields St. Cecilia's Catholic Church from the hardscrabble reality to which she ministers, just north of the Grand River on the city's northwest side. People call the two-story red-brick gym adjacent to the church "Ceciliaville," as if it were somehow apart from the municipality of Detroit. And it is, after a fashion. The basketball program here began in 1968, shortly after the riots, as a refuge from the streets.

For years, the sign over the back door read ST. CECILIA'S GYM—SPORTS CAPITAL OF THE WORLD. That wasn't just empty braggadocio. Michigan's finest ball players, from Spencer Haywood to George Gervin to Magic Johnson, came through that portal. Pistons like Dave Bing and Jimmy Walker entered their own teams in the league during the off season. As an ABA rookie with the Denver Rockets, Haywood had bought a long, new Cadillac, and when the season ended he drove it all the way back to Detroit just so he could park it outside the gym and let the homeboys see what the game had done for him.

Of course the high-school kids joined the summering pros and college players, and that attracted to St. Cecilia's an older, more calculating breed of parishioner, the college recruiter. The intersection of the ghetto with the big time turned Sam Washington, the league's founder and director, into a celebrity. The pictures lining his downstairs office were like those of a gregarious, big-city restaurateur. Here was Sam with Magic. Sam with Ice. Sam with former Michigan coach Bill Frieder, the mop-topped Freeds. At five foot four and 280 pounds, Washington looked more like a basketball than a basketball maven. But even as the high-profile coaches and pro headliners came by his gym, Sam was every pound the "godfather," as people affectionately called him. "If Sam wanted something done, people just did it," says Mike Cash, his longtime aide-de-camp. "He had that kind of magnetism." Sporting Detroit noted with sadness the day he died, in December 1988.

Sam had been discriminating about who he let in the league, as sponsor or player. A neighborhood business might pick up the $100 in entry fees for a roster of ten guys, and ball players had to be just that—ball players, not thugs looking to make a reputation by roughing up Motown's finest.

But after Sam's death his son Ron succeeded him. Fatefully, Ron Washington threw the league open to anyone. In the leadership vacuum, street players found berths on many of the twenty-five teams in Ceciliaville's elite college division. And some of those teams were now sponsored by local merchants of an altogether different sort, men willing to ante up as much as $500 and $600 for teams. They, too, had a business stake in the community. They were drug dealers.

A little cash on the side is a hoary Ceciliaville tradition. Ball players making the long ride in from Flint, say, or Grand Rapids, always expected a stipend for their gas and their trouble, NCAA rules notwithstanding. Small-time numbers runners would stoke a little action in the bleachers, and ringers on the college-division teams expected some scratch. But the crack lords took everything up a few notches. "You know the movie example of a guy who has too much money?" says one Detroit coach. "He lights cigars with it? Well, the equivalent among the Detroit drug crowd is you burn fireplaces with it. And so many of these kids receive something to play in college, why would they suddenly play for free in the summer?"

The dealers were cutthroat businessmen moonlighting as general managers. For hundreds of dollars a game they bought up coaches and players, both ex–Public School League (PSL) stars who hadn't gone to college and current collegians. It was a rich man's diversion to see who could put together the most powerful "franchise." Ceciliaville one-upsmanship, until now just a harmless part of the in-your-face pickup ethic, had taken on a frightful new dimension. Toward the end of summer 1989, when the playoffs began and the rosters were frozen, the bleachers would fill up with urban dandies wearing gold. The drug lords bet on their own teams and against one another, raising the stakes by $1,000 at a time, calling out higher and higher figures right in the stands.

A thousand people were shoehorned into the gym on August 5, 1989, for the college-division semifinal between the Players and Steve's Big Shots. The game was close for most of this Saturday afternoon, at least until the final quarter, when Lee Coward of Missouri, a guard for the Players, busted a few three-pointers and seemingly settled matters. With only a few minutes remaining, one of the Big Shots took a deliberate stroll down the sideline, apparently toward the water fountain at the far end of the gym. He was probably a provocateur. He stopped in front of the Players' bench and helped himself to a cup of Gatorade from their cooler.

One of the Players leapt to his feet to take up the challenge. Soon spectators had joined the players' scuffle.

Bottles flew. Fans, referees, and ball players alike fled the gym, filing hastily through the one narrow door to the parking lot outside.

Ron Washington decided to declare the game void. He designated the evening's scheduled second semifinal as the college-division championship. But tipoff time for that game was still several hours off, and perhaps two hundred people, including many of those just flushed from the gym, milled about.

In one part of the lot Steven Dale Goodwin, the coach and sponsor of Steve's Big Shots, was jawing heatedly with an unidentified man. Thirty-seven thousand dollars had been riding on the game, witnesses say, and the man wanted Goodwin to pay up. Goodwin argued that he didn't owe a cent because the game had been suspended.

"Oh?! So you ain't gonna pay me and I'm your bitch? And I supply you?"

Two shots rang out, each striking Goodwin in the chest.

Any doubts that the shooting was drug related quickly evaporated. It turned out that Goodwin had an arrest record for weapons charges, and a conviction for armed robbery. Several hundred people had witnessed the incident, yet police could identify no suspects. And Goodwin, who recovered from the wounds in the hospital, refused to answer questions.

Father Thomas Finnigan, the pastor at St. Cecilia's, closed the gym immediately. Soon new rules were drawn up for the college-division league. Henceforth all players and coaches will sign a contract agreeing not to wear gold chains, swear, or gamble. No teams will be sponsored by any entity other than the church or the college the team represents. And no one not currently enrolled in college will play.

They were sensible steps, a small price to pay if one of Detroit's great traditions were to be salvaged. But the shootout at St. Cecilia's revealed one problem for which there is no ready remedy. If the rule of law in this city is so tenuous, NCAA rules don't have a chance.

Cooley High coach Ben Kelso knows well the roots of the crisis facing high-school basketball in Detroit, for he was suckled by the streets. He grew up in Chattanooga, Tennessee, one of eleven kids in a two-room house, raised by a mother who sent young Ben and his siblings out daily with a wagon to panhandle for food. At fourteen he left home, fleeing north to Flint, Michigan, where a sister had settled. Again he beat the long odds of the streets. He earned a basketball scholarship to Central Michigan not by dazzling as a high-school player, but by writing letters to scores of coaches, asking them to come by a summer league and check him out. Kelso was a star for four seasons with the Chippewas, and a serviceable reserve for a couple of years in the mid-seventies with the Detroit Pistons, where he played with a cousin of Reggie Warford's named Bob Lanier.

The Kelso jump shot was a pretty parabola that belied the gritty beginnings of the man who squeezed it off. But today, as his hair thins and picks up flecks of gray, Kelso shoots straighter than most. He has seized a leadership role among the city's Public School League coaches since leaving Henry Ford High for Cooley in 1984. Three years after that he was named national high-school Coach of the Year, and won a state title despite suspending his star, Michael Talley, on the eve of the championship game for breaking curfew.

The Cooley he came to was in chaos. Authorities had just transferred the principal and released a number of teachers for improper fraternization with students. But Kelso soon discovered that the housecleaning wasn't complete. Two men would show up in the basketball office in midafternoon, just after school. They hung their coats in lockers there, right next to Kelso's. When the gym filled up with

Cooley ball players, they, too, took the floor. After practice they waited for the youngsters to shower up, then took them out to dinner.

"I don't see you guys around during the day," Kelso asked one of them. "What do you teach here?"

"Oh, I don't teach here," he replied.

"Well, what do you do? Do you work for the [school] board?"

"No, man. I go out, get players at a young age, and steer those players to Cooley."

These were the street agents Kelso had heard about, the middlemen who matched kids with colleges—only they were working the front end too. The high schools needed them. In defiance of Michigan High School Athletic Association rules that ban recruiting of any sort, they were hustling up the Cooley stars of the future, taking advantage of the "open enrollment" policies that don't restrict Detroit students to schools in their neighborhoods. Several PSL coaches, particularly Southwestern High coach Perry Watson, are notorious for recruiting. Even as rules provide for only one paid assistant coach, many PSL teams have three and four men in dress suits riding their benches, hanging on, looking for a break, hoping for a return on their investment.

Kelso indulged the two interlopers for a while, figuring he needed their help to right the Cooley program. But early in Kelso's first season, one of them arranged a weekend visit to Arkansas–Little Rock for two of his stars, Curtis Kidd and Paris McCurdy, without letting him know. Kelso felt himself losing control of the program. That Monday he went to his principal and A.D., and demanded the two be banished from his gym.

One of the exiled street agents was in his twenties, about 6 foot 1, with a faint stutter and full Jeri curl. He favored long coats and a beret, and billed himself as a singer and entertainment promoter. His name was Vic Adams.

"I got him out of my gym," Kelso says. "Within a week he was someplace else."

People who know Missouri coach Norm Stewart say he would never countenance rule-breaking. They say his principles take their place right up there with him on the pedestal he has occupied in that state since he played at Mizzou in the mid-fifties. Just as emphatically, the same people describe him as a competitor without peer, a man who didn't merely suffer from four straight first-round postseason losses during the eighties, but chafed under them, because he knew that many of the teams partaking of college basketball's prosperous new era were flouting NCAA rules. In 1983 Stewart concluded that his top recruiter, Gene Jones, hadn't been delivering the requisite talent. He replaced Jones with an affable, beetle-browed journeyman coach named Rich Daly.

Missouri needed to tap a lode, to get a few inner-city athletes who could mesh with the white role players Stewart has always been able to find in the small towns of the Show-Me State. Daly seemed to be the man to do it. He had scoured the basketball badlands for eleven years as a successful junior-college coach, and another five as an assistant at Tennessee-Chattanooga. He was persistent and persuasive—"He could sell you a pair of used underwear," Derrick Chievous, one of Daly's first marquee recruits, likes to say—and moved comfortably through big-city schools and grimy gyms. Daly set his sights on the Motor City, which turns out twenty-five to thirty Division I prospects every year. All he really had to do was pick off one a season, and the Tigers would stay near the top of the hypercompetitive Big 8.

That first year Daly made a play for a Detroit high-school star named Demetreus Gore, and lost out narrowly. But he did land a consolation prize, Lynn Hardy, a lightly regarded Cooley guard. Soon Daly signed Coward, another overlooked little guard, and Nathan Buntin and then Doug Smith, a couple of forwards with much bigger names—in all, seven Detroiters, more than one a year. People took notice. Rich Daly became known in the coaching fraternity as Doctor Detroit. His internist, everyone in town knew, was Vic Adams.

Adams and Daly had first hooked up in 1984, during Missouri's pursuit of Gore. Adams was still working Cooley then, and steered Hardy to Mizzou. No one put much stock in it at the time, for anyone could have "delivered" Lynn Hardy. But when Hardy panned out, it made Adams look even better. Now the "starving artist" who panhandled chump change from college coaches—no more than $10 or $20 at a time for meals—became more discriminating. "He suddenly became interested only in kids who were going to be good enough to play big-time ball," says former University of Detroit coach Don Sicko. "Before, Vic dealt mainly with juniors about to become seniors. Now he was cultivating relationships with ninth- and tenth-graders, taking a tremendous interest in these kids if it's just a hobby."

Adams "went exclusive," Sicko says, doing everything with an orange and black twist. He threw soda-and-pizza parties at his apartment, where kids all over the city knew they could see the Missouri highlight film. He met with Daly when Doctor Detroit came through town, and at least once even Norm Stewart himself sat down for a meal with Adams. More and more, people noticed, those Jeri curls came to rest on shoulders clad in a Mizzou sweatshirt.

Adams, who had taken up at Pershing High as a "volunteer assistant" after Kelso threw him out of the Cooley gym, was a terrific catalyst, someone who eliminated for Missouri all the problems that come with being an arriviste. Mizzou hadn't pried a player out of St. Louis in ages, but the Tigers were now the talk of Detroit, hotter even than Michigan. Come the summer of 1988, however, Missouri got a little heavy-handed. By then, Daly had set his sights on a terrific forward in the PSL, a senior-to-be named Daniel Lyton. There was only one problem: Lyton played at Cooley, where Ben Kelso had told Vic Adams to take a hike only a few years before. That summer, a source close to the Cooley program has told the NCAA, Rich Daly and a PSL coach—one who had already sent a player to Missouri—sat down with Kelso. Daly reportedly offered Kelso $20,000 cash if Kelso could influence Lyton to sign with Mizzou. The money was to be paid in $5,000 increments, the first upon agreement, with the rest to follow. The other coach was there as a reference, to vouch for the credibility of the deal, to assure Kelso that Daly could be trusted.

Kelso said no.

That wasn't what they wanted to hear, the same source says, so Missouri worked around Kelso. The source says that Adams and Daly tried to engineer a transfer for Lyton before his senior season, so they could find another coach with whom they could do business. That fall Lyton, who had already committed verbally to Southern Cal, suddenly —and unbeknownst to Kelso—signed with Missouri. Vic Adams brought the Mizzou letter of intent by the Lyton home himself.

Kelso declines public comment on the charges, and Daly denies any improprieties. "It's definitely not true," he says.

But Kelso will say, "Even with [high-school coaches in Detroit] standing up, forming an organization, trying to fight the situation, saying 'Hey, look, we've got to teach the kids there's more to life than the value of a dollar,' [the street agents] would say, 'The hell with you,' and find another way. It's very hard to fight a situation like this when parents and kids don't have the resources to refuse, say, twenty thousand dollars. Twenty thousand dollars to a poor kid in the city of Detroit is a great, great deal. And some of these guys are smart enough to know that, and if you turn them down, they just go right around you."

Kelso also wonders about the circumstances under which

Lyton met the college board score requirements of Proposition 48. Kelso had set up SAT preparation classes for his players, and Lyton attended every one. But several times Lyton was signed up to take the test and he didn't show. "Then one day he came and said he had taken it," Kelso says. "He didn't say where he went to take the test. I continued to ask him about it, and he said he went downtown somewhere.

"[Prop 48] has brought about people figuring out ways to get around it, because they can't get through it. And they can't get through it because they haven't been prepared in the first place. So then they figure, hey, I've got to get there the best way I can."

No evidence has emerged to implicate Adams in improperly helping Lyton meet his Prop 48 requirements. But Pershing High, Adams's current base of operations, was the site of two mysterious fires that damaged a counselor's office in 1987; a number of teachers and administrators no longer work there after instances surfaced of transcript tampering to help students get into the armed forces. And Adams has told at least two college coaches that he could solve any transcript problems. A source close to Marshall coach Dana Altman says that when Altman was at Moberly (Missouri) Junior College in the mid-eighties and pursuing Detroit high-school stars Johnnie Bell and Marvin Branch, Adams told Altman that he, Adams, could get either player "a GED, or anything you need." (Branch bounced around between three other jucos before flunking out of Kansas; Bell ended up at Arkansas–Little Rock.) Altman says, "I've made my comments to the NCAA, and for right now, that's where I'd like to leave it rest."

The image of downtown Detroit as a bazaar of contraband—score a gram of crack on this street corner; get your bogus transcript and board scores one block over—isn't far from the truth. Jerry Tarkanian says he got a phone call from someone who said he could guarantee that Anderson Hunt, the star guard from Detroit Southwestern High who sat out his first season at UNLV as a Prop 48 case, would meet the test requirement. The caller wanted $2,500. "I hung up on him," Tarkanian says.

PSL transcripts, meanwhile, look like ransom notes. "They're abortions," says former University of Detroit coach John Mulroy. "They'll have handwritten grades, then stickers, then places where there's been computerization—just a hodgepodge. What happens is a well-meaning friend, confidant, coach, approaches the kid's teacher and says, 'Hey, this kid's gonna get locked out of college. And what's the difference between a D and a C?' There were kids we recruited who were going to be close, and the principal told us, 'Don't worry about the boy's grades. If you can take care of the test, we'll make sure of the rest.' In other words, the high school's end is the two-point [grade-point average] and the core [curriculum requirements stipulated by Prop 48]. If you can solve the other end, the whole thing is covered."

But even if the secondary school won't actually falsify the transcript, a college can always modify its own standards. The better the player, the more a school is willing to bend. "I know if I have any kid who can play at all, I can get him into college," says one Detroit high-school coach. "I don't even worry about grade-point average. I know I can find a school that'll make a deal."

And it's not just the so-called "bandit" school that will go out of its way to be accommodating. A source at Cooley High describes a conversation that Kelso had with Arizona State's Bill Frieder, then at Michigan, in Kelso's office about Wolverine signee and Cooley star Michael Talley and his chances of meeting the requirements of Prop 48.

"I don't know," Kelso said. "I don't think Mike's strong enough to pass the test. I've already taken him through three or four pretesting classes."

"Well, hey, I'll tell you what," Frieder is said to have replied. "Don't worry about the test. Whatever we have to do, we'll do. We can work it out. We can get him through it."

"Is there something you can do that I haven't already done?"

"Just don't worry about it," Frieder reportedly said.

At that point, the source says, Kelso "got the picture." Kelso won't comment on the exchange, but doesn't deny the conversation took place.

"That's absolutely not true," says Frieder. "I might have said, 'Don't worry about passing the test, I can get him into Michigan.' I did with [former Prop 48 Wolverines] Terry [Mills] and Rumeal [Robinson]." Frieder, like Tarkanian, says he also got a call from someone asking for $2,500 in exchange for fixing Mills's test. "I called him a son of a bitch and hung up the phone."

Before going on to Missouri, McKenzie High's Doug Smith took the ACT and failed to meet Prop 48 requirements, then "flunked" the SAT, too, before finally scoring 700 or better on his third attempt, and going on to play his freshman season at Missouri. A PSL source says he was told by a McKenzie coach that Smith's standardized test was taken care of.

While he was being recruited, a copy of Smith's transcript was as rare as the Dead Sea Scrolls. "Some high-school coaches think that if they show a poor transcript early, the kid won't get recruited," says Michigan State coach Jud Heathcote. "They'd rather show it late, after the school can work things out. Principals and high-school coaches say, 'Coach, don't worry, he's gonna be all right.' We never saw Doug Smith's transcript, and he made an official visit."

Did Norm Stewart cut a Faustian deal when he sent Rich Daly into Detroit? And what does it mean that Lyton, after being grilled three times by NCAA investigators, suddenly said he wanted out of his Missouri letter of intent because he didn't want to play for a team that was going to go on probation? "Daniel is a perfect example of a kid who was ruined by a lot of people who couldn't have cared less about him," Kelso says. "He's come back to me so many times now and said, 'Coach, I should have listened. They all ruined it. They ruined it.' They weren't looking out for what was best for him, but to line their own pockets. Now the kid is out here doing nothing."

As Lyton found himself at loose ends, having been released from his Missouri letter of intent in December 1989, the Tigers and their proxies have fallen out of favor in Motown. Michiganers will make a run on Nissans before their next great high-school star, Chris Webber, chooses Missouri or takes a stall in Vic Adams's stable. Most every coach in the PSL tried to get Chris, a 6-foot-9-inch junior at Detroit Country Day, to choose his school when he came out of eighth grade, and a high school in Indiana offered his father, a swing-shift worker with General Motors, "lots of stuff" to transfer down, Chris says. Meanwhile, the street agents have pulled out wads of money and massaged it in front of him, and gestured toward their cars with no great subtlety.

But Chris Webber says he and the rest of the best of Detroit's class of '91 are taking a stand. "Most kids who turn to those guys are from one-parent homes where the mom doesn't know anything about basketball," he says. "We've seen a lot of players get screwed over. There's a pact between the kids to forget those guys."

In a perverse way, the freelancers who carve up Detroit perform a beneficial service. In the midst of a shattered social structure, they lavish paternal attentions on youngsters with no father figure. There's even something vaguely noble about ensuring that a kid will bring whatever the market will bear, provided the young man or his family gets to share in the proceeds. But what happens when the middleman is the high-school coach, someone with a salary, a title, and all the other trappings of legitimacy? Indeed, what happens when the power that only a coach can wield over a youngster is suddenly exercised on behalf of a university interested in the player's services? And what happens when a coach does this unbeknownst to his teenage charge?

"In Chicago there's a circle of coaches who control everything," says one college coach based in the Los Angeles area. "They're a lot smarter than the guys out here. They don't let these third parties get involved and they don't lose control of the summer situation. If there's any money to be had, they get it."

Inner-city Chicago is an academic wasteland. Two out of every five freshmen never graduate from the city's high schools, and a 1988 survey found Chicago had thirty-five of the fifty-five secondary schools with the worst ACT scores in the nation. Martin Luther King High is among them, a place where fifth-grade reading levels are the norm. In the midst of this human tragedy, Landon (Sonny) Cox coaches varsity basketball. He has gone 213 and 29 and won a state championship in eight years since taking over at King. As the 1989–90 season began, the Jaguars were ranked number one in the land by *Street & Smith's* and *USA Today*, and Cox had perhaps his best team ever.

Sharply groomed and turned out, never seen in public without a tailored suit, Cox wears shimmering cuff links that catch the glare of gym lights as he works a sideline. His teams run and shoot, but do so precisely. Cox, too, is a model of comportment, as if he's used to being watched intently. Like Vic Adams, he styles himself a musician. But unlike Adams, he's a gifted saxophonist whose band, Sonny Cox and the Three Souls, has cut a number of albums on the Chess label.

It has been years since Cox seriously picked up a horn, for basketball has replaced jazz as the sound track to his life.

He throws enormous amounts of time and energy into his team, and has sent such players as Efrem Winters, Lavertis Robinson, Marcus Liberty, and Jamie Brandon on to major colleges. The disappearance of street agents, commonplace around Chicago during the seventies, coincides almost exactly with the rise of Cox and King High.

Cox knows well the power he has. Recruiters seek him out. They might track him down at George's Piece of the Rock, a restaurant and tavern on West 87th Street where the city's black high-school coaches hang. There they toady to him, flattering him as needed. Individually they come by King and make the small talk that will keep them in his good graces. Many of the coaches who do business with Cox resent the condescending attitude he cops, yet they and he know he has what they want—that he controls the natural resource.

He gets that control early. As in Detroit, Chicago's fifty-six public high-school coaches fight over the city's best ball players. A youngster can live on the South Side and go to school on the North, or leave a home by the lake and take the el out to the West Side each day. Cox has been known to lure to King the best young talent both honorably and questionably. King is now a machine, a sort of schoolboy Georgetown, with a mystique and tradition that sells itself. (No other team in town has better warmups—a black set and a gold set—than the Jags.) Cox has sent more than thirty kids on to the college ranks, about four a year, a remarkable number considering that Prop 48 has been in effect for half of his tenure, and the Public League player who meets its requirements is rare. He's known for closely monitoring the college coaches who sign his players, making sure promises of tutoring or Pell grant money come through. And he has built an addition to his house, so any of his players can bunk in there if life at home gets too unpleasant, or personal problems spin out of control. During the 1989–90 season King forward Johnny Selvie continued to attend school and play ball as he awaited charges on drug trafficking. He wore an electronic device on his wrist at all times so the police could track his whereabouts; as his designated guardian, Cox was responsible for his every action.

But Cox's reputation isn't entirely that of the selfless, one-man ministry. The career record of which he boasts doesn't account for the games he had to forfeit in 1982 for using an ineligible player. That same year, Taylor Bell of the Sun-Times received anonymously in the mail a copy of Winters's transcript, which had been altered. Cox was never implicated in the grade fixing, but the King principal was demoted after an inquiry by the Board of Education. And after a decade of sudden transfers—Marcus Liberty won a city title at Crane High as a freshman, then up and left for King the following fall—coaches around the city have come to accuse Cox of improperly inducing players to play for him. He does so, they say, with promises of car transportation to and from school, and daily lunch tickets for the cafeteria. He uses his plush van to squire his players from summer-league game to summer-league game, giving young Jaguars the equivalent of three extra varsity seasons of experience—this despite Illinois High School Association rules that bar coaches from working with or transporting their players over the summer. Junior-high kids, when they enter the Cox home, see the stacks of Nikes there, and naturally assume they'll be theirs.

He isn't much more discreet in his message to the college recruiters who come calling. Listen to one Big Ten assistant coach, who insists on remaining anonymous because he still has to recruit Chicago, talk about how Cox does business:

"Anybody can go in and see a kid. Anybody. If you court Sonny long enough, you can get one of his lesser players. You've got to realize, one of his lesser players is good enough to make a mid-Division I team. It may not cost you.

Say, the eighth man on his team, he's recruitable by your mid–Division I's, your Miami of Ohios, your Indiana States. If you're all recruiting him, you're gonna get this kid according to your relationship with Sonny. According to how much you stroke him. If two of you are stroking him and your relationship is equal, Sonny's gonna pull one of these: 'Hey, man, you want my kid? You can have my kid. No problem. None at all.' But somewhere in the conversation he'll make it clear that this kid's worth a new set of uniforms, or fifteen or twenty pairs of shoes.

"If you want an 'ace in the hole,' it goes like this. If you want to sit down and talk to the kid there's gonna be a price. It'll run anywhere from five hundred to fifteen hundred dollars, just for the privilege of talking face-to-face.

"When I first got my [Big Ten assistant coach's] job, I was sitting in a gym in Chicago, watching some kids play. Sonny came by to congratulate me. He said, 'I got some players. You can watch 'em play as much as you want. But if you want to come in and talk to 'em, you're gonna need some talkin' power.

"'If you want a visit, you're gonna need some heavy, heavy talkin' power.

"'And if you wanna sign him, hey, come on through.'

"You've got to understand the lingo. Talkin' power is money. Money talks. In the ghetto, the old saying is, 'Money talks, bullshit walks.' Or, 'The power's in the green.' It'll cost five to fifteen hundred just to talk, just to say, 'I'm John Jones from such-and-such university.' It'll cost another five thousand to visit the kid's home, and ten thousand to get him to visit your campus. 'Come on through' means you've got to come heavy. Sonny told me, 'You been around long enough. You know what the fuck I'm talkin' about. You know what you gotta do if you ever want one.'

"We don't have one.

"If you get into Chicago and get to know the coaches, you'll find that they hate Sonny. But they're not going to talk about this. He's part of the community. Ninety-nine percent of the coaches in Chicago, basketball's all they got. And right, wrong, or indifferent, they're going to stick together. They'll tell Sonny, 'You're a dirty SOB.' But when it comes down to the nitty-gritty, they're going to back Sonny up."

Talk to other recruiters, and you'll hear other figures quoted for the Cox price list. One Big Ten head coach says one of his assistants was asked to come up with $15,000 just for access to one player. An assistant at yet another Big Ten school says Cox told him it would cost $5,000 to get Liberty to visit his campus. Jay Williams, a former assistant at Minnesota and Purdue, will go on the record, for he's now selling insurance in Minneapolis and beyond the long arm of the Code. "We were recruiting Efrem Winters for Purdue," he says. "I'll never forget it to this day. It was in one of the gyms in Chicago, I was sitting in the stands, trying to set up an appointment with Coach [Gene] Keady and the staff with Sonny and Efrem.

"[Sonny] gave me the special conditions [for the meeting]. It was forty thousand dollars just to sit down at a table. *Just to get to the table.* It could have been a table at a McDonald's somewhere. I was in just total shock. He cut right to the chase, gave me the facts of life right off the bat.

"I said, 'Well, we appreciate the time, we'll discuss this and be in touch. We'll give you a call back.' I got to the airport and ran into another recruiter. We both had these dumb-phonic stares on our faces. I told him, 'You must have just got done with Sonny.'

"He said, 'Can you believe that shit?'

"He said it was the same number—forty thousand—for them as it was for us. Just to get to see Efrem. He is so blunt about it. That's what turns people off. [But] it takes away the riffraff. He's dealing with people who can talk serious. I can tell you as an assistant coach, it's a great big poker game."

Williams says he played along with Cox, coming through with small-scale stuff—shoes, $10-an-hour summer jobs, and the like—to stay on his good side. But neither he nor the Boilermakers could handle forty grand. "Somewhere down the line Sonny will really slip and make a major mistake," Williams says. "He knows the limitations of various programs, [but] he's gonna push it to the limit."

Given the Cox price scale, a single blue-chip ball player could turn into quite a cash machine. Liberty chose Illinois over Cincinnati and Syracuse. Among the coaches visiting Liberty was Georgetown's John Thompson, who says that he, Cox, Liberty, Liberty's mother, and Hoyas academic adviser Mary Fenlon were meeting in Cox's home when Cox told Thompson, "We have to talk alone."

Thompson wouldn't do it. "I'm not conducting an investigation when I go recruiting," he says. "And there are no secret agendas. No secret bags of money passed to you. No need for private conversations. When you do that, you lose leverage, and my personality doesn't allow me to lose leverage."

Cox denies that he buys his players as junior-high-schoolers, only to sell them several years later. "I've never done anything like that," he says. It's so preposterous, I can't even believe that [accusation]. If you can find one person to say that, I'll stop coaching and teaching today." The charges that he auctions off access, visits, or commitments, he says, are the figments of jealous recruiters' imaginations. His door is always open, he says; many recruiters just aren't willing to agree to help his youngsters in legitimate ways—with pledges of such things as tutoring and additional aid—to satisfy him.

Illinois coach Lou Henson, who has wound up with virtually all of Cox's best players, dismisses the notion that any money changed hands to get Winters, Liberty, or Brandon. "Coach Cox would not do that," Henson says. "A lot of coaches are protective of their guys. They want to make sure the recruiters don't just come in and take over. But the players can still go where they want to go."

That's not what one former King player says. Kevin Williams, no relation to Jay Williams, is one of the better players to pass through Cox's program. On a hypothetical price list, he might fall somewhere between genuflection at George's and "come on through." A muscular but retiring youngster, he averaged 16 points and 10 rebounds before graduating in 1986 and embarking on a sorry odyssey.

Ill-prepared academically, Williams sat out his first season at Cincinnati as a Prop 48 case, then barely averaged three points a game as a sophomore. But Williams was miserable at Cincinnati, playing for Tony Yates, the former Illinois assistant who is one of Cox's closest friends. He had never been allowed to make decisions about his own career and, suddenly finding himself at loose ends, became a hoops refugee. He wound up at Arizona Western, a junior college, and in 1989 enrolled at Long Beach State, trying to sort out his life.

On this summer day Williams sits in the trailer that serves as the 49ers' basketball offices, his voice soft as he tells his tale. "I really didn't want to go to Cincinnati. I wanted to go to the University of Tennessee. [Cox] wouldn't let me take my visits. I only took visits to Illinois and Cincinnati.

"Deep down inside I'm still hurting about Cincinnati, how Coach Cox did his deal. I don't express it much. I try to work as hard as I can to work up a good mentality, to keep a strong mind about it. But I wish he was a man sometimes, and said, 'Kevin, I did this, and I was doing this.' But he never did."

What makes him think he was indentured to Cincinnati? "I couldn't prove it. But it's obvious. It's right in front of your eyes. No one said anything to me, but everyone knew about it. It was like, 'You're going to Cincinnati, son. Coach

Yates is going to take care of you.' You can tell, just like if coffee's cooking in the kitchen. You can smell it."

He felt he was chattel at Martin Luther King, but Kevin Williams considers himself free at last. "I really wish right now that I could go back into time and do it all over again."

On the afternoon of Friday, November 20, 1987, a portly, thirtyish man walked into the gym at Brooklyn Technical High School and up to basketball coach Mark Festberg. The Engineers were about to play a game, and Festberg didn't have much time to talk. But when the gentleman introduced himself as Syracuse assistant coach Wayne Morgan, Festberg knew instantly that he was there to see Brooklyn Tech's six-ten junior shot-blocker, Conrad McRae. Festberg had never met Morgan before, and was happy to exchange brief pleasantries.

The next day McRae failed to show up for Tech's mandatory practice. Festberg was at first mystified. Then it began to dawn on him. McRae had asked for permission to skip that morning's workout so he could go up to Springfield, Massachusetts, to watch the Tip-Off Classic between Syracuse and North Carolina. Festberg's telling him he couldn't go evidently hadn't dissuaded McRae from going anyway.

Indeed, a number of Festberg's players and friends would tell him that they saw Conrad during the Tip-Off telecast that afternoon. He was sitting courtside, right next to the very same man who had visited Brooklyn Tech the previous day. Only this man wasn't Wayne Morgan, Festberg soon learned. His name was Rob Johnson. He lived in the Queens Bridge public housing project and drove a leased Ford Taurus. He said he worked customs at Kennedy Airport, but, as one recruiter says, "The funny thing was you couldn't reach him at the job, but you could always reach him at home." And he was known throughout the city as a street agent.

Johnson is no Spook Stegman, no matchmaker of schools

and players according to need. He works for Syracuse almost exclusively. As Vic Adams is for Missouri in Detroit, Johnson is for the Orange in the Apple. "He's got what you'd call an obsession with Boeheim and Syracuse," says Arnie Hershkowitz, a New York high-school talent scout who knows Johnson well. "Boeheim's an idol to him. It's the one program that really accepts him."

Going incognito is nothing new for Johnson. He has pawned himself off as Larry Gay, the former Georgia and current Louisville assistant; he has phoned around to colleges, introducing himself as a New York City high-school coach, trying to drum up interest in "his kids." And here, during a recruiting noncontact period, after misrepresenting himself, Johnson had spirited McRae out of New York and up to the Syracuse opener. A year later McRae would sign with the Orangemen.

Festberg spoke to the real Wayne Morgan on the phone a week later. "I'm sorry this happened," Morgan told him. "But Robert Johnson isn't affiliated with us."

Basketball in New York City is fast, untidy, played in close quarters. It's rare to find nets on the baskets, rarer still to find ball players content to shoot outside jumpers without the reward of the *swish* only nets can provide. Thus city kids learn to go hard to the hoop. "A New York guard," the *Village Voice* once said, "will give up his gold and his girl before he'll give up his dribble."

Uncle-ing here follows accordingly. It's aggressive and confrontational, marked by wars for turf. A decade ago Johnson steered Tony (Red) Bruin, who played on a youth-league team he coached in Long Island City, to Syracuse. Now his allegiances are common knowledge around town, and kids jockey for orange Nikes, a trip to a Syracuse game, or Orangemen regalia. Johnson was "on my back" about Syracuse, says Andre McCullough, a guard from Our Saviour Lutheran High, now attending prep school. Jamal

Mashburn of Cardinal Hayes High, a year ahead of McCullough and a year behind McRae, is bound for Kentucky; he says Johnson came on to him even stronger. "He put the pressure on," Mashburn says. "He just kept on saying Syracuse this, you'll like that. He gave me a Syracuse poster, the one with Derrick Coleman, [Rony] Seikaly, and Stevie Thompson. He invited me to [the] B/C [All-Stars summer] camp. [Jim Sullivan, Festberg's successor as coach at Brooklyn Tech, sued and won in small claims court after Johnson overcharged Sullivan's players for transportation costs to attend B/C.] He implied, like, did I need anything. Stuff like that."

Johnson has solicited the business of schools other than Syracuse. Former NBA star Nate (Tiny) Archibald recalls that, when Archibald was an assistant at Georgia, Johnson "shopped" a guard named Eric Leslie to him. "He was talking about what the kid was worth," says Archibald. "I told him he was fucking crazy. I said all I could offer the kid was a scholarship. He was talking about other schools, that he felt Eric was going to go to Syracuse. [Leslie wound up at Rhode Island after a stopover at Villanova.] He just said he had some ins with some people up there, that he could work out some financial arrangements.

"He mentioned a couple of thousand dollars that would be paid to him, $10,000 to $15,000 as I remember. He would get a good stipend. That way he could take care of the kid, buy him clothes, get him 'hooked up for school,' as they say. The deal never worked out. When [Georgia coach] Hugh [Durham] heard about it, he was pissed."

For a street agent like Johnson, it's tougher to make a living in New York than in Detroit or L.A. For every Conrad McRae he can deliver, there will be many more McCulloughs and Mashburns who'll lend their ears to others. That's because power in New York is concentrated in the city's two AAU programs, the New York Gauchos and the Riverside Church Hawks, and both monitor their youngsters closely. The Hawks are based on the outskirts of Harlem, hard by the Columbia campus, in the basement of the church that rebel minister William Sloane Coffin once called home. Under the stewardship of coach Ernie Lorch, a church deacon and prosperous corporate lawyer, the Hawks comport themselves respectably and play the same way—with structure, as if they were a jayvee North Carolina. The Gauchos, by contrast, have a reputation for being loosey-goosey renegades that play defense with abandon, like UNLV. They're funded by an Argentine-born real estate magnate and Jaguar-driving Yale graduate named Lou d'Almeida, who in 1987 built the Gauchos a multi-million-dollar, 2,500-seat gym in a converted warehouse in the Bronx.

Lorch and d'Almeida are bachelors who treat their players like surrogate offspring. (Lorch actually paddles his players.) Both take their age-group teams on the same expectations-raising trips as Issy Washington's and Rich Goldberg's flagships. And each, according to players, coaches, and scouts in New York, provides his players with gifts. Sometimes they're in the form of cash, although players may receive clothing, jewelry, rent money for their parents, or several thousand dollars to cover tuition at a parochial school. Over the top players, they've been known to engage in bidding wars. The prevailing rate for the very best ringers, any wired-in New Yorker will tell you, is up to $2,500 for a big tournament, and $250 for a big game.

During the early eighties, St. John's star Walter Berry bounced back and forth between the Gauchos and Hawks. Georgia Tech's Kenny Anderson started with the Madison Square Boys & Girls Club Broncos, then moved to Riverside, before joining the Gauchos. Lloyd Daniels, the crack-addicted New York playground star, "always used to pick up money from the Gauchos," says Arnie Hershkowitz. "Lou would give him as much money as he could get away with." (D'Almeida denies ever giving players cash or jewelry, but admits he buys them clothing, and says he spends about $100,000 annually on parochial-school tuition for some thirty Gauchos.) Former Cleveland State star Ken (Mouse) McFadden stayed with the Madison Square Broncos, turning down one offer of $5,000 from a rival to jump. "It didn't matter what number they threw at you," says the Mouse. "They could cover it."

Beginning when youngsters are twelve or thirteen, the Gauchos and Hawks start scouting out talent. The Gauchos actually retain kids to hustle up ball players; street sources say they pay a finder's fee of $50 to $100 per delivery, which d'Almeida denies. The funneling process continues several years later, when the "outside organizations," as high-school coaches call the AAU programs, steer players to particular secondary schools. The Hawks and Gauchos all but determine who the next city champion will be.

Just as in L.A., the trips and inducements are a recipe for trouble. "So many kids get that New York City attitude," says Rich Kosik, a Brooklyn high-school counselor who has tutored and coached many of the best ball players to come through New York in the last decade. " 'I'm on Riverside,' or 'I'm on the Gauchos.' That's what happened with [former Syracuse guard] Pearl [Washington, for whom the Gauchos helped buy a motorbike]. If you'd told me that Pearl would be a flop, I'd have laughed in your face. But these kids don't realize that players in the Deep South and the Midwest are working all the time."

To protect its position in the rivalry, each program "warehouses" kids. The personal attention lavished upon them can be salutary, given the fatherless homes many come from. Yet youngsters who could be playing often, developing their skills on a lesser team, find themselves content to sit as a Hawk or a Gaucho simply because the perks, travel, and prestige make it worthwhile. "It's a tragedy, what happens to these kids," says Madison Square coach Paul (Doc) Nicelli, who has watched every salvo in the war as a third party for two decades. "They put their hands out the first time, and then all of a sudden they can't stop it. It leads to things like the point-shaving scandals. We've been down that road before. It's a different song, but the same dance."

In most big cities, the AAU coaches are Walter Mittys, angling for a piece of the action. But the Gauchos and Hawks are so well established that they have the position and influence to counterbalance the blandishments of street characters like Rob Johnson. And Lorch and d'Almeida are so well heeled that neither program must kowtow to any college or sponsoring shoe company. The "outside organizations" are paternalistic cocoons. In some ways they coddle, but in others they protect.

Dave McCollin, who handles most of the coaching chores for d'Almeida, says schools have made offers for Gauchos players. "I'm not about that," says McCollin. "And I'm not going to moralize whether they're ethically wrong for doing that either. Basketball is a business. I mean, they've got to fill up a gym, and it's coming down to their school and another school, and the economic fact of the matter is that those kids are generating income for the university. So therefore the university does have—I hate to use the word—a 'slush fund,' to deal with maybe giving that little extra turn.

"It's all still relatively the same. The same things they offered the kids back during the scandals [of '51] are what they're offering them now. You're talking about inflation, the cost of living, of course, too. But what does the average high-school kid aspire to when he turns eighteen? A car. A crib. A little bit of jewelry. They want to look like a successful athlete. Me being an adult, I look at that, and that's not a lot.

"It's a violation and all that, and you get into the morality of whether it should be offered. Then you get into whether it's morally right for a kid to be playing at, say, Syracuse, where he's filling up a gym with thirty thousand people, and regardless of how much money the school makes, the school can't pay for this kid to fly home. That's highly immoral. I mean, the coach has a golf course in his backyard. He's got a swimming pool. He's got three cars. The kid knows the coach is making maybe a million dollars a year with all his benefits—and they can't give him any money when he's scoring twenty-five points or grabbing thirteen rebounds? That's why all this happens."

If a Gaucho comes to him or d'Almeida and says a school has made an improper offer, McCollin says, it isn't their place to tell him it would be wrong to accept it. "If you want to take the chance, I'm not going to get involved in that. But I'm not going to sit here and tell you you're wrong either." It's when a third party comes calling that McCollin steps in. He'll contact the patron school and tell it to call off the dog. And he puts his players on notice.

"I tell them point-blank: no individual out there is doing anything because he likes you. You break your leg tomorrow, that person isn't going to be calling you, offering you things, looking to give you rides or take you to a Knicks game. You've got to realize you're being used. I tell the kids not to underestimate an adult. A lot of teenagers think they're one step ahead. But just when the kid thinks he's using him—and that's usually when they'll say, 'Don't worry, Dave, I got it under control, I just go to a couple of games, I ain't taking nothing significant'—I say, 'Yeah, but that's the thing. That's the bait.' Just when you think you're running a game on him, you find out you're hooked. And I'm gonna start looking at your list of schools, and if I see his school is on it, I'm gonna ask you why."

Before Rob Johnson really got his hooks in him, Conrad McRae was a polite and awkward young man trying to make sense of his body. Brooklyn Tech is a demanding school, and Conrad was a bright student, albeit a sluggish one, the kind of youngster who could have played at Duke if he had only applied himself a bit more.

By the end of his sophomore year McRae was already 6 foot 7 and acquiring a reputation. In early July, Mark Festberg says, McRae called him, asking for a ride to LaGuardia Airport, so he could fly up to Syracuse to attend a summer camp there. A prepaid ticket was waiting for him at the airline check-in counter. Festberg, suspicious of the trip and the circumstances of its arrangement, declined to give McRae a lift. Weeks later, Festberg says, Rob Johnson called him up, pleading with him not to divulge his knowledge of the trip. If Johnson, a Syracuse booster, or Syracuse itself paid for the airline ticket, it would be an NCAA violation.

The rest of that summer—a time his coach felt would have been best spent in summer school—was McRae's coming out. He made two other stops on the camp circuit, and when he held his own against Alonzo Mourning at Five-Star, schools like Villanova, Temple, Georgia Tech, and Louisville began to take notice. But McRae was already spoken for. He had seen Syracuse. He loved the behemoth Carrier Dome and was impressed with the players, stars like Thompson, Coleman, and Sherman Douglas. On one of his visits, he told his coach, he had been introduced to the man the players said provided them with cars.

It was the following fall, even before Conrad blew off that Saturday morning practice to catch the Syracuse game with Rob Johnson, that Festberg noticed changes in his star. The coach would catch him hanging out in the cafeteria when he should have been in class.

"How many lunch periods do you get?" Festberg would ask.

Chastened, Conrad would leave the cafeteria, ostensibly

headed for class. As soon as his coach was out of sight, he would head back. Festberg couldn't discipline him. The team went 3–9 in its league and Conrad did poorly in the classroom. He had played right into the hands of the system.

In March 1988 the Lakers came through Madison Square Garden for their only New York appearance of the season. It was a hot ticket, but Howard Garfinkel, the erstwhile middleman who now runs Five-Star, was able to score a couple and invited Conrad to be his guest. They settled into their seats. Garfinkel bought Conrad several hot dogs. The game began, and McRae, spotting some friends, went off to join them, leaving his host all alone. When Festberg heard the story he wasn't surprised, and told Garfinkel so. "A twenty-five-dollar seat," Festberg says. "Hot dogs. Then twenty minutes later he's gone. Garf was doing for Conrad what everyone else was doing for him. What did he expect?"

Around Christmas of that same season, McRae became upset with the playing time he was getting with the Hawks. Just before Tech took its holiday break, he met Lorch in lower Manhattan, and Lorch took him out and bought him a beautiful $450 black leather coat with a fur collar. Still, Conrad was irritated. Six or seven kids on the team were getting more than he was. Why, Conrad had to ask for things. He felt he was "getting jerked," as the kids in the city say, and by the end of January, Conrad had gone "uptown," to the Gauchos.

Rob Johnson has squeezed his 260 pounds into a booth in a New York City coffee shop. His face is soft, even allowing for the crescent-shaped scar above his left eyebrow. He's wearing a sweat suit, a Carrier Classic wristwatch—a gift, he says, from former Syracuse player Eugene Waldron—and a look of careful bemusement. As a calling card, he produces a sheaf of letters from such college coaches as

Dean Smith, Rick Pitino, and Wade Houston. All are dated 1979 through 1981, and all thank him for his help in recruiting players.

Johnson concedes he has heard all the stories about his activities—the Wayne Morgan impersonation, the McRae travel arrangements, even the one about him having been involved in an episode of child molestation, which he says is a malicious rumor started by a rival coach jealous of Johnson's ability to attract players to his youth-league team. "Not true" is his mantra, his reply to them all, even to the NCAA, which is probing his activities.

"I'm just a big fan of the Syracuse program, because I like Jim Boeheim," he says. "If someone asks me about the program, I tell them it's a good program. The kids seek me out. I don't seek them out. Syracuse don't cheat. Everybody thinks they do, but they don't."

Didn't Conrad fly up to camp at Syracuse?

"Not true. Syracuse did not fly him up to the camp. It's a violation. Why would they do that?"

Didn't you tell Mark Festberg not to tell anyone about the airline ticket?

"Not true."

Didn't you introduce yourself as Wayne Morgan?

"I heard that one too. Not true."

Isn't Syracuse your primary interest?

"I get a lot of calls from a lot of coaches."

Which ones?

"You want to know every school that calls?"

Just the top ten or so.

"Syracuse. I have friends at the University of Akron. Georgia Tech. Who else calls me? I said Georgia. . . ."

Ten, twelve seconds pass. Johnson has wrapped his yellowing letters of reference into a baton and stuck them under his chin as he watches the predatory New York traffic out the window.

"Akron . . ."

Another interregnum of silence.

"Uh, South Carolina . . ."

You can hear the clatter of dishes being cleared, and a waitress asking a diner if he wants butter on his toast. But you hear nothing more on the subject from Rob Johnson.

Opposites are supposed to attract, and that may be what turned Wayne Simone into a player in the recruiting game. Little else would account for it. Simone is wan, doughy, privileged, and obliging. The kids he now moves easily among are, for the most part, black, sinewy, poor, and obstinate. Patron and clients sometimes make a curious match.

Simone is in his mid-twenties, from the affluent Connecticut suburbs south of Hartford. Upon graduating from Villanova in 1986, he took a large sum of family money and started an ill-fated basketball magazine, based outside Philadelphia, called *Off the Glass*. One of Simone's employees was Chip Boyce, a New Yorker who knew a highly sought-after young player in his Queens neighborhood, a star at Christ the King High named Jamal Faulkner. Boyce began bringing Faulkner down to Philly from time to time, and Simone took an interest in the young man. "He needed a steadying influence," Simone says. "His dad was absent and his mom would let him do what he wanted. Jamal is an honest person, but he lies, if you know what I mean. He lives in a fantasy world, without many responsibilities. I'm close to his age—I can relate to him. He likes to go out, pick up girls, have a drink and a good time. So do I. But I wouldn't bullshit him. If something was wrong, I'd say so."

Faulkner's high-school coach, Bob Oliva, had tried that tack. Oliva had been disappointed by his star's indifference toward his schoolwork and got firm with him. But Faulkner, immature and insecure, perceived Oliva's discipline as rejection. When Simone took an interest in him, and broached the idea of helping Jamal pick a college, Faulkner bought in.

At the time, Faulkner was only considering two schools, Temple and Pittsburgh. Simone persuaded Faulkner to expand his options. He began calling around the country, contacting coaches on Faulkner's behalf, introducing himself as the party running Jamal's recruitment, "putting a lot of mustard in the pudding," as Oliva says. Clemson and Texas soon entered the picture, and that, Simone admits, "pissed Pitt and Temple off."

One day before Faulkner's senior season, Jamal told Simone that a gentleman named Sam Albano wanted Simone to call. Albano, a friend of Oliva's, owns several bakeries in Queens and lives in Howard Beach. "I didn't call him," Simone says. "I told Jamal that if Sam Albano wanted to talk to me, he could call me. So he calls me out of the blue. I didn't know he was looking for trouble. He starts talking shit to me, like 'I don't know why you had to get involved.'"

Then, as Simone tells it, someone seemed to pick up on an extension. "Hey, Simone," the other voice said. "You stay away from Jamal or I'll break your fucking legs." Click.

Simone called Albano back.

"You heard what I had to say," Simone says Albano told him. "This conversation is over."

Simone refused to bail out. And he baby-sat Faulkner the day before he signed, having dinner with him, going over the pros and cons of each school until midnight. "From the minute I picked him up to the minute I left him, Jamal said he wanted to go to Texas," Simone says. "I drove back to Philly that night, exhausted out of my mind, happy it was over. When I got home there was a message on my machine that Jamal had signed with Pitt. So I called him. He said, 'Wayne, I signed with Pitt.'

"I don't know what happened with Pitt the last day.

When I left him—and I had spent five hours on Sunday with him—it was Texas every step of the way.

"I knew Albano was [at the home]. He delivered [the letter of intent] to [Pitt]. Somehow he either did something or said something to Connie Faulkner to have her switch her mind, to have Jamal not go to Texas."

(Texas coach Tom Penders seems to corroborate Simone's account: "Jamal said he was coming right up until the day he signed. He said he was definitely signing with us. I don't know what happened. It was like a bomb."

Who lit the fuse?

"A third party."

Oliva says Jamal became "very frightened" at the end. All Connie Faulkner will say is that Sam Albano had nothing to do with the recruitment of her son.)

Albano is a St. John's graduate, and John Sarandrea, the Pitt assistant who recruited Faulkner, coached St. John's star Malik Sealy at Tolentine High in the Bronx. Simone believes Faulkner was a gift, Albano's way of paying back Sarandrea for Sealy's choosing the Redmen.

Albano calls Simone "a frustrated individual" whose account of the threatening phone call is preposterous. "Wayne is obsessed with the Jamal Faulkner thing," says Albano. "He would make up any story to make himself look good." In fact, Albano says he was the target of a threat—a 6 A.M. phone call made just before Thanksgiving, shortly after Faulkner had signed with Pitt. The caller told Albano, "You and your cousin Joe are gonna have your legs broken."

"I don't even have a cousin Joe," says Albano. "I called Penders. I told him I suspected one of his assistant coaches, Dave Miller, who had been recruiting Jamal, had made the call. Miller had called Bob [Oliva] and said that [Jamal's decision] had ruined his career. I told Penders I could have his phone records subpoenaed, that I could sue him. That's the only threat I know that happened."

Faulkner wound up failing to meet Prop 48 requirements,

and enrolled at Cheshire Academy, a Connecticut prep school, in the fall of '89. Albano wrote a $6,100 check to pay for Faulkner's first semester there. Why? "Because I'm a nice guy," Albano says.

Just the same, Jamal is now talking about attending Arizona State—where Dave Miller is now an assistant to Bill Frieder—for the 1990–91 season. Pitt isn't pressing the issue. "They've given up," Simone says. "They're afraid to set Jamal off, where he'll go blabbing his mouth. I know they've given him things, given his mom things.

"Recruiting is as dirty as hell from every perspective. It's not fair to the kid. It makes good people bad."

But Simone would do for another blue-chipper what he did for Jamal. In a minute. "I'm gonna help them because they don't have anyone else."

The Las Vegas Invitational falls during the twenty-one-day evaluation period in July, the look-but-don't-touch intermezzo in a recruiter's summer. Coaches are forbidden to speak to prospects, even over the phone, and the NCAA is there, somewhere, to take note of those who do. For many of the recruiters on hand, the week is one long challenge to find the most ingenious ways to express their interest without crossing the cops.

Here is nonverbal communication worthy of a doctoral dissertation. A long hallway links the two gyms on the UNLV campus where the tournament takes place, and after the best teams finish up each day, the procurers form a gantlet. They hold up the walls, hanging out, their indifference legislated as the players file by. The game is see and be seen. Eye contact is okay, and even a nod or "hello" is kosher, for the NCAA permits pleasantries within a so-called "rule of civility." But Emily Post stuff won't really distinguish you, won't help you stand out in the crowd.

To make an impression, one assistant has rented a white Suzuki Samurai because he knows inner-city teenagers think it's hot. UNLV has obligingly left stacks of four-color Runnin' Rebels annuals in the hallways, hoping they'll be picked up and perused. (They are.) Other schools contrive "bumps"—that's recruitspeak for "chance" encounters— by the hotel pools, and leave phone messages (conversations are verboten, but messages aren't) for the kids. And the T-shirts shout like megaphones. Each coach wears one billboarding his school's most impressive recent accomplishment. GREENSBORO FINAL FOUR says the shirt on the man from Siena, which reached an NCAA subregional in 1989. Another reads COLORADO STATE/LEAGUE CHAMPS, just in case the youngsters here had forgotten. An assistant from Columbia wears a powder-blue shirt graced with the New York City skyline—proof that even a school that makes you pay your own way and will never be on TV can find a selling point. Steve Fisher, Michigan's new coach, was in a plain polo the first day, but soon catches on to the nuances of sartorial salesmanship, slipping into another shirt reading NATIONAL CHAMPS.

If this is a big dance, the biggest of the summer, the players are jailbait. With a Wayne Simone, however, the coaches can converse as much as they want. And Simone is here. He has sunk $12,000 of his own money into funding a team of inner-city New England high-school kids, most of them from Connecticut. He has already sent a number to competition summer camps to help them get exposure; Vegas is the next stop on the circuit.

Team Connecticut is a team in name only. It has no uniforms and little organization. The players wear bermuda shorts and T-shirts, and tote around changes of clothes in plastic shopping bags. They barely make the ten P.M. tipoff for their first game, arriving in twos and threes at the gym straight from the airport. Nevertheless, they play a terrific first game, upsetting a highly regarded team from Kansas City. A deft lead guard named Travis Best penetrates and scores at will; Bill Curley, a widebodied rebounder and inside scorer, throws his weight around to good effect under the glass. On the sidelines, Simone's primary job isn't to coach, but to act as depository for team jewelry.

In the quarterfinals Team Connecticut pulls off the biggest upset of the week, knocking off the defending-champion Gauchos by a point. "This is your town!" shouts Len Gordy, an assistant at Clemson, afterward. He gives Simone a congratulatory shake. "Talk to you tonight."

Moments later, just outside the locker room, Ray Lopes, a recruiter for UC–Santa Barbara, sidles up to Simone.

"We like John," he says.

"He's available," Simone says, as if he has played the game all his life.

"Is it . . . Wayne?"

"Yeah."

"And the last name?"

"Simone. S-i-m-o-n-e."

"Where you staying?"

"Room 2910. The Alexis Park."

"Okay. Good job, Coach."

Wayne Simone, *coach*. He has been accepted, been welcomed into the fraternity. He enters the locker room, where the team is jubilant, except for a few guys bitching about playing time.

"We've got to play again in four hours. We'll go back and meet in my room."

No one hears him in the din.

"Stop!" Simone says. "I'm talking!"

"Yo, Wayne," says a player. "You got the car keys?"

That afternoon Connecticut upsets another favorite, a team from Utah featuring Shawn Bradley, the 7-foot-4-inch shot-blocker bound for Brigham Young, to move into the semis. The Conn Crew is now the talk of the tourney. The $2,000 on meals and pocket money that Simone has spent this week alone seems entirely worth it. "It adds up, twelve kids," he says. Then he sighs. "I have money—my money from before. Besides, I want to get into coaching. I'm getting a lot of exposure."

Before his team's next game, while his players are dressing, Simone stops by the scorer's table for a word with the P.A. announcer. "It's suh-*moan*, not *sigh*-mun."

Simone has hardly called as much as a time-out all week, leaving the technical aspects of the game to a quiet Bostonian, Jack McMahon, who has coached at schools around New England for more than twenty-five years. "He knows a hell of a lot more about coaching than I do," Simone allows.

But McMahon had to leave town unexpectedly, and Simone is on his own now. He paces the sideline in a peach golf shirt and loafers with no socks. Several gold chains, vouchsafed to him by his players, are draped around his neck. The players' instincts, not Simone's genius, give them a lead of five at the half.

During the break, Sonny Vaccaro comes out of the stands to huddle with Simone at midcourt. If Connecticut wins, Vaccaro wants to put Nikes on the players' feet for the tournament final, which will be played in UNLV's glittery Thomas and Mack Center and televised live on ESPN.

"If we can keep 'em, we'll play in 'em," Simone says.

"No problem," says Vaccaro.

Connecticut seems to have found a formula. With Best leading the break, his team maintains its lead, and Simone rests Best and Curley with a minute and a half to play in the third quarter. Their substitutes help push the margin to eleven at the buzzer.

But in the fourth, Milwaukee creeps back. The Connecticut lead is only five with almost five minutes to play, and still, inexplicably, Best and Curley sit. Milwaukee presses all over the court, and Simone's indecision can be seen in the panic of his players. One calls a time-out as he struggles to bring the ball over midcourt, only Connecticut is out of time-outs. Technical foul. Simone's team is coming a cropper.

Simone sends Best back in, but it's too late. Milwaukee is back in the game, and Simone, without McMahon's guidance, is at a loss. Milwaukee wins by five, and Connecticut's run is over.

For several minutes afterward, Travis Best doesn't move. He just sits on the bench, a towel draped over his head. Simone, too, is in a daze, and silently passes out jewelry and money clips to his stewing players. "The breaks just went their way," he finally whispers. "Travis seemed tired. I thought . . . my responsibility was to give these kids exposure. I wanted to get all the kids in. We had a big lead and I thought I could get more kids more time. They came back so quick.

"I'm pissed off at some of these kids. The bitching, yelling, and moaning. Some of them can stay home the next time."

But Simone will be here again, for the kids. He's going to help them because they don't have anyone else. It's their only way out. And for Simone, it's his only way in.

Even after losing Steve Miller to Dwane Casey in fall 1983, Reggie Warford continued to work the high schools of the East on Pittsburgh's behalf. And even after the Irv Stewart fiasco, Warford kept on enlisting the help of third parties.

The following year he went after Doug West, a willowy scorer from Altoona, not an hour and a half from Pittsburgh. One of the first times he saw West play, Warford made sure to pull a Pitt cap out of his RX7 and hand it to a friend of West's named Victor Thomas.

At first blush, Thomas seems to fit perfectly the profile of the inner-city hanger-on. He has a bit of the rapscallion about him. Several years older than West, with a discolored eyetooth and a cocky disposition, he had been quite a player himself at Mount Aloysius Junior College before returning to Altoona, a cozy city of 57,000, to take a job with the highway department. He still played ball to keep the edge on his game, but his attitude had mellowed noticeably. Someone had clocked Victor good in an argument, and he was never, a friend says, quite as full of himself after that.

Doug West was just beginning to establish himself as a local high-school star when Thomas finished up at Mount Aloysius. Victor took an interest in him, sharing ball-handling tips and providing rides around town in his brown Mustang. Doug's parents were separated, and when recruiting began in earnest, Thomas became an adviser and confidant.

Victor was right where Reggie Warford wanted to be. Plus, he was no mercenary latecomer, no Irv Stewart who would have to be enlisted to gain a foothold. Warford kept in touch with Thomas through the summer and into the fall, calling him three or four times a week to monitor what Doug was thinking and where he was leaning. Several times Doug and Victor made the drive up to Pittsburgh for football weekends, bunking in at Warford's place over the Friday night; once, Victor remembers, Reggie gave him money to cover the cost of gas.

And Doug liked Pitt. Yet he knew himself well enough to be suspicious of that attraction. The players had a lot of fun, and the Oakland section of town near campus was full of diversions. Would he find time to study? In the final weeks of West's recruitment, Villanova, the other school he was considering, shrewdly played on those doubts. The Wildcats put Atlanta Hawks coach Mike Fratello, a former assistant to Villanova coach Rollie Massimino, up to calling Doug and making their case. And they planted a seed in West's mind about Pitt's interest in Jerome Lane, a player of similar size from Akron, with whom West might compete for playing time.

Shortly after his official visit to Villanova, West had been in Pittsburgh to visit a friend, and took the occasion to drop by the Panthers' basketball offices and tell the Pitt staff that he intended to sign with them. But Villanova's guerrilla tactics—the Fratello phone call and the mention of Jerome Lane—had caused a problem. Even after the pleasant surprise of West's unannounced visit, neither Warford nor Roy Chipman felt comfortable with West's verbal commitment.

It was about this time, Victor Thomas says, that Warford reached him by phone. He had been trying in vain to reach Doug, Warford told Thomas. He had something urgent to talk to him about.

Thomas said he would probably see West later that day, and could relay a message to him. Good, Reggie said. "He said, we would like you—he used the word *we*—to get Doug and bring him to the University of Pittsburgh, to the offices at Fitzgerald [Field House]," Thomas says. "I asked him what it was in reference to, and then he said to me, 'Well, I feel as though I can trust you.'"

According to Thomas, Warford said that a certain doctor, a Pitt alumnus, wanted to meet Doug, offer him $25,000 in cash, and provide his father with a job. Thomas was taken aback, but told Warford he would let Doug know. Later that day he tracked Doug down at a friend's house. "C'mon, we got to talk," he told him.

For fifteen or twenty minutes, as they tooled around Altoona in Victor's Mustang, Victor told Doug about his conversation with Warford. West thought Thomas was crazy. Thomas assured him he was serious—or that Warford seemed serious.

Several days passed. It was now November 8, a Thursday. That morning Altoona High coach Larry Betar called the Pitt coaching staff to tell them West had decided on Villanova, and ask that they not call West anymore.

But Villanova hadn't honored the verbal commitment Pitt felt it had received from West, and the Panthers weren't going to go down without clawing. Sometime during the day, Warford reached Thomas at work. He told him much the same thing he had said several days earlier, only now Doug needn't come to Pittsburgh. He should expect a call later that night. Again Victor and Doug drove around town, discussing the latest developments in the privacy of the Thomas Mustang.

Doug returned home shortly after eight that evening. And around nine P.M., just as Victor had told him, the phone rang. On the line was Dr. Joseph Haller, a prominent oral surgeon and businessman in Altoona and a Pitt trustee.

As West tells it, Haller first identified himself, then said that West should have been expecting his call. He said he had been in touch with a member of the Pitt staff, and went on to offer West $10,000 and a car. He said he could improve the quality of life for Doug's family.

West says he told Haller he didn't like what he was hearing, and hung up on him. Then he called Warford to tell him he never would have considered Pitt if he had known he would be offered an improper inducement.

"Things like this happen," West says Warford told him.

At a press conference at Altoona High the next day, Doug West announced he would attend Villanova.

Roy Chipman says he had asked Joe Haller to phone West, talk up the school, and offer him a lucrative summer job—all permissible under NCAA rules at the time—if he came to Pitt. Haller says that's all he did, and that when West told him he had chosen Villanova, he thanked him for his time and wished him luck. Reggie Warford denies entirely the two phone calls that Victor Thomas describes.

As part of its series the following fall, the Lexington *Herald-Leader* published initial, sketchy detail about Pitt's recruiting improprieties, including Warford's offer of an inducement to Steve Miller, and Haller's phone call to Doug West. The story sent the Pitt program reeling. Haller filed a libel suit against West, and to this day the feud between Villanova and Pitt is a persistent embarrassment to the PR-conscious Big East.

One day in fall 1985, Chipman's young son, Geoffrey, came home from school and asked his father, "Daddy, are you going to jail?" A short time later Chipman announced he was quitting at the end of the season. As is the custom in college basketball, his staff left with him.

Reggie Warford hasn't held a job in the game since, and he considers the *Herald-Leader* responsible. He sued the newspaper for damages, charging libel. A judge found in favor of the *Herald-Leader*, but the case was still on appeal as of mid-January 1990.

Roy Chipman decided he had had enough of basketball. Today he sells paper packaging.

Standing on Bleecker Street in Greenwich Village, looking through the restaurant's doorway, you can see him from the sidewalk on this muggy June day. He's leaning back in a wooden chair, working a stogie in his left hand. The face is unforgettable, even without the signature widow's peak he wore in his most famous TV role. But the address is no longer 1313 Mockingbird Lane.

The sign above the restaurant says GRANDPA'S. Is Al Lewis, Grandpa from "The Munsters," really "the most knowledgeable roundballer who ever lived"? That's what he calls himself. In one breath he denies ever having brokered players, or "butchered" them, which is the term he uses. He's just a basketball junkie, a free-lance talent scout, a Brooklyner who never could let go of the rhythms of the city's game, even when he went west to make his name in show business. (Few middlemen have Lewis's credentials, which include a Ph.D. in child psychology from Columbia.) But in the next breath he says he could have been the best at it. "I know every trick that was made and invented. There ain't a spook alive who knows more about tricks than I do."

Lewis owns up to influencing the college choices of players from Chuck Cooper and Solly Walker to Sidney

Green and Stuart Gray. It could be dangerous being a bird dog in the old days; once during the Rupp era he had gone to Lexington to watch a high-school tournament, and the Baron's people somehow got wind of it. "I wasn't in my hotel room ninety seconds when two Kentucky troopers big enough to block out the sun asked me to pack, and took me to the train station."

Who he worked for he won't say. Nor will he share any of the secrets he has been privy to over the years. "I'm no Joe Valachi," he says.

But he will say this: "I don't buy players, but if a school came to me and said, 'We definitely want this guy,' I would find out what the going rate was and I would say, 'You have to raise the price or you can't play in the poker game.'

"I don't recruit, see. I don't tell a kid to go to this school or that. I say to the kid, 'School X is willing to pay you this amount of money if you go there. If you agree, here's your bona fide cashier's check.'

"A kid would be crazy not to take the biggest offer. If a guy is paying, ya take it! If somebody comes with a better offer, and the kid can count money, why would he take the least amount?

"Butchers of dark meat, they're all over. As long as you make the pot of honey big, you'll always find mosquitoes, pirates, and thieves around. There's more and more money, so you get more and more spooks. There are thirty thousand guys out there, turning over rocks, looking for a 6-foot-9 black spider with four arms."

You can't help thinking that if he found a Herman Munster with a soft touch tomorrow, Al Lewis would be right there, in the home with him, whether the prospect were in New York or L.A.

Does Lewis know anything about Chris Mills? "I didn't get involved in that deal," says Grandpa the uncle. "I backed out of it."

243

8

L.A. Lawyer

THE DOCUMENTS have piled up for nearly a dozen years now, filling sixty crates in the Los Angeles County Hall of Records alone, and untold more space in the offices of law firms around L.A. All owe their existence to a single case. Though it has never gone to trial, it's the legal equivalent of an M. C. Escher drawing, a nightmarish morass of depositions, suits, and countersuits.

The case, called Willow Ridge, is at once simple and complex. Distilled to its essence, it's an effort on the part of some 1,500 people to recoup $35 million they lost to a Los Angeles financier named Barry Marlin in a series of investment schemes gone bad. Marlin was a persuasive and fast-living tax lawyer who between 1969 and 1975 enticed hundreds of investors, mostly United Airlines pilots, into backing his real estate deals and precious metals and banking transactions. He promised, and seemed to deliver, extraordinary returns, some guaranteed up to eleven percent.

But Marlin's sure thing turned out to be a classic Ponzi scheme, in which investors are paid off with contributions from still more investors rather than with a hard return on their original stake. For a time Marlin stayed one step ahead of the posse, but in 1977 grand juries in three states returned indictments on a variety of charges, including fraud. Marlin pleaded guilty on six criminal counts and spent two years in federal prison.

That hardly pacified the investors, who were still out a collective fortune. So a number of the swindled pilots filed lawsuits, hoping to recoup their losses, and the suits were consolidated under the name Willow Ridge, after one of Marlin's ill-fated limited partnerships. The plaintiffs, however, had a problem. There was little point in suing unless they could recover some money. And whom could they sue? After all, Marlin was in prison, broke. The pilots decided to name as co-defendant a former business partner of Marlin's, a multimillionaire Beverly Hills attorney named Leonard Ross. Ross was emphatically free, breathtakingly prosperous, and, most important, well insured.

For two years, beginning in 1969, Ross and Marlin had been collaborators. Ross, fresh out of UCLA Law School, graduated at the top of his class. He applied his business acumen to finding investment opportunities and setting up deals. Marlin, meanwhile, crisscrossed the country, using his considerable charisma to hustle up investors. Their company, Marlin & Ross, Inc., financed a number of projects, including All-Pro Management, a sports agenting business run by Leonard's older brother, Al—the man who would appear in Chris and Claud Mills's life years later. But in 1971 Marlin and Leonard Ross had a falling-out. The fraud for which Marlin would be indicted began in 1973, after Leonard Ross left the partnership. But the long, inevitable unraveling of Marlin's financial empire was partly the result, Marlin says, of extortion by his erstwhile partner, Leonard Ross.

Deep in the avalanche of paper that is Willow Ridge are statements, given by Marlin under oath, in which he describes being abducted by Leonard Ross, Al Ross, and two armed thugs, Walter Siefert and Bobby Clark, on May 25, 1971, and held for twenty-four hours in Leonard Ross's Hollywood apartment. There, Marlin says, he was forced to sign over to Ross everything they had previously owned jointly, and coerced into surrendering most of his personal property and signing a multimillion-dollar promissory note. He says he was left with $34, his clothes, and the furniture in his apartment.

Marlin goes on: "When I requested an opportunity to discuss the matter and review the documents, I was threatened [by one of Ross's associates and told] that if I did not immediately sign the documents without reading them he would blow my head off, drink my blood, and break both my arms and legs. . . ."

Leonard Ross has denied these allegations, and his attorney has described Marlin's statement as a "palpably ridiculous" story designed to divert attention from his own legal troubles. Federal authorities, however, considered Marlin's account serious enough to warrant bringing the principals before a grand jury. Neither Ross was indicted. But Clark was later convicted of perjury for denying to the grand jury that he had a pistol, and for denying that Al Ross had a firearm in his possession.

Willow Ridge would ultimately take a series of complicated turns. When Leonard Ross's insurers balked at paying the cost of defending him, Ross hired a litigator named Lynn Boyd Stites to reverse a potentially disastrous legal position. Stites won for his client bad-faith settlements from insurance companies totaling about $20 million. But in 1984 Ross and Stites parted company bitterly. Stites wanted a percentage of the bad-faith awards. Ross considered the more than $5 million in legal fees, already paid Stites from insurance company coffers, compensation enough. Lawyers being lawyers, they worked out their differences by suing each other.

Stites, the man who had represented Leonard Ross in the taking of the deposition in which Barry Marlin alleged extortion, soon alleged that he, too, had been the victim of similar threats by the same man. In a complaint filed in February 1988, Stites charged that Ross was a member of organized crime, and sued him for, among other things, attempted murder and infliction of grave bodily harm. (Sixteen months later, Stites would drop Leonard Ross as a defendant in that suit.) In turn, Ross charged Stites with constructing a network of lawyers, called the "alliance," to manipulate litigation and generate a continuous loop of billings to insurance companies.

As the eighties drew to a close, the Willow Ridge mess was well into its adolescence. Not one of the 1,500 plaintiffs had seen a penny from the case, even as spawn after spawn of countersuits and cross-claims generated more than $70 million in payouts to lawyers. Barry Marlin was out of prison, staked to a new life by the federal witness protection program in exchange for his testimony in a kickback case involving the Teamsters Union. Lynn Boyd Stites was reported living in Switzerland, where he refused in 1989 to speak with Mike Wallace of CBS for a "60 Minutes" segment on the "alliance." And Leonard Ross was safely free of the outstanding Willow Ridge litigation, an even wealthier man because, as a basketball coach might say, he had made the transition smartly from defense to offense. He owns a nine-bedroom, 15,800-square-foot, $25-million Beverly Hills home that once served as a set for The Godfather.

Leonard's brother and former business partner lives in the neighborhood, in a single-story, hacienda-style manse with a basketball court in the backyard. It's by Lucille Ball's old place on North Roxbury Drive, and the Hollywood tour buses meander past his home too. But Al Ross, the man who packed a pistol on that day back in May 1971, has had to regroup.

At one time Al Ross was the hottest sports agent in the business, only he would wince if you called him an agent, for he styled himself much more than that. He was a financial adviser, one of the first of a new breed of lawyer who would do more for an athlete than just negotiate a contract. He banked the paychecks, worked out a budget, disbursed an allowance, and paid all the bills. He sold insurance and prepared tax returns. He found tax shelters and investment opportunities too. Sometimes they were limited partnerships in which he acted as the controlling general partner, who would in turn purchase property from his kid brother, Leonard. For the usual ten-percent cut, Ross's All-Pro Management offered the athlete one-stop shopping.

Ross prospered during the early seventies, a time of enormous change in pro sports. He was a pioneer in negotiating contracts with deferred payments, deals that secured a ball player's financial future and allowed franchises to pay out astonishingly large total amounts over time. The NBA and ABA were then joined in their pre-merger sparring, and Ross became notorious for finding loopholes in the existing contracts of basketball players and striking bigger, better deals elsewhere. As Ross helped Spencer Haywood, Jim McDaniels, John Brisker, and Charlie Scott make lucrative jumps from the ABA to the NBA, Mike Storen, general manager of the Kentucky Colonels, called him "the ABA's worst enemy."

That, players quickly realized, made Ross their friend. His first big catch was Carl Eller, the Minnesota Vikings' lineman, whom he met at a party in L.A. before the 1970 Pro Bowl. Eller's finances were a mess. Ross turned them around so thoroughly that several years later Eller, in gratitude, gave Ross the Defensive Player of the Year trophy he had won. Word of the Ross touch made its way through football and basketball locker rooms, and soon clients were coming to him. At one time or another Ross represented football players Marlin Briscoe, Duane Thomas, Diron Talbert, Jim Marshall, Gene Washington, Deacon Jones, and Marv Fleming, and such basketball stars as Bob McAdoo, Jim Chones, Elmore Smith, Rick Barry, Elvin Hayes, Garfield Heard, and Happy Hairston.

They were heady times. All-Pro (later Al Ross & Associates, and then First United Management) had a sumptuous suite of offices on the Avenue of the Stars in Century City, featuring inlaid tile floors and a built-in sauna. Ross's black Eldorado was equipped with a phone long before such things were fashionable. He was 6 foot 3, young, and wore his hair stylishly long. He moved just as easily among members of the exclusive Hillcrest Country Club as through the gyms around town, where he played pickup basketball several times a week. He was a shooter, a good shooter, and would tell you so.

One day in 1972 he phoned Mitch Chortkoff, a columnist for the Los Angeles *Herald-Examiner*. "Chorty, this is Al," he barked. "What's the matter with you? Here you've got the most exciting personality in the country and all you do is sit on your typewriter."

Ross was talking about himself, of course. He was direct, brash, streetwise. Black athletes in particular were drawn to this expatriate New Yorker who dealt unalloyed soul shakes. So many black ball players came by the home Ross and his wife, Sheila, then shared in Bel Air that neighbors took to calling it the Bel Air Black Hilton. For his part, Ross liked to say that the color of his clients' skin shouldn't affect the color of their money.

Ross grew up as Al Rosenberg, one of five children of George Rosenberg, a cab driver who lived on Henry Street in lower Manhattan, and his wife Rebecca. Al had been an

All-City forward at Seward High, then gone on to Michigan State in 1954, where he played two years of basketball under Forddy Anderson and earned a degree in phys. ed. He has said he was on scholarship, but Michigan State has no record of him having been so. Like most other New York ball players of that era, he spent summers at the resorts in the Borscht Belt, busing tables and playing ball. He says he came to L.A. to try out for the Lakers; once in town, he picked up graduate degrees in psychology and education, and in 1968 a law degree by going to night school. He spent the sixties looking for a calling, and by the end of the decade had found it.

Ross's greatest moment was the landmark Spencer Haywood lawsuit. Haywood had signed a six-year, $1.9-million pact with the Denver Rockets of the ABA when he came out of the University of Detroit. The Rockets' owners billed the contract as the best in sports. But Ross studied the deal and believed it was worth considerably less. Only about $400,000 of that figure was to be paid over the six years; the rest was deferred, with much of the money contingent on the panning out of a variety of investments the club had set up. Haywood wouldn't be eligible to reap the full value of the contract unless he played in Denver for ten years, and he could be seventy by the time he would receive the last penny. Ross believed in deferred payments, but this was ridiculous. He successfully challenged the Rockets' pact, then engineered Haywood's jump to Seattle, a move that led to the NBA ending forever its ban on underclassmen going pro early.

Al and Sheila Ross took Haywood into their home for three months as the case was adjudicated. Al played one-on-one with his star client to help keep the Haywood skills sharp. Soon Ross struck a $1.625-million deal with Seattle over six years, and Haywood departed the Bel Air Black Hilton. Ross says Haywood's eyes welled up with tears the day he left. Four years later, Ross and Haywood would be suing each other for millions.

A number of Ross's other clients began bolting around 1973. By then, one of them, former NFL running back Clint Jones, was ready to retire and wanted to cash in a $50,000 real estate investment. He says he had been promised Marlinesque returns, in the double digits. But when he called Ross from a pay phone and asked for his money, Jones says, "Al told me he couldn't do it. He tried to stall me off. I became so angry at him, I literally considered terminating him. If there was any way I thought I could get away with it, I would have. I tore up the phone booth. People must have thought I was nuts."

Jones sued, eventually recovering $15,000 after attorneys' fees. Jim Chones would eventually sue Ross, too, alleging among other things fraud and securities violations. Soon Charlie Scott followed. Elmore Smith, Bob McAdoo, John Brisker, Marlin Briscoe, and Jim McDaniels sued too. Most of the complaints charged fraud, mismanagement, or securities violations, and a number alleged that Ross concealed the extent to which he and Leonard were in business together. All were settled with nondisclosure clauses that kept the details of the agreements confidential.

By the end of the decade, Al Ross was no longer representing athletes. He had filed countersuits totaling nearly $100 million against the players who sued him, alleging that they conspired to "induce breaches of contract, interfere with advantageous relationships, and commit trade libel and defamation." Just as positive word of mouth had helped build his sports management empire, the grapevine brought it down.

The experience embittered him. Ingrates, Ross called his former clients. Haywood, he said, demanded Ross renegotiate his contract with the Sonics simply because Ross had also hammered out McDaniels's deal with the team, and McDaniels was making more money. "No matter what you do for them it's not enough," Ross said. "It's, 'What have you done for me lately?'"

As steeped in sports as he was, Ross seemed happy to be rid of the men who played the games. He turned to investment and real estate deals. He serviced a number of entertainment clients, including the Sylvers, a Jackson Five–style family act popular during the disco craze, who would eventually sue Ross too. And he tended to his Thoroughbred interests in Kentucky.

"The horses," Ross said, "don't talk back."

It's April 1987. Nearly a dozen years have passed since Al Ross kissed the athlete-representation business good-bye. The Aloha Classic, a week-long all-star tournament designed to showcase college seniors for NBA scouts, showcases something else: that there are a lot more agents where Ross came from.

Honolulu is teeming with them. They come to practices, sit with players in the stands, and loiter outside locker rooms. They track their quarry down in hotel lobbies and on Waikiki Beach. The players are so fed up with their pitches and platitudes that they'll say anything—"Yeah, right, dinner at seven"—just to get them off their backs.

Ross, now fifty, is one of these solicitors. He flits from player to player, reconfirming dinner plans, dropping off brochures, promising he'll follow up with phone calls. Next to some of the agents here, Ross seems too discreet. The agenting game has changed since the seventies. Scottie Pippen, a wiry kid from Central Arkansas, is the week's sensation. A few months earlier not an agent in America knew who he was; now they can't keep away from him. One night around eleven P.M. Pippen walks up Kalakaua Avenue, Waikiki's main drag, on his way back to the hotel. Ross is several steps behind him, struggling to keep up.

For several years now Ross has been trying to get back in the business. As before, he shrinks from the term "agent."

Rather, he's a full-service attorney and financial adviser. In 1984 Ross approached former Maryland coach Bob Wade, then a high-school coach directing one of the teams in the McDonald's High-School All-America Game, seeking introductions to Georgetown stars Reggie Williams and David Wingate, both of whom Wade coached at Dunbar High in Baltimore. Wade told him he wasn't the Georgetown coach.

At roughly the same time, Kentucky center Melvin Turpin had finished his eligibility, and was about to become a first-round NBA draft pick. Leonard Hamilton, then still a Kentucky assistant, suggested to Melvin Boyd Cunningham, a friend of Turpin's, that Ross might be able to come out of retirement and make Turpin his only client.

But there was a problem. Ross wasn't fully certified as an agent by either the NBA or NFL players' associations. His work for the Carl Ellers and Spencer Haywoods had been done long ago, back when the landscape of pro sports was different. And the rancor with which Ross and many of his former clients parted still lingered. In 1987 Ross was granted interim certification by both unions, the first step toward getting back in pro athletes' good graces. But before NBA Players Association executive director Larry Fleisher died in 1989, Fleisher said, "I would look very carefully over what [Ross] has done in the past ten years because there are some very unpleasant allegations in those lawsuits. His handling of players at that time was less than honorable in my view."

Ross didn't pick up any clients during his first year of interim certification, so the NBA didn't act on his provisional status. But from the time he tried to rejoin the profession, Ross was around prospective clients of a different sort. They weren't collegians, at least not yet. But John Williams, Tom Lewis, Sean Higgins, and Chris Mills, the very best high-school basketball players in Los Angeles, would all be choosing colleges soon enough. And each, as an agent would say, had a great upside.

Ross says, "I never met John Williams in my life." But people close to the L.A. hoops scene say Ross and Williams hung out together at UCLA, attending pickup and regular games there until Williams left Crenshaw High.

Several people place Ross around Tom Lewis as Lewis was coming out of Mater Dei High. Jim Hatfield, the Kentucky assistant who recruited Lewis, says, "Al's desire was to negotiate pro contracts. He got involved with high-school players because he wanted to get them back. Whatever school the kid leaned toward, he would support that school." Another source says that Ross, Lewis, and Pat Barrett, Lewis's guardian, had a meeting in Ross's office at which the terms of Lewis attending UK were discussed. "An offer [of money] was made," the source says, "but money was never presented."

Ross was in the middle of the Sean Higgins chase, too, especially at the close. In its probe of the Higgins recruitment, the NCAA developed enough evidence to bring two separate allegations: one that Ross was acting on Kentucky's behalf, and another that he was acting on UCLA's. According to one of the NCAA's charges against UK, Dwane Casey offered inducements—a $300 monthly cash allowance and a BMW among them—to Higgins directly during Higgins's visit to Lexington, and reiterated the offer to Clifford Benson-Bey while Casey and Benson-Bey sat in the stands at the Forum, watching a Lakers preseason game with the Chicago Bulls, about a month before the November signing date in 1986. The allegation went on to say that Ross, in a phone conversation with Higgins, told Higgins that whatever Casey offered Higgins would indeed be provided.

"Sean Higgins's allegation had been around for two years," says Casey. "The NCAA didn't believe it then, so why should they believe it now?"

But the NCAA's David Didion, who was involved in the case, says the allegation never led to a finding of a violation because no one in a position to corroborate Higgins's claims—least of all Al Ross—would talk to the NCAA about them. "The committee wouldn't be able to make a finding with one half of the story," Didion says. "Our hands were tied."

The NCAA also charged that Ross had picked up Higgins at the Benson-Beys' home, taken him out for a meal, and then driven him to Pauley Pavilion to attend a UCLA intrasquad scrimmage—and thus Ross was a representative of UCLA's athletic interests.

At the time of that intrasquad scrimmage, Bruins coach Walt Hazzard was confident he would land Higgins. Hazzard had visited the home several weeks earlier, and just the day before, Higgins had told Hazzard he wanted to attend UCLA.

But after the scrimmage, Ross tracked Hazzard down. It was a tense meeting: Ross and Hazzard hadn't been cordial since the early seventies, when Ross represented Hazzard briefly while Hazzard was playing for the NBA's Golden State Warriors. "The only time telephone service in this house has ever been cut off is when First United was 'paying our bills,'" Hazzard has said.

But in Hazzard's office, they had other matters to discuss. Ross told Hazzard that Higgins wasn't going to sign with the Bruins.

"What do you mean?" Hazzard asked.

"The kid doesn't like you," Ross said. "He doesn't like your personality and he doesn't think you're an X and O coach."

"What the fuck are you talking about?"

"The kid's lying to his [mother and stepfather], telling them he's going to UCLA. But he's not coming to you."

Of course, events would prove Ross to be absolutely correct. He knew exactly what Higgins was thinking. First Ross said he could help improve Hazzard's position with Sean by "facilitating communication." Then he began "shopping" Higgins to Hazzard, according to someone close to the events of that day.

Hazzard was furious. He had spent hundreds of hours on the Higgins case, preparing for any eventuality, and here, in the last stages of the game, an interloper was dealing this wild card. Having just spoken at length with Sean the night before and detecting nothing to alarm him, Hazzard didn't think Ross's services were necessary.

The meeting broke up. Moments later, Hazzard and Ross came across Clifford Benson-Bey out on the floor at Pauley.

"What the fuck are you doing with that motherfucker?" Benson-Bey demanded of Hazzard.

"He tells me he's your family lawyer, representing the family," Hazzard said.

Benson-Bey got up in Ross's face. "You don't have shit to do with us. Don't go around saying you represent us. You stay away from my kid."

Ross says he took Higgins to the scrimmage because Sean had called him and asked for a lift. He says he never told Hazzard he represented Higgins, only that he was a "family friend." He denies emphatically that he takes on high-school kids as clients, or that he represents the interests of any particular school. Indeed, the NCAA dropped the allegation that he was a UCLA booster too.

But people around the recruiting scene don't claim that Al Ross looks after the interests of any particular school. They say he looks after Al Ross. If that means accommodating someone in the process, fine. "He wanted to get back into the action," says a former UCLA recruiter. "The action had left him behind. He came up to me and said, 'You want Higgins?' I said, 'Yeah, we want Higgins.' He said, 'This is what it will take.'"

When Ross wouldn't help them in their probe of the recruitment of Higgins, NCAA investigators asked Merritt Jones—the Michigan booster, of all people—to phone Ross and ask him about a conversation Ross might have overheard between Sean and Steven Antebi. Had he heard any improper offers being made? Ross was reluctant to answer, according to NCAA sources, and then asked Jones, "What's it worth to you?"

Joe Bill Campbell, Dwane Casey's lawyer, says Ross wanted several thousand dollars to give an affidavit on Casey's behalf in the suit against Emery. Campbell said thanks, but no thanks.

"When the shit goes down, Ross is there," says L.A. City College coach Reggie Morris, formerly of Manual Arts High. "It's not inappropriate to call him a broker. He steers kids to programs. I don't think one particular program. It's LSU one time, somebody else the next. I don't know how he gets in, but he does."

One prominent black major-college assistant coach explains how Ross gains and uses influence. He says that over the summer of 1988 Ross called him and "begged me" to come by his Beverly Hills home. The coach did.

"He told me he was in the brokering business, a fact that was well known among coaches," the coach says. Ross indicated he could "deliver" James Moses, the guard who ended up going to Iowa, "in exchange for getting him back" as a client when Moses graduated. During the course of their conversations, Ross also offered to donate $250,000 to the fledgling Black Coaches Association. "He said he would fund it in exchange for the rights to talk to [black] coaches so he could get players," the coach says. "He wanted influence with black coaches around the country."

Ross, the assistant said, told him he didn't mind investing money "if he could get them when they came out [of college]." He understood that no coach could guarantee that players would be funneled back to him, but Ross said he liked the odds. "He said all he had to do was get one or two players with million-dollar contracts, and it paid for the money he'd invested in the other players."

* * *

Perhaps the most intriguing details about the Bills 'n' Mills affair are the four phone calls, made from the Kentucky basketball offices or charged to credit cards issued to the Wildcats' staff, to Al Ross between July and November 1987. That's the very period in which Kentucky overhauled UNLV in the Mills sweepstakes. It's shortly after Ross asked Tarkanian for access to UNLV seniors Armon Gilliam and Freddie Banks, and implied that he could then help out Claud Mills financially. And it's soon after Tarkanian told Claud that he didn't like Ross's appearance on the scene.

The first of the phone calls was dialed from the Los Angeles Airport Marriott on July 23, while Dwane Casey was in L.A. on a recruiting trip. The last was made from Casey's extension in the UK basketball office on November 12, the day after Mills signed.

The first three times, Casey says, he was returning Ross's calls, inquiring about pro prospects Tellis Frank, whom Casey had recruited to Western Kentucky, and Pippen. Casey says he made the November 12 call to needle Ross that UK had signed Mills. "If Ross would call, say, about Tellis Frank, he would say, 'You're never gonna get Chris Mills, he's going to UCLA. He's not gonna leave the West Coast,'" Casey says. "It was an ongoing thing with Ross. It was just kidding around. Then the day after he signed I called to tell him we got Chris. And he said, 'You're kidding.'"

Ross says that it was Casey who initiated the first three calls. He says Casey called him to ask questions about Chris—"What kind of player he is, what kind of individual," Ross says—and for advice to pass along to UK seniors intending to pursue pro careers.

Regardless of who initiated those calls, Ross's ties to Kentucky evidently go back to the days of Casey's predecessor, Leonard Hamilton. One college coach says it was UK that alerted Ross to Fairfax High's dispute with high-school authorities—the imbroglio that first brought Claud Mills and Ross together—because the 'Cats sorely wanted Higgins and Mills to travel with the Lions basketball team to the Bluegrass. Tom Lewis told the NCAA that when he returned to Mater Dei High after an away game, Jim Hatfield and Ross were at the school, waiting for him. They exchanged pleasantries with Lewis, then got into the same car and drove off together.

Several former Kentucky players say they were introduced to Ross on campus, and Rex Chapman has told *Sports Illustrated*'s Curry Kirkpatrick that he met Ross in the Wildcat Lodge itself. Eddie Sutton says Hamilton introduced Ross to him when Ross came through the UK basketball offices in 1985-86, Hamilton's last season there and Sutton's first.

Hamilton says he hadn't met Ross until that season. But two years earlier, at a time Ross was uncertified, Hamilton was touting Ross as a possible agent for Mel Turpin. And at least one ex-UK player remembers Hamilton introducing Ross to him, near Memorial Coliseum, before the fall of 1985.

In the wake of the trial of Norby Walters and Lloyd Bloom, and sundry revelations about the nefarious activities of agents, college coaches all over the country are trying desperately to keep agents away from their players. But Hamilton took his entire Oklahoma State team over to Ross's Beverly Hills home in November 1986, during the Cowboys' visit to L.A. to play Pepperdine. They ogled nearby mansions and ate Kentucky Fried Chicken in his backyard. When Derick Mills, Chris's half brother, was coaching an L.A. area all-star team, he remembers Ross telling him that he, Ross, knew the coach at Oklahoma State, and that if anyone on his team needed a scholarship, Hamilton would take a look-see.

"I don't work for high-school athletes," Ross says. "I'm not even in the agent business. I'm a developer. I'm into real estate, law. If coaches like to come to my house, listen, they're friends of mine. I'm an athlete, a ball player. I played ball. I have very good rapport with coaches. If I took one penny—one penny—I would tell you. But I never got compensated one iota."

Claud Mills says, "I don't even know about Al Ross. He don't associate with me. I don't know his business but he's a multimillionaire so what would he have to do with a person like me? I'm the one who picked what school Chris would go to. I wouldn't listen to no man on earth trying to tell me where Chris should go. I'm a basketball genius. I don't need to talk to Al Ross."

Yet five months after Chris signed with Kentucky, when Claud learned one Friday evening that the Los Angeles *Daily News* was about to publish its account of the Emery Air Freight envelope coming open, he phoned Al Ross. Ross in turn called the *Daily News* and Emery, and made several public statements about the case on the Millses' behalf. "One [Emery employee] said the package was open, one said it was partially open, and another said it wasn't open at all," Ross told the *Courier-Journal* shortly after the incident. "And the Lexington carriers said it was sealed tight. This is getting ridiculous."

Street talk is cheap. But if you care to give it currency—and in L.A., what's really going down in the ten-foot culture can be picked up in the parks and gyms and summer leagues—the Mills recruitment poses several intriguing questions. Did streetwise Derick Mills open Claud's eyes and make him realize there were vistas beyond UNLV, beyond a sinecure at Lorimar and having the power of the pen in Vegas? Did Chris's natural mother, Karen, suddenly pay Chris a visit before his junior season because she was sent from Milwaukee by one of the colleges in the hunt to dope out the situation? Did Dwane Casey ultimately add his voice to Jerry Tarkanian's, and tell Claud to disassociate himself from Al Ross? And was the deal with Kentucky really for $250,000 over four years?

When pressed, Al Ross will say this: "Maybe down the road, when the father and Chris decide to come into the pros, *then* I would be interested. You know, if it's like a relationship, if it lasts, down the road, who knows?"

But to people around the L.A. recruiting scene, Al Ross is a man actively looking down that road, trying to reestablish himself in the business, and using the terrific high-school basketball talent in his backyard as leverage to do so.

If Ross is indeed peddling influence, he surely isn't the only agent who has figured out that you can't start scouting clients too early. A New York *Newsday* series in spring 1989 linked agent Lance Luchnick to payments to high-school and college coaches, reportedly for access to stars of the future.

Whether the office is a suite in Beverly Hills, or a luncheonette counter across from an inner-city school yard, the game is the same. Secure your investment early. Send it off for appreciation. If it comes back to you, you've got a valuable commodity.

Al Ross is on the line. "You want a great headline? Say I got a million dollars for delivering Chris Mills. Seriously. In hundred-dollar bills. Is that good? Wouldn't it make it more interesting?

"But make sure you say that Emery didn't deliver it."

9

Closing the Envelope

DAVID ROSELLE'S PLAN for saving basketball at the University of Kentucky required reeducating the masses. It required cooperating fully with the NCAA. But it also required, as a show of good faith, cleaning house over at Memorial Coliseum.

Getting the resignation of athletics director Cliff Hagan, on whose passive watch the improprieties had occurred, was relatively easy. As a replacement Roselle set his sights on C. M. Newton, the basketball coach at Vanderbilt, who had been a reserve on Rupp's 1951 national champions. Roselle slipped down to Elizabethtown, Kentucky, one foggy morning around Christmastime to meet Newton and try to talk him into taking the job. Newton was skeptical. He had grown up in Lexington, ultimately graduating from Transylvania University in town. He knew the SEC well, going back to his years as coach at Alabama. Yet he loved Vandy, and his wife, Evelyn, was happy there. Finally,

Evelyn made her husband an offer: she would give up Nashville if he gave up the bench.

But if reform were to go forward, Roselle knew, he also needed to replace Eddie Sutton. And that wasn't going to be as easy. Roselle had been alarmed at the number of academically deficient players brought in during the Sutton regime. Joe Hall may well have recruited just as many, but Hall operated in another era, back before Proposition 48 came along and made academic risks so conspicuous. Since Roselle took over, Sutton had brought to campus a parade of recruits—Shawn Kemp, Sean Woods, Reggie Hanson, John Pittman, and (it would turn out) Eric Manuel—who came up short on Prop 48. The president's concern wasn't grounded in elitism, but in his oft-enunciated philosophy of being fair to the kids. Students ill prepared in high school, and then thrown into the breach of the biggest of big-time programs, had little chance of earning a degree.

By mid-March, with the season over, Roselle began turning the screws. A Lexington TV station carried a report that Sutton had offered to fire his entire staff—the secretaries, equipment manager, and trainer, in addition to his assistants—to save his job. Sutton denied it, and the report was never substantiated. On March 17 Sutton and Roselle met in the living room of the president's house, and Sutton vowed he would stay on. The next day Sutton reiterated that vow on CBS, doing so over a live hookup during coverage of the NCAA tournament. But on March 19, a Sunday, Roselle told his coach that he had called a meeting of the athletics board for Tuesday to discuss the future of the basketball program. "And Eddie," Roselle said, "I've got the votes."

Later that day—again on national TV—Sutton announced his resignation. Three of his assistants, including Dwane Casey, would soon follow. At an Easter service at Southland Christian Church the next week, more than

2,000 parishioners gave Eddie and Patsy Sutton a standing ovation.

Ed Dove had been in passionate form at the meeting of the NCAA's Committee on Infractions in Charleston, South Carolina, in early May. Schools have the right to appeal sanctions meted out by that body, as do coaches. Under NCAA rules, however, students don't. Dove skewered the committee on that point. "It was the only time they ever gave us anything," Dove says. "'Good point. Thank you. Next case.' Of course, if you get into the facts—Eric's facts are not the most favorable. But procedurally, the thing sucks."

Two weeks later, on May 19, Dove was fighting through a thicket of reporters and minicams to get to Manuel's room in the Wildcat Lodge. He found Eric sitting on his bed. "I mean, how do you tell someone he's getting the death penalty? He just dropped his head and stared at the floor for a while. I've done a lot of termination cases where people lose their kids. It was basically the same feeling."

Six of the state's TV stations cut into their programming with live coverage of the press conference at which the sanctions were announced. The program got one year without live TV, a two-year ban from tournament play, and a limit of three scholarships for each of two seasons. In addition, the NCAA stripped Kentucky of its wins and revenues from the 1988 tournament for having used a player, Manuel, the school should have known was ineligible. For receiving $1,000 in an envelope, Claud Mills would never see his son play for Kentucky again. For sending the envelope, Dwane Casey was banned from coaching for five years. And Manuel's death penalty meant he would never again play at an NCAA school. Over and over, Roselle and the NCAA's Steve Morgan emphasized that the entire program might have been shut down if the school hadn't been so cooperative. But that day it seemed the NCAA had in fact assessed the ultimate sanction: it stripped the 'Cats bare, and then made them play.

Joe Bill Campbell, Casey's attorney, scoffed at the notion that the program might have been suspended. It was spin control, he said, a "smoke screen," a way of trying to sell to the fans ex post facto Roselle's strategy of abject surrender. Indeed, that night callers to the talk shows wore the "little mathematician" out. A letter to the *Herald-Leader* likened Roselle to Panamanian strongman Manuel Noriega. Among lawyers in town the line was that Brown, Todd & Heyburn, James Park's law firm, had pocketed more than $350,000 for a guilty plea.

Eddie Sutton didn't have his job anymore. But the NCAA gave Sutton, who was never named in an allegation, a letter certifying his complete exoneration. Sean Sutton, despite admitting he provided false and misleading information to investigators, wasn't sanctioned either. That raised eyebrows. "Sean lied," Dove says. "It's dropped because he's white. Why else you think? All the white guys. Who do they hammer? Casey and Eric."

As Sutton descended from the rostrum after meeting the press on Sanctions Day, someone asked him whether he had anything to say to his successor, whoever that might be. Sutton's voice took on a mock-conspiratorial tone. "I'd tell him," he said, "all the deep, dark secrets."

Through the last twenty of his thirty-seven years, Rick Pitino's genius has always been his consistent ability to beat his age. Wherever youth might be a liability, Pitino seemed able to turn it to his advantage, to cop the benefit of the doubt. Pitino had been young for every job he held, starting as an assistant at Hawaii and then Syracuse; as a head coach at Boston University; as an aide to Hubie Brown with the NBA's New York Knicks; as head coach at tradition-encrusted Providence, which he guided improbably to the Final Four; and in New York again as the Knicks' top man, the position he always said was his ultimate goal. When Kentucky hired him at the end of May to take Sutton's place, Pitino was a well-traveled thirtysomething. "Rick Pitino coaches fast-break and pressing basketball, and that's always been a part of the Kentucky tradition, if you go back before Eddie Sutton and Joe Hall," David Roselle would say. For someone who wasn't supposed to care about sports, the president knew a lot.

The 'Cats had inquired about Lute Olson, Mike Krzyzewski, and a former UK player, the Los Angeles Lakers' Pat Riley. They had earnestly courted Seton Hall's P. J. Carlesimo, who, if the talk shows were to be believed, would never work out because he wears a beard. Pitino's was a terribly big name to find so late in a search, and Roselle and Newton were lucky and grateful he could be had. Pitino had no real interest in the job when Newton first called, for the Knicks were still in the midst of the playoffs. But when he mentioned Kentucky's feelers to New York general manager Al Bianchi, Pitino was alarmed that his boss made no real effort to talk him into staying in New York. His relationship with Bianchi wasn't the best, but now doubts and insecurities came flooding back, resurrecting a persistent feeling that he should have never left the colleges in the first place.

Pitino had been a good high-school guard on Long Island, a coach-on-the-floor type who worked his first recruiting pitch on his parents, persuading them that tuition to send him to basketball camp was an investment in his future. At the University of Massachusetts he captained the team and played briefly with a fellow Long Islander named Julius Erving. Even as social chairman of his fraternity at U. Mass, he showed a recruiter's ingenuity, phoning campus women to invite them to the frat house for a Friday-night champagne-and-buffet spread. When they showed up, they'd find beer and no food.

He was the youngest head coach in Division I when he took over at Boston University. The Terriers had gone 17–36 in the two seasons before, yet he launched the season with a midnight practice and free champagne. This wasn't "midnight madness," but insanity; four people showed up. The athletic director who hired him called him the Boy Coach. The players soon began calling him "little Mussolini." At BU he began a habit he would continue at Providence, scheduling three-a-day practices in season: a two-hour, six A.M. session; then mandatory individual instruction between classes; and a standard three-to-five reassembly in the afternoon. His intensity took some of his players aback. After one upset victory at Rhode Island, Pitino was so juiced he ordered the team bus to stop at a strip joint on the way back to campus. There he led his players in wolf whistles, even disbursing dollar bills so they could stuff them into the dancers' G-strings.

One night BU was hosting U. Mass, the Pitino alma mater, in a game that began as a back-and-forth affair. With ten seconds to play in the first half, the Terriers had the ball in their forecourt when Pitino called time-out to draw up a play. It was designed for Glen Consor, a senior guard and co-captain, to take an in-bounds pass and find teammate Steve Wright for a final shot. But when Consor got the ball he saw a clear route to the hoop. He went in for a basket at the buzzer, and the team retired to the locker room, feeling good.

Once inside, Pitino exploded. He was furious at Consor for insubordination. He threw chalk, slammed down a clipboard. "I told you what I wanted!" he screamed. "And I'm the coach!"

In the second half, the Terriers pulled away and won easily. Whether it was Consor's shot or Pitino's tirade, something had ignited them. But after the game Pitino sent Consor, still wearing his uniform sweats, out to the track. "I'll come and get you when I want you to stop running," Pitino said. Miles later, well into a New England night in the middle of winter, Pitino let Consor back inside. Says one former Terrier, "It was definitely a power thing, an ego thing."

Over the summer of 1987, just after Pitino took over as the Knicks' head coach, the NBA put a moratorium on new player signings. A collective bargaining agreement hadn't been hammered out yet, and the Players Association was threatening to sue to eliminate the college draft. Pending resolution of those issues, the league banned clubs from holding workouts with unsigned free agents or draft picks. Pitino held one anyway, and the NBA fined him an undisclosed amount.

Pitino demanded an enormous amount from his players, but he gave a lot of his time and energy himself. For someone so totally immersed in the game, who had spent his wedding night interviewing with Jim Boeheim for a Syracuse assistant's job, the line between work and family blurred. Tragedy twice encroached suddenly on his world, first at BU, when a Terrier player named Arturo Brown died of a heart defect while playing in a pickup game. Later, Pitino's infant son Daniel would die of a similar heart problem, only a few months into his young life. A state trooper flagged down the Providence team bus as it made its way across the Rhode Island line, back from the 1987 Big East tournament, to deliver the news.

At each stop on his résumé, some new professional challenge pulled at him. He eventually overcame qualms about the propriety of leaving each one. Pitino walked out on existing contracts when he left BU, Providence, and the Knicks—three in seven years. Yet he says, "I've never broken a contract in my life"—because each time he left, to pursue happiness elsewhere, his bosses let him go in the name of that happiness.

Naturally enough, the question came up: what does Rick Pitino really want? When he was a bright young assistant with the Knicks, the conventional wisdom held that he was really "a college guy." Soon after he took the Providence job the word was, "He's a pro guy. He really wants to coach in the pros." So he took over the Knicks, earning more than $400,000 a year. Skeptics watched his preternatural enthusiasm run up against the grizzled stolidity of Bianchi, an NBA lifer, and players like Mark Jackson and Patrick Ewing, who outearned and outshone him. They concluded that he wouldn't be happy until the team changed its name to the New York Ricks.

Eventually Pitino said his heart was still on campus. Leaving Providence was an enormous mistake. Being a college coach was more conducive to family living. He was tired of the clashes with management and the constant attacks on the back pages of the New York tabloids.

And so it was that he came to Kentucky. For $6 million over seven years, Pitino took the least family-friendly and least-collegiate college job there is, where thousands of self-appointed GMs and scores of second-guessing wags in the media will follow his every move. He got a preview of the privacy he could expect soon after buying a $245,000 lot in the fashionable Tates Creek section of Lexington. Genuflecting locals took souvenir soil samples from the Pitino property, which was still just a hole in the ground, and for the 'Cats' home opener against Ohio University fans brandished Pitino face masks. During the first year or two of probation, a grace period of lowered expectations, Pitino will be a ration of manna from the big time. After that, however, the fans of the commonwealth will revert to their impossible-to-please selves. "If he thinks New York is vicious," cracked New York Times columnist George

Vecsey, who used to work for the *Courier-Journal* and knows well the pathology of Big Blue fever, "he should try losing to Tennessee at home."

"I think the University of Kentucky will get turned around in a very short period of time with me as coach," Pitino said at the first press conference after his hiring.

No one who has followed Pitino's career doubted for an instant that he's right. The only extraordinary thing about that statement is that Rick Pitino didn't refer to himself in the third person.

Rick and Joanne Pitino flew into Lexington on May 22, a Monday, for a quick tour of the city and campus. Serious talks with UK officials weren't scheduled until the next day. But Tuesday morning's *Herald-Leader* carried a story that devoted followers of UK basketball—and skeptics of the hometown newspaper's motives—would consider a cancel-my-subscription classic. In 1977 the NCAA cited Hawaii's basketball program for sixty-eight rules violations. Under head coach Bruce O'Neil, a number of Honolulu business-men had lavished an excess of the "aloha spirit" on several Rainbows. Eight of the findings, the *Herald-Leader* reported, named Pitino.

As an assistant to O'Neil for two years in the mid-seventies, Pitino arranged for a Honolulu Ford dealer to receive two season tickets in exchange for providing two players, Reggie Carter and George Lett, with an Oldsmobile. Pitino also provided free airline tickets to Carter, Lett, and another Rainbow, Henry Hollingsworth, between New York City and Honolulu. He had done these things as part of a "knowing and willful effort" to contravene the rules, the NCAA concluded. In March 1977 the Committee on Infrac-tions recommended Pitino's "permanent and complete sev-erance of any and all relations . . . formally or informally with the university's intercollegiate athletic program."

The disclosure blindsided the commonwealth. O'Neil,

long since out of coaching and now running a video production company in Oregon, began fielding inquiries about what really went down in the islands a dozen years earlier. He seemed at first anxious to protect Pitino, telling one reporter that his young assistant really hadn't done much recruiting. But in his autobiography, *Born to Coach*, Pitino fondly recalls his duties at Hawaii: "I loved it. Loved the competition for players, the thrill of the chase, selling myself—everything. I loved living on airplanes and making thirty calls a day, doing the one hundred and one things that go with being a college recruiter."

Pitino's initial explanation was even more intriguing. He said he wasn't involved, in spite of what might be in the NCAA's findings. "I think that at the time they were going down, and the head coach and I had a falling-out because of it. And he tried to make me a part of it." Usually head coaches plead ignorance of shenanigans their assistants are up to. Here was an unusual role reversal—an assistant saying hanky-panky was all the head coach's.

At that, O'Neil told the *Herald-Leader:* "If Rick is smart, he wouldn't bring that kind of stuff up. . . . He's got to be real careful. He's always had trouble with loyalties. He talks about stabbing people in the back. That can go both ways."

Well after the uproar over the revelations subsided, O'Neil was again asked who arranged for the flights home and the players' cars, as cited by the NCAA. And he said Pitino did, albeit at O'Neil's direction. "If he wanted to," says Dana Pump, a friend of O'Neil's who runs a scouting service, "Bruce could bury Rick."

"Rick's always been real brash," says O'Neil. "I still remember when Garf [Five-Star camp director Howard Garfinkel, Pitino's patron] brought him to me after an NIT game at the Garden. He told me, 'I've got this guy I want you to meet. He's a future star in coaching.' I talked to Rick that night and hired him as a graduate assistant. Obviously I thought a guy with Garf's connections could help us get players. I felt he was a better coach than I was, and I was only twenty-eight. We had a real New York connection going.

"When a program comes out of nowhere like we did, everyone wants to jump on the bandwagon. And the thing with airfare to the mainland—what are they going to do? Swim? Most of my kids didn't even know *how* to swim.

"One thing sticks in my mind—Rick wanted to move up real quick. My other assistant left, and he became my head assistant. He said, 'Within five years I want to be a head coach.' I told him, 'Rick, you've got to be loyal. You can't bad-mouth people. You've got to take your time.' And when things went down at Hawaii, he jumped ship and took all the oars."

Today Pitino won't even concede that he committed youthful indiscretions. He says all he did was pass out free McDonald's hamburger coupons to players. He says he's linked to more serious violations because of grudges held against him by O'Neil, and several players interviewed by investigators.

O'Neil believes Pitino went behind his back, to the school's administration, to have O'Neil suspended and replaced with himself for the final few games of the 1976 season. "Rick didn't realize how much loyalty there was to me in the community," O'Neil says. "I had tenure as a full professor, and they couldn't fire me. Eventually I would step down without a fight. But Rick would not get the job [on a permanent basis]." Pitino denies he went behind O'Neil's back, but doesn't dispute that the circumstances of O'Neil's exit are the source of the rift with his former boss.

For his part, O'Neil is the first to praise Pitino's abilities as a coach. "He's matured a lot," he says. "I sense something about Rick now that I haven't sensed in thirteen years. That he wants to build something positive. There'll be no pressure on him at first. And I think he is a good enough coach."

Hawaii was old news; even the *Herald-Leader* conceded that. But however whiskered Pitino's indiscretions were, as long as the university didn't know about them—and inexplicably, neither Roselle nor Newton did—they were absolutely relevant to any deliberations over whether he was fit to run a born-again program. UK seemed about to hire a terrific basketball coach, but an enormously ambitious one, whose past is marked by examples of the ends justifying the means, and who has an NCAA rap sheet longer than Dwane Casey's. He had even been cited for breaking NBA rules. Had the "little mathematician" badly miscalculated?

That wasn't going to be the issue. The *Herald-Leader* would be the issue, for the newspaper's disclosures had touched off more hatred. An intemperate and inaccurate editorial by WKYT-TV executive Ralph Gabbard ripped the paper for making a big deal about nothing more than a few free hamburgers, and helped inflame passions. Invective from other quarters criticized the story's timing. Why dredge up ancient history just when Pitino, the only good thing to come down UK's pike in months, was in town?

In fact, the *Herald-Leader* had brought the story to light just as soon as it possibly could. In his lawsuit against the newspaper, Reggie Warford argued that the story implicating him in recruiting improprieties had prevented him from finding a position in coaching. As part of its defense, the *Herald-Leader* asked the NCAA for a list of any basketball coach ever named in a violation who had gone on to get another job. The list, a long one, had been kicking around the newsroom. And one of the names on it was Rick Pitino's.

When Pitino became a candidate for the UK job, Jerry Tipton, the reporter who covers Wildcat basketball, decided to find out exactly the extent of Pitino's involvement in the Rainbows' scandal. An assistant athletic director at Hawaii told Tipton that Pitino had not been named specifically in any of the NCAA findings, but promised to send him a copy of the infractions report. When a week passed and the report hadn't arrived, Tipton called back. The assistant A.D. said his boss had told him not to send it.

At this point, Tipton was busy chasing down a more pertinent story: UK's wooing of P. J. Carlesimo. Nonetheless, Tipton asked the *Herald-Leader*'s librarian to get a copy of the report from the NCAA. The report arrived on Friday, just as Kentucky's NCAA sanctions were announced, and Tipton was too busy to open it. But by the following Monday, Carlesimo had declared he wasn't interested in the job, and Pitino was again a candidate. So it was that Tipton opened the envelope on the very Monday the Pitinos came to town.

To be fair to all parties concerned, Tipton asked each for comment. He found Pitino and Newton dining at The Coach House, a Lexington restaurant, and shared with them what he had found out. Later that night Pitino offered to withdraw his name from consideration. Call off the press conference scheduled for the next day, he told Newton; he and Joanne had their reservations about the job anyway. But neither Roselle nor Newton would let him. They couldn't afford to let him. Things done as a graduate assistant a dozen years ago could be forgiven. By now UK needed Pitino desperately, if only as a gesture to the faithful.

And so Pitino faced the public the next day as brash as ever. "There's no one in this business with more integrity than Rick Pitino," he said. "You won't have to worry about cheating with Rick Pitino." In a way, he said, his past was a positive, for he knew what could go wrong in a program. To those remarks he would add, "I didn't make any mistakes. I don't care what anybody says."

As the uproar over Pitino's past carried on, and it looked as if Newton might whiff on yet another coaching candidate, a familiar figure got his hopes up. If UK needed to find someone, he knew just the right man for the job. The man was available. He was intimately familiar with the program.

And he was personally unsullied by any NCAA violation. The figure and his candidate were one and the same: Eddie Sutton.

Is it possible to find anyone in major-college basketball without a past? "C.M. wouldn't give a seeing eye dog to a blind man if it broke a rule," says Jock Sutherland, who was briefly Newton's assistant at Alabama. Yet it's whispered around the SEC that after Newton and Sutherland went 4–20 in their first season in Tuscaloosa, a loose confederation of 'Bama boosters took a vow that such humiliation would never be visited upon the Tide again. They called themselves the Four-and-Twenty Club, and put up money to make good on that resolution.

There's no proof that the group existed, much less that Newton knew of it or its activities. Yet Roselle never insisted on purity, only on putting basketball in perspective. He made concessions where he had to, particularly late in the game, when he had already played his strongest cards.

In early May, before Pitino had become a serious candidate, Newton said that henceforth the school would negotiate all coaches' shoe and broadcast contracts. "We want to get the coach out of being an entrepreneur and put him in the position of coaching basketball," Newton said. "That just makes sense." Then Pitino's agent, Mitch Dukov, came to town, and sanity suddenly made less sense. Dukov explained what his client would cost: $105,000, plus ancillary income—from camps, shoe and broadcast deals, and commercial endorsements—worth six times the base salary. In all, it would be a package more than quadruple the income of the football coach at the time, Jerry Claiborne. Roselle and Newton had to relent. They let Pitino and Dukov hammer out their own deals, and guaranteed a certain minimum in outside income.

That was a minor concession. More ominous was the narrow scope of the Park investigation. As vigorous as it was, it never really touched the boosters, who consider it their fundamental right to express love for the Wildcats any way they please. Many are still resentful of the way they were treated after Hall left in 1985. "We didn't find that boosters were a particularly large part of the problem," Roselle said. "They had been banned from the locker room after the last investigation."

The president was being naive. One of the salutary by-products of the football scandals in the Southwest Conference during the eighties was the exposure and humiliation of the offending boosters. Texas enacted a law holding anyone whose actions resulted in NCAA sanctions liable for lost revenue. Of course, such a bill could be enacted in that state because loyalties are divided among eight big-time schools. In Kentucky, no such Balkanization exists; Bluegrass politicians will vote to repeal tobacco price supports before they'll back legislation calling someone who just loves the 'Cats a crook. In the meantime, UK administrator John Darsie's view—that a booster who violates NCAA rules not only ought not be prosecuted but ought not even be identified—will prevail. And boosters determined to be involved with the program will go ahead and involve themselves, notwithstanding the best intentions of a president. Indeed, the Webb brothers threw a welcoming party for Pitino soon after he came to Lexington. Roselle quickly fired off to his new coach copies of the Herald-Leader's stories detailing the Scott Courts imbroglio. Nonetheless, Don Webb put in an appearance at one of the 'Cats' first practices, shaking the usual hands.

UK basketball will be back again, of course. In 1953–54, after sitting out that one season with a suspension, the 'Cats went undefeated, and in 1985–86, after the Herald-Leader series, they went 32–4 and won the SEC. Pitino quickly signed a big recruit, Jamal Mashburn of New York City, who raised eyebrows because he hadn't met his Prop 48 requirements when he committed. (What's more, Mashburn played

276

AAU ball for the spendthrift Gauchos; if UK really is playing by the rules, Jamal will probably be scaling back his life-style.) But even if he gets no one else of consequence, Pitino's success will outstrip the talent he has to work with. He's the coach, after all, who took nobodies at Providence to the Final Four in 1987.

Alas, Kentucky fans tend to judge a coach as much by the horses he brings in as by the outcome of the race. "Joe B. accepted that he wasn't a great coach," says one Lexingtonian. "He didn't try to prove his critics wrong. People here don't want to hear how you can coach. They want to know who you're gonna get. People here don't have no faith in 'sleepers.' They don't turn nobody on.

"See, when Joe left, the program left with him. It was like, 'I resign, and these ten thousand other soldiers behind me, they resign too.' You take that away from these people . . . that's what they're here for. 'I'm not gonna give [the Athletics Association] a hundred thousand dollars if I can't come into the locker room anymore with my kid and get Sam Bowie's autograph. You take that away from me, and I don't have no reason to give you a hundred thousand.'"

NCAA enforcement director David Berst considers the unreconstructed booster the biggest problem facing his office. For the next five years, all it will take is one outlaw fan to earn the program the death penalty. Rupp's Wildcats served that sentence in the early fifties for payments to players and academic irregularities, the very things the program is doing time for now. And everything about UK basketball—the passion for it and import of it, even Judge Streit's description of it as "the acme of commercialism and overemphasis"—has held steady over thirty-five years. As the 1989–90 season began, the only real difference was in the outlook of the man at the top. "I can't possibly know if there's an assistant coach or booster out doing the wrong thing," Roselle said. "But after going through this, I'm convinced a president can make a difference."

Roselle did, if only by surviving. Somehow, sound principles made for good politics. Even the big screw-up—not vetting Pitino's past—worked out in its way. Knowledge that Pitino wasn't some innocent helped soothe the ready-fire-aimers who only a week earlier had been calling for Roselle's head.

Yet why, barely into Pitino's first season, did Roselle abruptly announce he would leave UK to take over the presidency at the University of Delaware? He attributed his decision in vague terms to the basketball investigation. "You can only do one of those," he said cryptically. By that, did he mean he expected another?

Roselle also said he had made up his mind to leave even before the NCAA's probe was complete. If so, why had he signed a contract extension in late June, well after the basketball mess had been resolved? "He said he was too identified with cleaning up the program," said a disappointed Bret Bearup. "But what's wrong with that? What's wrong with being known as a problem solver, as someone with integrity?"

In fact, athletics may have been only a convenient pretext. Roselle was losing his struggle with the governor to secure the funding he felt the university needed to fulfill its potential. In one of his last comments before announcing his plans to leave, the president called "piss-poor" the amount of money Kentucky politicians were willing to spend on higher education. With the board composed more and more of Wilkinson loyalists, and the governor ensconced in the statehouse for two more years, it may have been the attitude of Wally and his followers that finally wore Roselle down.

As he yielded to Wilkinson's hand-picked successor, Charles Wethington, Roselle took with him a national reputation similar to that of John Oswald, the UK president of the fifties, who fought Rupp and was run out of town by boosters—only to end up at Penn State. "Replacing David

Roselle with Charles Wethington," said one crestfallen faculty member, "is like replacing Secretariat with Mr. Ed."

Kentucky's page sure isn't stainless. But without David Roselle, will it really be turned?

In June 1989, Bob Minnix, one of the NCAA's senior enforcement directors, a graduate of the University of Washington Law School, and a former football player at Notre Dame, addressed the annual convention of the Black Coaches Association. Like most of the people gathered in this hotel ballroom in Dallas, Minnix is young, bright, and congenial. He's also black. Enough of the phony solidarity, Minnix told his audience of several hundred. I need your help. College athletics needs it. When you see something improper going on, call me. Those of you who know me know you can trust me. You can count on complete anonymity. Like it or not, most of you are recruiters, and the integrity of the game is in your hands.

Minnix said his piece and left the dais to tepid applause. Then up stepped Dwane Casey. When I was investigated, Casey said, the NCAA poked into every aspect of my life—into my finances, into my past, into my friends. They talked to everyone who ever knew me, and I found out who my real friends are. People I thought were my friends stabbed me in the back. I hope that what happened to me will never happen to you. To help make sure that it doesn't, we've got to stick together.

Whether in endorsement of the Code, or out of sympathy for Casey's lot, the room filled with applause.

Like Eric Manuel, Dwane Casey still says he is innocent of the violation found against him. If $1,000 was indeed in that envelope, he says, someone else put it there.

The Casey case is this: more than seventy-five employees at Emery's LAX facility had access to the package. Any one of them could have found out if a specific shipment was in the Emery system by calling up information on a computer console. This would have alerted someone, at least four hours prior to the package's arrival, that Casey had sent something to the Mills home.

Further, Campbell says, back in November the UK basketball office had sent a letter of intent to the Mills family via Emery that was misdelivered. And the Mills family had received several phone calls from UCLA boosters during the days leading up to the incident, each suggesting that Chris claim he was improperly recruited so he could get out of his Kentucky letter of intent and sign with the Bruins.

To accept the scenario that Emery employees conspired to set Casey up, however, you would have to believe in a complex conspiracy. You would need $1,000 in seed money, a warehouse full of colluding employees, and perhaps Cecil B. De Mille to choreograph the whole thing. And you'd still have to reconcile Claud Mills's denial that there was any money in the package—"I don't know nothing about no money"—with testimony of a half-dozen Emery employees who separately told the *Daily News*, the NCAA, and court reporters taking depositions for Casey's lawsuit that they saw and delivered $1,000.

But there is another possibility, a theory Casey and Campbell have only recently espoused, for it implicates the program. It holds that a single booster, acting alone, slipped the money into the envelope before it left the basketball office. To accept this theory you would need only one suspect. He would have to be wealthy, brash, and enamored of the 'Cats. He would have to have free access to the UK basketball suite, and the hubris to think he would never be caught if he were to go by secretary Larnetta McDowell's desk, see the videocassette lying on top of the unsealed envelope, notice the name "C. MILLS" on the air bill, and slip $1,000 into the sleeve of the tape.

There is someone who fits that profile—fits it almost perfectly.

Jimmy Hamilton is described by acquaintances as someone who could have stepped out of a Jerry Jeff Walker song. He's a high-energy, high-living businessman in his early fifties, about 6 foot 1, with a rugged face and a taste for stylish black clothing. A cellular phone is never far from his ear. Among his holdings are substantial mineral rights, real estate, and a transportation firm that owns Wildcat Cab Company, where Eric Manuel worked the summer before enrolling at UK. Hamilton and Eddie Sutton had met through Alcoholics Anonymous, and quickly became friends. They are partners in a shopping center in Ashland, Kentucky, and Jimmy usually sat near Patsy Sutton during Wildcat home games.

Today Eddie Sutton declines comment on his relationship with Hamilton, or any aspect of his tenure at Kentucky. "It's history as far as I'm concerned." But on the day the Los Angeles *Daily News* story broke, Hamilton met with Sutton for hours in the back room of the basketball office, an area usually off limits to all but UK basketball personnel. He looked shocked, witnesses say, and his normally hyperactive personality was in overdrive. "He looked like a Mack truck had just hit him," says one person who watched him that day. "He was acting extremely upset. I could understand it, for he was Eddie's close friend. But he looked like he was personally wounded."

Several weeks after the incident came to light, Hamilton told Dwane Casey that he could get him "the best lawyer in the country." Casey, of course, had already retained Campbell, who today says, "He's a prime suspect. I told him he's a suspect. The same day, he got very upset. He told Dwane he was going to California to learn how to pass a lie detector test.

"When [the Emery issue] first came up, Dwane asked [UK assistant] Jimmy Dykes who had been in the office that day," Campbell says. "He first told him Hamilton was in the office the afternoon the package went out. Then, when

Dwane asked him about it later, Dykes said he didn't recall saying that. And when the university asked, he said he didn't recall him being in there.

"It was all over [Hamilton's] hometown [of Springfield, Kentucky]," Campbell says. "His brother was bragging that [Jimmy] put money in the package [while it was] sitting on the secretary's desk." Campbell says he has no evidence, only "information," which he passed on to the NCAA in a long letter, outlining a scenario in which Hamilton would have put the money in the envelope, unbeknownst to Casey. UK investigators, who received a copy of the letter, went to Springfield to pursue the reports, and submitted written questions to Hamilton through his attorney, Joe Terry. Yet their interviews in Springfield turned up nothing conclusive, and Hamilton, in a written response to the university's questions, denied any involvement. The NCAA wanted to interview Hamilton, David Berst says, but Hamilton was first unavailable, and later refused to sit for questioning. Terry insists the NCAA never so much as contacted him or his client.

Hamilton had been the unnamed booster charged by the NCAA with improperly paying UK assistant coaches, including Casey, cash bonuses. Terry thinks that's why Campbell is bringing his name up. "Jimmy was in the office a lot," says Terry. "He's a friend of Sutton's. He was a convenient fellow to reach out and put the blame on. But Jimmy told me he didn't know who Claud Mills was, or even who his son was, until all this stuff broke. So much of this is Joe Bill Campbell's imagination. He's the only one who has alleged anything with respect to Jimmy. The guy's gone bonkers."

On the subject of Jimmy Hamilton, however, Campbell sounds no crazier than Ed Dove. "If he's innocent," Campbell says, "why didn't [Terry] let his man talk to the university?"

* * *

Dwane Casey and Eric Manuel could have probably saved themselves, or at least copped a plea, by telling the NCAA all the deep, dark secrets. But to do so would have brought the program, and a number of powerful personages associated with it, down with them. Neither one has the temperament of a stoolie. Both were brought up in the South, to do what they were told. Each chose to deny everything, from their own involvement to the complicity of anyone near them. As they protest tenaciously that one of the most money-driven college basketball programs of the modern era wasn't even the slightest bit corrupt, they corrode their credibility. "I guarantee you," Casey says. "You can go to any school in the country and see violations far more serious than what Kentucky might have done."

Yet everywhere the NCAA found a seamy violation—an assistant coach sending cash to a recruit, or a youngster cheating on his college boards—there's an even seamier possibility. That Casey didn't put the money in the envelope, but a renegade intimate of the head coach or a vengeful rival school did. That adults putatively dedicated to education were party to Manuel's academic fraud. Neither of the theories that would exonerate Casey can be completely ruled out, and that they can't is a chilling commentary on the game today. Yet Casey, in his craven and blind devotion to the Code, won't testify to the tawdriness of college basketball, least of all Kentucky basketball, even if it would support his theory that he was set up. "The classless thing to do is to go out and point fingers, to say this guy did this or that one did that, to say 'I'm a scapegoat, I'm bitter, I hate the University of Kentucky,'" he says. "That's the easy thing to do. But the university's been good to me. I've never been one to go around and have a lack of class. It's harder to stand up and be a man and fight on your own ground."

What of the abuses afflicting the game—the chicanery,

the money, the dirty deals? Asked on a Lexington TV show during the spring of 1989, after the sanctions came down, Casey scoffed at the very talk of them.

"It's all rhetoric," he said.

Those who prize loyalty will give their sympathy to Dwane Casey and Eric Manuel. No doubt those who prefer integrity will save their admiration for others. But those who believe justice is when all the guilty have been found and punished—they'll look at the Bills 'n' Mills affair and just avert their eyes.

"A set of rules in mathematical terms constitutes an envelope." David Roselle sat in the president's office over summer 1989, talking about rules, the one thing mathematics, ethics, and college basketball have in common. "The ethical box you live in is defined by the rules you live by. People with higher ethical standards, their envelope is smaller."

A smaller envelope is a nice idea. But the David Roselles are rare and exceptional people, and few in the game who don't have to are listening to them. In college basketball, now as ever before, the size and type of envelope doesn't matter. All that matters is how much is inside.

—— 10 ——

A Full-Court Mess

THIS MONDAY is the first in October, the traditional start of a Supreme Court session, but today a justice of a different sort is at his desk. An open briefcase on an adjacent chair holds a copy of Thomas Paine's *Common Sense* and an NCAA datebook; a stack of black three-ring binders—the results of the University of Kentucky's investigation—sits on the floor nearby.

For twenty-five years D. Alan Williams has taught American history. His specialty is the Colonial period evoked by the building he is in now, a structure in the Jefferson style on the campus of the University of Virginia. Williams also spends three months of the year tending to NCAA-related work, including the business of the Committee on Infractions, which he has chaired through much of the eighties. Spend enough time on matters of crime and punishment in college sports, and a close observer—particularly one with an academic's predisposition to analyze—will begin to make out a trend here, a pattern there.

"In basketball you may have a substantial violation, or a couple of violations, but they may involve only two or three people," he says. "On the surface it doesn't look nearly as serious as a football violation, where to succeed you're probably going to have to commit violations for five to ten people in each entering class to get a pool of players, if that's the route you wish to take. In basketball you don't need to do that. And therein lies the problem. The smaller numbers make cheating more difficult to detect. And you have fewer dissatisfied customers. In football, it's harder to identify in high school whether or not a player is going to succeed. A number come in and things don't work out. They transfer. Transfer students are, generally speaking, unhappy campers. Unhappy campers tend to talk. Happy campers don't, until they're out."

Once they're out, the NCAA must guard against former players who exaggerate what they received to play in college, because they're loath to admit they did it all for free. Williams calls it the "teenage sex syndrome." And he has noticed another sort of peer pressure. When one school in a conference cheats, others follow suit. "It goes out in concentric circles, regardless of who started it. Like in the Southwest Conference in football, people begin to bid on players. The classic example is the player [Oklahoma State's Hart Lee Dykes] who took four schools down with him.

"Eight or nine years ago we had a bunch of academic violations [at Southern Cal and New Mexico]. That started with one group of coaches. Then the coaches moved out individually from there, and the next thing you knew there was this very serious series of academic violations occurring in the West and Southwest. You can trace it all back, like a virus.

"It used to be that assistant coaches were expected to do improper things as part of their learning process. When you

286

became a head coach, you didn't have to do things because your assistants did them. Assistant coaches did them because the word was out that if you didn't go along to get along, you'd never get along. And those who reported infractions or got caught would be to some extent ostracized."

Williams says "it used to be" because he thinks that may be changing. When he gets his copy of the *NCAA News* each week, one of the first things he does is riffle back to the job listings, to see how many of the coaches the committee has sanctioned get back into the business. He's noticing fewer and fewer are, and they're taking longer and longer to do so.

"You have to punish the offender. Go back to William Penn's injunction for Pennsylvania: that the chief end of government is to reward those who do well and punish the evildoers. That's not the exact quote—his word is to 'terrify' the evildoers. Clearly the NCAA is trying to terrify the evildoers. And to some extent, it's working."

From their ivory towers, people like Williams do what they can. But talk to those in the trenches and you'll find out exactly the extent to which the enforcement process is working—just enough to make everyone more prudent, and not enough to deter. There'll be fewer balloon notes on cars, less cash through the mail, no more pinch hitting late in the game, when someone might notice a suspicious jump in a youngster's test score.

To be sure, NCAA executive director Dick Schultz has done good work in muting the cry of selective prosecution that was raised under his predecessor, Walter Byers. In the late eighties the NCAA nailed the football programs at Oklahoma and Texas A&M, two schools widely thought to be untouchable, and hammered Kansas and Kentucky, the very cornerstones of college basketball. "There was a feeling out there among coaches that if you were big enough, you could do whatever you wanted," says Arizona's Lute

Olson. "That only the lesser programs were going to get hit. That there was too much money involved, and they couldn't afford not to have them on television. But that perception's been totally reversed the last couple of years."

Still, a coach looks at a college community restless for wins. He looks at an athletic director who has already budgeted in a line item for a tournament share. He looks at his station, his perks, his wife and kids, and weighs against all this the likelihood that the NCAA's woefully underfunded and understaffed enforcement division will ever catch him. And he becomes a careful evildoer, not a terrified one.

The NCAA has been maligned ever since it set up an enforcement arm in the fifties. "Judge and jury," it has been called; "punishment without proof," it has been charged with dispensing.

The Committee on Infractions does indeed act as both judge and jury. But members of the committee don't sit in Olympian detachment. They ask questions of the accused, who in turn can ask questions right back. In many ways, a panel of six well-educated adults, all experienced in hearing such cases and deciding on equitable punishment, is more likely to reach a fair verdict than would a standard jury. Just as in a criminal trial, a guilty verdict is reached by judging that the subject of the process was culpable, and not necessarily by "proving" it.

It's the NCAA's standard of evidence, which differs from a criminal court's, that draws so much criticism. The committee uses a widely accepted standard of administrative law: "the kind of evidence upon which reasonably prudent people rely in the conduct of serious affairs." This is emphatically not "clear and convincing evidence beyond a reasonable doubt." The NCAA doesn't even bring an allegation until it has developed enough evidence to believe there will be a finding of a violation. Thus only a small fraction of schools, coaches, and players that go before the committee are ever "acquitted."

From afar, those statistics make the enforcement process look heavy-handed. But if the NCAA didn't seize every available advantage at the judicial end, few schools would ever be sanctioned. That's because the investigators themselves face such a daunting task. They have no subpoena power. Unless he's one of the targets of the probe, any person can refuse to talk to the NCAA without fear of prejudice. Investigators are usually viewed as lepers when they come in on a case. Thus the NCAA gathers information as it can: by using limited immunity, the threat of revoking an athlete's eligibility, anonymous tips, or old files from previous investigations. Often a case is built with a list of seemingly picayune infractions, and sanctions don't always reflect actual findings of wrongdoing. In what could be the most ironic finding in the history of the Enforcement Division, the NCAA's most recent probe of UNLV is focusing on, among other things, a charge that Jerry Tarkanian's wife, Lois, spent $24 on graduation caps and gowns for players. "Frequently you'll see where there's been an NCAA investigation, and a school is going on probation because some kid got a T-shirt," says Jerry Roth, a Los Angeles attorney who helped UCLA in its in-house probe of the Sean Higgins affair. "Public opinion comments on the absurdity of it all. But what the NCAA has done is make a subjective decision. They feel the university has done something wrong, but they can't prove it. They believe it. So their punishment fits that subjective decision." The NCAA's thinking isn't unlike the feds' when they went after Al Capone: if we can't get him on murder or extortion, we'll get him on tax evasion.

The work of the Enforcement Division is made all the

more difficult by its heavy caseload and high staff turnover. Its files were filled with allegations about Reggie Warford's recruiting practices at Pitt, but the NCAA chose not to pursue them, even though Berst believes the accounts of Doug West and Victor Thomas. That's because Warford and Roy Chipman had left the school, neither was back in coaching, and more urgent cases awaited the staff.

Even as the NCAA's annual gross from the tournament pushes past nine figures, Berst supervises only fourteen full-time investigators and a budget of just $2 million. Enforcement representatives are paid so poorly—salaries start in the high twenties—that most are young and inexperienced, and few stick around for more than a couple of years. "We were just street policemen," says Kevin McCormick, the former NCAA investigator. "We couldn't possibly catch everybody." When Berst himself collapsed of exhaustion after a press conference in 1987 announcing sanctions against SMU's football program, there was no better symbol of how stretched his department is.

What does it mean that the NCAA publishes a thick code of rules but is unwilling to commit the resources to enforce them? "The relatively modest, rather ineffectual enforcement mechanism is the product of a series of small choices," says John Weistart, a professor at Duke Law School and the author of The Law of Sports. "The enforcement budget is one of those choices. If they really wanted to take charge, there are things the NCAA could do better in its investigative policies, like forcing boosters to pledge that they'll cooperate fully with the NCAA or be disassociated from the program. Right now, with the furor for reform in college sports, if the NCAA went to the state legislatures and asked for subpoena power, it'd probably get it."

They won't ask, of course; the NCAA's current party line holds that there is no crisis in compliance, and progress is being made. Take Dick Schultz at his word when he says that "ninety-five percent of what's going on in college athletics today is good." But be sure to point out that the good is squirreled away in the lower divisions, with the club sports and women's lacrosse teams, and in the few Division I leagues that don't offer athletic scholarships. The showcase and cash machine for which the NCAA is best known, and from which that organization gets its operating budget, is the basketball tournament. And from the Sweet Sixteen on, most every team in it has compromised values or mocked higher education.

Ninety-five percent of college athletics may be good. But ninety-five percent of money-making college basketball is rancid. The NCAA knows it, but the policy-making membership—the colleges chasing the tournament millions—has too much vested in the status quo and the new billion-dollar deal with CBS to call for the necessary changes. Schultz has talked of the need to share that dazzling wealth, because "the public perception is there's an enormous incentive to cheat." In fact, the *reality* is there's a tremendous incentive to cheat. Perception, of course, is easier to alter, and thus becomes the focus of the NCAA's concern. Enforcement, compliance, infraction, probation—the NCAA talks a good game. But ultimately it's like the airline that says "We would like to be the first to welcome you to Cleveland" and never actually welcomes you to Cleveland.

"I'm a little different," the man says. "I've coached forty years. Maybe I'm a sort of Ray Meyer now, looking back at all the changes there have been. But I'm concerned about cheating. I ran into it at Washington State, at Montana, and here. I've been able to endure bad years because we did win that national championship. But you can't live on that forever. I happen to work for an athletic director who believes in a lot of things other than wins and losses, and a president who recognizes how hard you have to work in the toughest league in the country. In a different situation I might have been fired. How many guys have their two worst years ever, and then get a contract extension because their bosses think it's the right thing to do?"

The answer is, not many. Jud Heathcote sits in his office in Jenison Field House, a plaque commemorating Michigan State's 1979 national title gracing the wall behind him. The winning coach in the game that launched college basketball's moneyed decade is the outgoing president of the coaches' association. The lines in his sun-tanned face seem to tell the story of the past ten years.

"At the premier schools, coaches' salaries have escalated to a point where we're working for money rather than teaching kids. We're out of balance right now. If you take the entire profession, Divisions I, II, and III, there is a lot of teaching going on, a lot of coaches who care about the welfare of students. But if you look at the top programs, the coaches there are more concerned with winning. Their image. Their TV contract. Their perks and their total salary. Look at the provisions in Bill Frieder's contract at Arizona State—the incentive clauses. Is that where we're headed? Or are we supposed to do the best with the players we have?

"The things I stand for and believe in, I've done a pretty good job of standing for and articulating. But I don't think I've done as good a job as I could to change what's going on. I could name names. Instead, I shake their hands and play golf with those guys, and I know what's going on in their programs. And we kind of look the other way. We kind of tolerate that when we shouldn't."

Why?

"I don't know. There's been a Code forever. And there's a system. A lot of athletic directors are involved. See, I could call the NCAA. I could say 'so-and-so is cheating.' But a lot of guys don't. Because a lot of athletic directors don't want you to get involved in that. 'If you've got a grievance, take it to me, I'll handle it.' And a lot of times one A.D. calls another and says, 'My guy's a little upset about your guy. Could you look into it?' 'Oh, we'll take care of it.' And we never get down to what's really going on.

"You know [former Memphis State coach] Dana Kirk? Likable, fun-loving guy. We're at a Division I coaches' meeting, and Dave Berst is explaining how his people do things, and I ask Dave what happens when he sees things in the newspaper—like when [former Memphis State center William] Bedford had his third speeding ticket driving a booster's car. Well, Dana comes up to me afterward, almost pounds me in the chest. 'What right do you have to mention my program?'

" 'Maybe I shouldn't have singled you out,' I say. 'But I'll tell you something else, Dana. There's something fucked up in your program.'

"Somehow, some way, we have to get to the point where we police our own profession. Which we could do if every guy who knew or suspected something said, 'Hey!' But the cheaters know how to cheat. It's all cash money that you can't find."

Every time the ills of college athletics come up, a ritual list of proposed cures gets reprised. Make freshmen ineligible. Get rid of jock dorms and booster groups. Give coaches tenure. Take away their shoe contracts.

The one problem that rises above all these, however, is the money the game is producing, and how that pie gets divided. Money leads to cheating. Address the imbalance in how it's distributed, and the game will take a step toward sanity. There isn't a coach who'll deny that. Listen to people talk about "talkin' power":

"This one-billion-dollar TV contract is the paramount

example of the injustices in the game," says LSU's Dale Brown. "Look at the money we make off predominantly poor black kids. We're the whoremasters."

"It's gonna get worse," says Gary Colson, who's now an assistant at California but is still trying to get back in as a head coach. "It's got to, if you look at the money involved. It's like Sodom and Gomorrah. Eventually it'll destroy itself."

Sonny Smith, who left the SEC for Virginia Commonwealth after eleven years at Auburn, says: "Basketball runs the NCAA. Money from television revenues runs it. It is the deciding factor for administrators, the deciding factor for coaches, the deciding factor for players. The administrator has got to make money, and the president won't allow that money to stop coming. Now I coach for money. What the SEC took away from me was love of the game. It gave me everything else I got, but it took away my love for the game."

"Cheating is a bigger problem than it's ever been," says former Miami coach Bill Foster. "Two hundred ninety-two schools are chasing that dream now, and Final Four teams last year got a million three. Consciously or not, institutions push the coaches. The guys selling players know they've got a great deal going. In some cases colleges pay lip service to 'doing it right.' The bottom line is they want it done."

"We all know the root of all these problems is money," says Cooley High coach Ben Kelso. "I don't give a damn about all the other stuff. The bottom line is the money. No question. And when it comes to dealing with the money, people are going to do whatever is necessary to get by."

With his clout in the coaches' association, Heathcote is in a unique position to do something about the money. He has introduced a proposal to the NABC membership that would address the most compelling economic incentive to cheat. About half of the $70 million generated by the 1989 NCAA tournament went to the competing teams and conferences. Heathcote's plan calls for distributing only $6 million to participating teams, $100,000 for each tournament win. The other $20 million or so would go in equal shares to each of the 292 schools in Division I. That's about $70,000 per campus, guaranteed—whether you're North Carolina or North Carolina A&T, whether your conference has six teams in the tournament field or one lonely automatic bid.

Heathcote's is just one voice, and his organization doesn't have a vote on the floor of the NCAA convention. But others in the fray have concrete solutions to redress some of the problems.

Purdue coach Gene Keady would like to shut down the summer auction circuit. "Confine recruiting to September till the end of May," he says. "We don't get to know the kids anymore, don't get to be around them enough. I liked the old way better, where you met the parents, could go to the school as much as you wanted, talked to the janitor, to the high-school coach. Now the rich get richer. The kids go to the schools they see on TV the most.

"Everybody coaches these kids now. Doctors, factory workers. They're not really coaches. I call them hosts. It seems what we're developing now is a bunch of social idiots. They know how to eat fast food and travel in vans, and that's it."

Terry (Fat Chance) Kirkpatrick, the former Houston assistant, says: "If Nike wants to pay a coach, fine. But don't let them sponsor summer leagues. Let them donate their money and shoes to the city of Los Angeles. It's a tax write-off. Then let the high-school coaches run the league."

Sonny Vaccaro says that he is all for that. "The Federation of State High School Associations should take control. Kids should be able to take only one summer trip. They should be able to play only in their neighborhood. And they should be coached by someone who works in the school system— someone who, if he does something wrong, will have his job on the line."

"Just give every coach the same amount of money," says

Abe Lemons, the coach at Oklahoma City and a former NABC president, "and tell him he can keep what's left over."

In his usual droll way, Lemons is advancing the old argument that colleges should pay their players up front. Stipends, however, won't forestall bidding wars. And if they're paying players, schools and coaches may feel even less compelled to educate them. What's an ex-athlete to do after four years if he didn't come away with anything but a few thousand bucks? Certainly not play in the pros; current odds on a college ball player hooking on with an NBA team are 500 to one. As David Roselle says, "If you grant that there are a lot of problems in college sports, why in the world should we add a loss of purpose to that list?"

John Thompson, who was offered money coming out of high school, thinks the public must stop sympathizing with the Eric Manuels and Chris Millses. "The biggest hole in the system is not making the player responsible," he says. "The player is far more sophisticated than most people give him credit for. As a kid goes through the recruiting process, what began as sincerity and innocence goes away. It starts off as sincere interest, but then they go to the Nike camp, come to Vegas, travel around to summer tournaments, and the entourage follows them. With the athlete, the innocence becomes craftiness. He's conditioned to living in a comp world.

"Sometimes I wonder what dishonesty is. Is it dishonest for a kid to be paid . . . or is it just against the rules? Who's to say that when Landon Cox wants to have a private meeting with John Thompson that that's wrong? Certainly part of what he's trying to accomplish is wrong. Wrong because a player could lose his eligibility, be banned for life. We've put ourselves in the position of enforcing the law rather than thinking about whether what we're doing is right."

Thompson is touching on matters of entitlement, a theme

that echoes again and again. Recall L.A.'s Don Fields, speaking on behalf of John Williams, saying, "The allowance has to be paid with dignity." Lexington's Irvin Stewart telling Steve Miller, "You're an All-American basketball player. You should have money in your pocket." Dave McCollin of the New York Gauchos saying, "The kid knows the coach is making maybe a million dollars a year—and they can't give him any money?"

The NCAA's critics argue that the rules don't have a moral foundation worth supporting. Indeed, college basketball in particular is caught between the go-for-it law of the streets and the quixotic ethic of amateurism the NCAA is pledged to uphold. "Every NCAA meeting," Al McGuire likes to say, "should be held in a fourth-floor tenement house in Brooklyn."

If coaches and boosters were merely Good Samaritans, and the pox on the game were only humanitarian excesses —the free flight home for Grandma's funeral—these pleas would hold some truck. But the motives of the rule breakers are usually grounded in self-interest. There's no real difference between the Rick Huckabays who invoke "Christian principles" to defend rule breaking, and the inner-city Robin Hoods, the Landon Coxes and Vic Adamses, who have turned the brokering of teenage boys into a vocation, however well-meaning they may be. "Everything is based on need and nothing on want," one coach confesses. "So we can have some pride left."

In short, coaches buy kids to buy wins to buy time.

"We're clean," says Syracuse assistant coach Bernie Fine. By that he means the Orangemen don't violate NCAA rules. But what's more immoral? Syracuse taking care of its players? Or Syracuse not taking care of the stars who pack the Carrier Dome, generate humorously large sums for the school, and don't necessarily graduate? If Fine is to be believed when he says Syracuse is clean—and as long as Syracuse gets involved with Landon Cox's best players, is on the shortlist of virtually every high-school star in L.A., and has Rob Johnson working the streets of New York on its behalf, he probably shouldn't be believed—the Orangemen may want to keep that virtue a secret. Oh, Syracuse can tell the NCAA and the outside world it's straight; of course, the school has to. But give that impression to the inner-city eighteen-year-olds whose hands have been out since grade school, and the Orange won't get a second look.

"Bernie Fine and I are pretty good friends," says Jerry Tarkanian. "Bernie always tells me they're straight at Syracuse. [Former UNLV forward] Sid Green told me that's a bunch of shit, because they bought [ex-Orangeman] Red Bruin a car. So I kid Bernie about that, when Bernie's telling me they're straight."

By July 1989, Eric Manuel has already announced he will enroll at Hiwassee Junior College in Tennessee, Eddie Sutton will soon sign on with Nike to do promotional work, and depositions are proceeding apace in Dwane Casey's big-ticket lawsuit against Emery.

Far from Lexington, at Cal State–Los Angeles, the college summer league is going forward on one of those breezeless, withering evenings that come with stage-one smog alerts. You can tell just how far along the night's action has gone by weighing the air. Come the nightcap, it's heavy with carbon monoxide and evaporated sweat.

Pat Barrett's team features such players as UCLA's Trevor Wilson, Syracuse's Stephen Thompson, and, of course, Tom Lewis. Their opponent is Team Mills. Chris, who has just announced he'll attend Arizona, is the star; Derick is the coach, assisted by Claud, who looks dapper in a Nike warmup suit. The game is close until the second half. That's when Thompson goes on a binge around the basket, Lewis drains a few jumpers, and Barrett's team breaks things open. They're up fifteen in the final minute when Chris nails one of Barrett's players, a junior-college star named

Joey Cubit, with an elbow. Cubit takes issue with it. Chris, frustrated, comes back with a punch.

Claud bolts from the bench, ready for action. Fortunately, he runs into Wilson before he can get to Cubit, and players from both teams calm him down.

But here again, after intervening months of trouble, is Claud's love for Chris. The boy may not be his blood, but he's his nonetheless. And it makes you wonder: if Claud had never changed Chris's name from Ford to Mills, would anyone in the Emery warehouse have made the connection between the envelope from Kentucky, which was addressed to "C. MILLS," and Chris, who was previously Chris Ford? Would the *Daily News* have ever gotten the story? Would Eddie Sutton and Eric Manuel and Dwane Casey all still be in place? And would David Roselle be just another obscure academician?

While Chris's world crumbled in Lexington, his high-school teammate, neighbor, and one-time rival was winning a national title in Ann Arbor. And tonight Sean Higgins is also in the gym, watching from midcourt. He's in a Michigan T-shirt, his neck swathed in gold, his head topped with a white hat reading NATIONAL CHAMPIONS. From where he sits, literally above the fray, he has the look of an Ethiopian monarch.

Sean might have been a UCLA Bruin. His mother and stepfather clearly wanted him to be, and there may indeed have been a coercive atmosphere in the Benson-Beys' apartment during the fall of 1986. Yet would Vickie have really permitted her husband to threaten her only son with a baseball bat? DePaul forward David Booth was a high-school star at Manual High in Peoria, Illinois, when he made his visit to Michigan in fall 1987, and Higgins, then a Prop 48 freshman, was one of the players who showed him around campus. Booth had heard the story of the baseball bat, and knew of Sean's struggle to get out of his UCLA letter of intent. As he and Sean walked to their seats in

Michigan Stadium for the Wolverines' football game with Michigan State that Saturday, Booth broached the subject. And Booth says Higgins told him he had made the story up.

"He said he had to find a way to get out of it," Booth says. "He said, 'There's a way out of everything.'"

Amid all the exploitation in college basketball today, Sean Higgins may be more than just another player in the game. He may be a winner at it. Someone who learned well. Someone who exploited back.

EPILOGUE
Compliance and Defiance

THE 1990 COLLEGE BASKETBALL SEASON ended with issues of the game's integrity dominating as never before. Florida, Missouri, Illinois, Nevada–Las Vegas, and North Carolina State were all facing the wrath of the NCAA. Meanwhile, the exaltation of sneakers as status symbols had touched off a national debate about the responsibility of companies like Nike and Reebok as they pitch and purvey their expensive products to teenagers. NCAA Executive Director Dick Schultz, referring to the $1 billion television contract with CBS, confessed anxiety about "the $300,000 free throw" and its potential damage to the game. As if to highlight the wormy turn everything had taken, the NCAA's least favorite miscreants, Jerry Tarkanian's UNLV Runnin' Rebels, beat choirboy Duke in the championship game in Denver for their first national title. The breathtaking emphasis with which Vegas won the Monday-night final highlighted once again the primacy of talent at college hoops' elite level. *Just give 'em the horses.*

Ed O'Bannon soon announced his college choice, UNLV, but shrewdly declined to sign a letter of intent until the NCAA announced exactly what sanctions, if any, the basketball program would receive. (The "Two-Ay," as the NCAA is known around the Rebels' athletic department, had had Rebel fans worried ever since it embarked on its investigation into UNLV's controversial courtship of Lloyd Daniels, and scored its Supreme Court victory in *NCAA v. Tarkanian*.) When the NCAA punished UNLV by prohibiting the school from defending its title, O'Bannon signed with UCLA.

Elsewhere, much was happening, too.

Heading the NCAA's letter of inquiry to Missouri was an allegation that a street agent, presumably Vic Adams, acted as a representative of the school in Detroit, and delivered Mizzou's letter of intent to the home of Daniel Lyton. Lyton enrolled at the University of Detroit, where he'll play for Kevin O'Neill's erstwhile recruiting sidekick, Ricky Byrdsong.

The troubles at North Carolina State included persistently poor academic performance, and an admission by former Wolfpack player Charles Shackleford that, while a student, he accepted $60,000 from two men, including an agent. In addition, an unnamed Wolfpack player told ABC News that he and as many as three other players, including Shackleford, participated in a scheme to shave points in four games during the 1987–88 season. Shackleford denied the allegation. The player said the enormous wealth reaped by then-coach Jim Valvano, and the players' frustration at not getting compensated for their time and effort, helped them justify what they had allegedly done. Valvano resigned soon after the revelation, only to accept a $300,000-a-year job with ABC Sports and ESPN as a college basketball analyst.

Oklahoma State hired one of its alumni, Eddie Sutton, to replace Leonard Hamilton, Sutton's former assistant at

Kentucky, when Hamilton moved to Miami to take the head coaching position there.

California assistant coach Gary Colson, after being frustrated for several years in his attempts to get back into the game as a head coach, was hired to direct the program at Fresno State.

Georgetown coach John Thompson, the admiral of Sonny Vaccaro's Nike flagship, turned down a $6 million offer to be the Denver Nuggets' general manager—a package that was only marginally more lucrative than what he was already making.

LSU coach Dale Brown, whose shoe contract with Converse was up for renewal, announced that he would ask shoe company executives to sit down with him and Schultz to discuss the possibility of putting coaches' shoe money in a pool for needy players, to be used for emergency travel, medical treatment, and other matters relating to "human dignity." Soon thereafter, Brown and L.A. Gear agreed to a deal worth $300,000 a year, a sum believed to be the highest ever paid a college coach.

An audit revealed that thousands of dollars of what a state investigator described as public funds were diverted to athletes from basketball camps run at little Central Washington University by longtime Wildcats coach Dean Nicholson. A total of $65,000 was reportedly paid to 49 athletes over three years. Nicholson resigned under pressure after 26 seasons, and the school was eventually put on a two-year suspension.

Rudy Washington, who had piloted the Black Coaches Association while an Iowa assistant coach, moved from Iowa City to Des Moines to take over as head coach at Drake. He replaced Tom (The Alphabet Man) Abatemarco, the former recruiting wizard for Valvano at N.C. State. A university investigation found that Tom Butler, one of Abatemarco's assistants, supplied at least two players with prewritten term papers and encouraged them to hand them in. One player, Terrell Jackson, is suing the school, charging intentional deprivation of education, and claims that Abatemarco knew of the scheme. Abatemarco was nonetheless hired as an assistant by new Colorado coach Joe Harrington, whose departure from Long Beach State left a vacancy that was filled by former 49ers assistant Seth Greenberg.

One player still at Long Beach State was Kevin Williams, the former star at Chicago's Martin Luther King High School who had originally wanted to play for Tennessee, but said his coach, Landon Cox, wouldn't let him visit there. Williams is one of nine returnees on a team that won 23 games in 1989–90. Cox and his Jaguars completed an undefeated state-championship season, finishing No. 1 in USA Today's national high-school poll.

Against the advice of virtually all parties, including NBA Director of Scouting Marty Blake, who called the decision "a colossal mistake," Sean Higgins forswore his remaining college eligibility and declared for the 1990 NBA draft. He had no degree, but said he had accomplished everything he set out to at Michigan. On June 19, he was the 54th and final player chosen, by the San Antonio Spurs. He is only barely still a player in the game.

During the spring of 1990, Jerry Roth, the attorney for former UCLA coach Walt Hazzard and a number of other figures close to the Bruins' basketball program, was contacted by an NCAA investigator looking into Jim Harrick's alleged improper visit to the home of Don MacLean. Soon thereafter, Roth fielded a phone call from a highly placed member of the UCLA administration. The caller told Roth it "would not be to Walt's advantage" for Roth to talk to the NCAA, and counseled Roth, if he were asked again about MacLean's recruitment, "not to comment" any further about the matter. At about the same time, Hazzard was in Washington, D.C., interviewing for the vacant head coaching position at Howard University. He did not get the job. (There is no evidence that the two episodes were related.)

Pat Coyne, Don MacLean's mother, is one of four sources who has related to the authors of this book the circumstances of Harrick's visit. When asked if the UCLA coach had visited her home, Coyne said, "I really don't know what to say about that. . . . He wasn't there long—about fifteen minutes. We didn't know it was against the rules. I didn't know all the rules." And the purpose of Harrick's visit? "I guess to tell Don he really wanted him."

Coyne said her son had not made up his mind, but was leaning toward Georgia Tech as of that Sunday morning. "Don was looking at who would help his basketball career. Later he made his decision. He didn't say much. He just said his choice was UCLA."

As MacLean prepared to begin his junior season at UCLA, the NCAA had not yet begun a formal probe of the incident.

Arnold Hershkowitz, a follower of the New York City basketball scene, reported that Rob Johnson had gotten involved with several prospects in the class of 1991, including 6'7" Crafton Ferguson of Andrew Jackson High School in Queens and 6'10" Wilfred Kirkaldy, a former star at Boys & Girls High in Brooklyn who now attends Oak Hill Academy in Mouth of Wilson, Virginia. By the summer both had wised up, distancing themselves from "R.J.," as Johnson is known around the Syracuse basketball office. Even the loosey-goosey Gauchos, Lou d'Almeida said, had banned Johnson from their gym. Johnson did, however, succeed in steering former Georgetown guard David Edwards to Texas A&M.

Bill Rapp is a Syracuse car dealer who sat on the Orangemen's bench until questions about the propriety of his presence were raised in newspaper stories in early 1985.

He told the Syracuse *Post-Standard* that he knows Johnson and considers him "a great guy. He's a very nice man who loves kids and loves the games."

Jim Sullivan, Mark Festberg's successor as Conrad McRae's coach at Brooklyn Tech, didn't agree with Rapp's characterization of Johnson. "I would like to make it my life's work to put him out of business," Sullivan told the Syracuse *Herald-Journal*. "He's a basketball prostitute."

At a press conference, Syracuse coach Jim Boeheim acknowledged that Rob Johnson is a supporter of his program, has access to the Orangemen locker room, and sits regularly in seats just behind the team's bench. Yet he said there isn't "an ounce of truth" to the evidence that Johnson steers players to Syracuse, or to characterizations of him as a street agent, and called suggestions that Syracuse had broken any NCAA rules "a travesty, an outrage." He said that Syracuse has had minimal success recruiting players from New York City. "Of all the kids [Johnson] had known," he said, "we've successfully recruited just one player—Conrad McRae." (During Boeheim's tenure at SU, the Orangemen have also signed, among others, Derek Brower, Eddie Moss, Eugene Waldron, Tony [Red] Bruin, Rafael Addison, Wendell Alexis, Dwane [Pearl] Washington and, most recently, Adrian Autry, from New York City's five boroughs and the immediate metropolitan area. At least four of them knew Johnson before they arrived at Syracuse.)

Although Syracuse doesn't release graduation rates, Boeheim defended the academic performance of his team. Its graduation rate, he said, is "conservatively" about 90 percent. (This didn't prevent Syracuse star Billy Owens, early in the 1989–90 season, from telling Mike Waters of the Syracuse *Post-Standard*, "I always think about leaving. I can't hack school no more, and getting up and going to classes.")

Boeheim added that Jerry Tarkanian had assured him that any comment Tarkanian made to the effect that former

Runnin' Rebel Sid Green had mentioned that Syracuse had bought Red Bruin a car was "a joke," something made in jest to a third party and overheard by one of the authors of this book. (The comment, which is on tape, was made in person, directly to the co-author in question, who wouldn't characterize Tarkanian's mood at the time as lighthearted or jocular.)

"We have never broken an NCAA rule," Boeheim said at a press conference, "and we never will."

Several months later, in a column in *Eastern Basketball*, Syracuse sportswriter Bob Snyder quotes Boeheim as telling him, "No school is squeaky clean."

In keeping with its record of virtually never reversing a decision of the Committee on Infractions, the NCAA's Steering Committee turned down Dwane Casey's appeal of the five-year restrictions on his employment as a college coach. Casey and his attorney, Joe Bill Campbell, had claimed, among other things, that the penalty was based on insufficient evidence and was out of proportion to sanctions brought against other assistant coaches in similar cases.

The Steering Committee reiterated the belief of the Committee on Infractions that Casey himself had put the money in the envelope. In support of its finding it pointed to two things. One was the question of exactly when and by whom the Emery package was sealed. When asked on several occasions whether he had sealed the package himself, the NCAA noted, Casey's answer moved from uncertainty about whether he had done so (his reply when first interviewed on April 9, 1988) to certainty that he had not (his stance later, on April 26). Likewise, comments by Larnetta McDowell, the secretary in the basketball office on whose desk Casey had left the package, evolved from "no recollection" one way or another as to whether the package was already sealed when she handled it, to a specific recollection that she had sealed the package herself.

The NCAA's other point dealt with Casey's response to questions about large amounts of cash to which he had access. On February 2, 1988, Casey cashed a check for $10,000, and was able to account for only $8,250 in miscellaneous expenses. In addition, before sending the infamous overnight envelope, he received two checks totaling $8,472 for speeches and work at a basketball camp. In spite of this, Casey denied to NCAA investigators that he had access to unusual amounts of money, or had possessed unusual sums over the six previous months, or knew of anyone associated with the program who had access to unusual amounts of cash. Casey says he hadn't meant to mislead the committee on this point; he simply interpreted the questions about access to large amounts of cash as referring to money that would be used improperly—a slush fund. "So I said no," he says, "because that money wasn't for a slush fund. It was for personal use."

Casey, the NCAA affirmed, wasn't unduly hamstrung by the sanctions levied against him, for he could still be hired by any NCAA institution, so long as the school appeared before the Committee on Infractions to discuss the imposing of "certain limitations on the athletically related duties of its new assistant coach due to his involvement in a previous infractions case. . . . The committee has no reason to believe that he would be precluded from obtaining a position, it being understood that it is likely that some limitation will be imposed on him for a designated period of time at a new institution."

Notwithstanding the vistas of possibilities limned by the NCAA, Casey found the job pickings stateside rather slim. Over the summer of 1990 he left for Japan, where he would coach an industrial-league team. "I'm not going to say anything derogatory about the NCAA," says Casey. "But if they want you, like a prosecutor, they can get you. I'm hanging in there. I'm looking at people like Tates Locke, who bounced back."

A 15-member NCAA *ad hoc* committee adopted a proposal for spending the CBS billion. But it wasn't the Heathcote Plan, the Michigan State coach's initiative for sharing the wealth equally among all Divisions I teams. The committee settled on a revenue-sharing formula that, while including a catastrophic health-insurance plan and directing more money to winners of championships in Divisions II and III, still divvied up the Division I spoils in a manner that rewarded winning by taking into account NCAA tournament success over the previous six years. Indeed, other criteria under consideration by another NCAA committee —tying a school's very eligibility as a Division I basketball institution to such factors as the number of sports and athletic scholarships the department funds—would also reward size and commitment to the big time.

"I don't think you should have a socialistic, communistic sharing of the wealth," Georgetown athletic director Frank Rienzo told *The New York Times*. "They tried that in Eastern Europe and it didn't work."

Jud Heathcote does look a little like an aging Politburo member. But Rienzo's rantings are nothing more than the shrill voice of self-interest. Universities aren't publicly-held corporations, with expectant stockholders and a fiduciary duty to generate the largest profits possible. The Hoyas make a fortune from their affiliation with the Big East alone, through licensing fees, other TV revenues, gate receipts, and more. The school's national profile has been enhanced immeasurably by its basketball success. For Rienzo to say that an institution would have less incentive to field a top-flight basketball team if a limit were placed on the size of one slice of its pie—all Heathcote asks is that a school forsake a chance to win a million-dollar jackpot, and settle instead for a guaranteed $300,000 or so annually—is preposterous. Basketball factories would lose nothing but some of the powerful incentive to cheat. And the players enrolled at that school, many of whom are autitioning for their own NBA payday, are going to play just as hard. . . even if nothing's at stake but a troply.

Nowhere was the untidiness of the recruiting underworld better reflected than in the rancorous, high-stakes imbroglio between Illinois and Iowa over a young star named Deon Thomas. The case had all the elements of an espionage novel—international intrigue, secret tape recordings, physical reprisal, and conspiracy theories, with college athletics' version of the firing squad looming at the end.

The two Big Ten rivals each badly wanted Thomas, a 6'9" forward from Chicago's Simeon High School who was named the state's "Mr. Basketball" as a senior. He reportedly gave Iowa a verbal commitment early in 1989, only to sign with Illinois in April. But Thomas never played for the Illini during the 1989–90 season, which would have been his freshman year. The school voluntarily held him out of action pending the outcome of an NCAA probe.

The NCAA charged that, among other things, Illinois assistant coach Jimmy Collins promised Thomas $80,000 and a Chevrolet Blazer to enroll in Champaign. In addition, the letter of inquiry, sent to the Illini in the spring of 1990, alleged that Collins made a similar offer—$20,000 and a Blazer—to Notre Dame's LaPhonso Ellis two years earlier, with the cash to be disbursed in $5,000 installments. The NCAA brought the allegation about Thomas partly as a result of a tape recording, made by Iowa assistant coach Bruce Pearl and legal under Iowa law, of a phone conversation between Pearl and Thomas in which Thomas seems to confirm that Collins made him an improper offer.

"When I first heard the charges, I thought it was just a joke, just street talk," says Collins, who was banned from recruiting off-campus until the case was resolved. "To tell you the honest-to-God truth, I laughed. Because I thought it was a joke. But now a year later I'm talking about it, so it's obviously not a joke. But it is a lie. The allegations facing me I didn't do. And I'm not ever going to admit to them. I feel like I've been shanghaied."

Pearl, though not the target of any investigation, has been shunned by his peers. Ripped by Dick Vitale, the game's cultural commissar, for doing something so "totally unethical" as taping the call and something so stupid as committing "professional suicide," Pearl didn't make the trip to Illinois on March 3 for Iowa's season finale. He takes solace in letters of support from such coaches as Lute Olson and Dean Smith.

Pearl admits he was "uncomfortable" taping the call, but says he did so only after returning from the coaches' convention at the 1989 Final Four in Seattle, where a number of other recruiters told him of rumors they had heard that he had broken NCAA rules in his pursuit of Thomas. Pearl says he taped Thomas only after Simeon coach Bob Hambric, who has sent such stars as Nick Anderson and Ervin Small to Illinois, phoned Iowa coach Tom Davis to charge that Pearl had made improper offers to his star.

"Nothing could be further from the truth," says Pearl. "And only one person could clear me—Deon. I called him and asked about our recruiting effort."

The 14-minute conversation, one of at least nine said to have been recorded by Pearl, took place shortly after 7 P.M. on April 9, 1989, soon after Thomas had backed out of a campus visit to Iowa. According to Pearl's transcript of that call, in addition to asking about Iowa's recruiting effort, Pearl took the opportunity to ask about Illinois's.

"Okay, baby," Pearl said. "I just want to go over a couple of things and ask you a couple of questions."

"Uh-huh," said Thomas.

"Okay, when you went down to the Indiana game [on an informal visit to the Illinois campus in late January of 1989] . . ."

"Uh-huh."

". . . and you talked to Jimmy and Jimmy offered you $80,000 and the Blazer, that upset you, didn't it?"

"Yeah, somewhat."

"Tell me how . . . what your reaction to it was."

"Nothing. I was just more amazed, you know."

"Yeah."

"I didn't say anything about it to him."

Yeah."

"You know, I just laughed it off."

"Really? I felt at the time, Deon, that . . . at the time, I really felt like even though you were leaning towards Iowa, I felt that Illinois was in decent shape. . . . And I thought you were going to take a look. But when they offered you the money, didn't that turn you off a little bit?"

"No. No, not really."

"It didn't?"

"You know. I just thought about it a little bit more, that's all. It didn't really turn me off."

Thomas has said that he was just "talking trash, not paying a lot of attention" to Pearl. He has said that he agreed with Pearl in order to end the call more hastily, because he didn't want to speak to the Iowa assistant coach at all. (In October 1990, one of the authors of this book was advised that the University of Illinois and the NCAA had obtained a second transcript that was reported to give a different version of this tape. The second transcript is said to have contradicted Thomas's apparent agreement with Pearl's questioning of Collins's recruiting practices.)

In fact, Thomas would go on to charge that it was Pearl,

not Collins, who offered him $80,000 and a Blazer. Indeed, whereas the NCAA charges that Collins offered to refurbish the home of Thomas's grandmother, Bernice McGary, or move her into a better building, McGary says it was actually Pearl who made the offer. Everett Johnson, Thomas's stepfather, says that Pearl offered to move Deon's mother to Iowa City, and that Pearl told him (Johnson) that if Deon didn't sign with Iowa, he (Pearl) would make allegations "that will ruin Deon's career."

"The things that are basically in the allegations against Illinois were made by Iowa, and they were just twisted around," says Thomas.

Pearl denies all improprieties. "The defense is just trying to discredit the witness," he says. And he maintains that only when NCAA investigators came to Iowa City in August 1989 to raise questions about his conduct—and when he felt matters might well come down to his word against Thomas's—did he excuse himself from the room, fetch the tape, and tell his interrogators, "I think you'd better listen to this."

Illinois partisans and Illini coach Lou Henson charge that Pearl went beyond merely cooperating with the NCAA. They say he actively turned the Illini in, and cite some 120 phone calls, made over five and a half months beginning in May 1989, between Pearl and Rich Hilliard, an NCAA enforcement representative. Indeed, in May 1989 Pearl wrote a memo to the Iowa athletic department outlining how Iowa might go about taking Illinois to the authorities and still be successful in recruiting Thomas. Davis took up the matter with Chalmers (Bump) Elliott, Iowa's athletic director, who decided not to roil the brotherly waters of the Big Ten—even though Pearl says Thomas had told him about improprieties by the Illini on several earlier untaped occasions. Thomas says this never happened.

Pearl says he didn't tell NCAA investigators anything until they tracked him down to question his conduct in the recruiting of Thomas. "I'm hopeful people will respect me for doing my job," he says. "Which is, when called upon, to cooperate with the NCAA."

Even with the tape recording, the NCAA needed a second source if it expected to bring the charge against Collins and get a finding from the Committee on Infractions. To corroborate, investigators came up with Renaldo Kyles, a senior at Simeon High who was close to Thomas and whom Pearl shrewdly befriended. Kyles is a genial, overweight member of his Baptist church choir whom Thomas now calls "my so-called friend." Hambric calls Kyles "a butt-sucker from Day One," and says Thomas told him that Pearl paid Kyles for help in recruiting Deon, a charge that both Kyles and Pearl deny. Because of his links to Iowa, and perhaps because he wore a Hawkeyes jacket around school, Kyles had received several threats, gotten into a fight with an adult who charged him with double-crossing Illinois, and had to be kept out of Simeon for a week during the 1989–90 academic year until things cooled off.

"It's a case of sour grapes," says Hambric. "Iowa's trying to wipe out Jimmy Collins as a recruiter. But it's not going to be able to do that because the high-school coaches in Chicago know how Iowa operates. Iowa's not going to get anybody out of here. And if you're in the Big Ten, you need Chicago.

"Everybody in the Top 25 cheats. Everybody breaks some rules."

Illinois included?

"Everybody."

"Pearl came over to Europe," continues Hambric, who took his Simeon team to Amsterdam in March 1989 for a tournament. "He suddenly showed up while we were there. He said he was on vacation."

Pearl, who spent more than $1,700 of Iowa's basketball budget to make the overseas trip, says he was only "baby-sitting" Thomas during a recruiting contact period. He says there's no truth to Thomas's charges that Pearl gave him $100 in Amsterdam and took him and three Simeon teammates to lunch. "The kid was coming [to Iowa]," says Pearl. "Just to be able to phone his mother from Amsterdam, to demonstrate my concern, I thought it was worth the trip."

By the summer of 1990, the relationship between Illinois and Iowa had become so nasty that Collins was calling Pearl a liar and Thomas was calling him a snake. But the Illini and the NCAA had entered into almost as contentious a relationship. Illinois decided to challenge vigorously the NCAA's charges, out of a belief that evidence gathered in the case was unreliable and inconsistent. Among the questions raised were:

Why would LaPhonso Ellis suddenly implicate Illinois, after originally telling the NCAA, during an Operation Intercept interview, that the Illini had done nothing improper?

As much as Henson would like to believe in a conspiracy among such rival coaches as Digger Phelps and Big Ten rival Bob Knight to put his program away, it's probably because Ellis, even as a high-school senior, knew enough about the Code not to drop a dime on anyone. It took the prompting of the reformist Phelps two years later to persuade him to come clean.

Why hasn't Kyles publicly corroborated Pearl's account of the alleged offer of $80,000 and a Blazer from Illinois, even though he is believed to have done so in his original statement to the NCAA?

As much as the Illini would like to believe that Kyles is a pathological liar, it's probably because he's subject to fear and peer pressure, given the incidents that have taken place at Simeon since the Thomas affair became so public and ugly.

Why has the NCAA's conduct infuriated so many of the

lawyers, private investigators, and former judges enlisted by the besieged figures in the case?

As much as Illinois fans would like to believe that the NCAA is unfair and unfeeling, it's probably because most of the professionals involved in the case are used to working with experienced people in the legal profession, and following standards of due process and civil procedure. Suddenly they're finding themselves dealing with greenhorn Clouseaus and the NCAA's peculiar brand of administrative justice.

A good example of the tensions at play is the fight that almost broke out between Steven (Randy) Rueckert, one of the NCAA gumshoes assigned to the case, and Robert Auler, an attorney representing Ervin Small, a former teammate of Thomas's at Simeon. Auler had a number of reservations about Rueckert's interrogation of Small on January 11, 1990, a session that Auler sat in on. When Rueckert later returned to Champaign with a statement for Small to sign, Rueckert became enraged when Auler began reviewing Rueckert's notes to compare them with notes of his own.

"You're not going to copy my report!" Rueckert said, according to Auler.

"Then how am I going to get a copy of this little gem?" asked Auler, who says he feared he would be struck.

"You can see it with the rest of the public at the NCAA office."

"You mean my client and I can drive to Kansas?"

"Yes!"

"Then stick this up your ass!" said Auler, ripping the document up. "It's a lot closer than Kansas, and almost as small!"

Until Illinois, no school had contested every major charge in an NCAA "indictment," much less gotten off. Yet here was a school hiring a pricy private attorney and a retired federal judge, and spending nearly $500,000, to defend itself. For the Illini, whose basketball program had generated $2.5 million in television and ticket revenues during the 1989–90 season, the economics of the game left them with little choice but to fight back. Like most big-time athletic departments, Illinois has two revenue-producing programs (football and basketball) that support fifteen other, money-losing sports. Yet it's a delicate line the Illini are walking, as they try to defend themselves while still giving every appearance of "cooperating" with the NCAA. Indeed, the NCAA frowns on aggressive defenses; witness the Dwane Casey decision, in which the Committee on Infractions chided Joe Bill Campbell for his "adverserial" posture. The "cooperation" that it encourages and rewards seems really to be contrition.

More than any other, the Illinois case underscored the perils of running an enforcement division on the cheap. Even as Rueckert and Auler nearly came to blows over the contents of Rueckert's report, the NCAA won't tape-record its interviews, because it says it can't afford the staff or cost to transcribe them. And even as the Illinois case dragged on—and many cases outlast the typical enforcement officer—the NCAA membership still won't increase salaries and manpower to provide itself with swifter, more reliable justice. The NCAA is already on the defensive for its unwillingness to provide due process to its accused; by continuing to devote only 2 percent of its budget to enforcement, the organization puts its credibility even more profoundly at risk.

No wonder Mark Goldenberg, Collins's attorney, promised legal action if his client were injured as a result of the entire affair. And no wonder Illinois was one of four states whose legislatures were considering bills that would require the NCAA to bring its enforcement practices more in line with civil procedure. (The other three, not surprisingly, are Missouri, Florida, and South Carolina, all of them home to schools in trouble with the NCAA of late. Nebraska has

317

already passed such a law.) Yet the NCAA, which won its Supreme Court fight with Tarkanian over the very issue of whether or not it is a "state actor," continues to argue successfully that it isn't bound by due process—because it's a "voluntary" organization, not aligned with any particular state. Of course, if a school wants to play in the big time, there's nothing at all voluntary about being a member of the NCAA.

Because the Illinois football team was placed on probation in 1988—Illinois had suffered through five NCAA sanctions since 1967, and a Henson program was sanctioned in the early seventies while he was at New Mexico State—the school was subject to the death penalty if the charges of major violations held up. Collins and Henson figured to lose their jobs. And in the clannish and cutthroat world of player procurement, Pearl stood to be a big loser, too.

But Deon Thomas, who hasn't yet played a minute of college ball, had already lost. At worst, all anyone had accused him of doing was listening to an improper offer. For that, he has lost a season, and much of his innocence. "I get very angry that I had to sit out, because of a lot of 'he say, she say.' I got caught in the middle of big business, which I didn't understand it was. I was just thinking, 'Okay, this is just basketball and a chance at higher education.'

"I didn't see it for the big business that it is."

VALVANO

Jim Valvano
with Curry Kirkpatrick

A provocative memoir by one of today's most outspoken and colorful sports figures who takes readers inside the pressure-cooker world of championship-level college basketball.

Jim Valvano became one of the best known coaches in college basketball during his long, successful career guiding the North Carolina State Wolfpak to national prominence. Now, for the first time, with his unique court-side perspective and with his flair for outspoken observations and outrageous humor, Valvano tells his story his way.

Available in Hardcover From Pocket Books In February, 1991.

POCKET
BOOKS